# RESOURCES AND EVERYDAY CONFLICTS IN RURAL UKRAINE

RUSSIAN AND EAST EUROPEAN STUDIES

JONATHAN HARRIS, EDITOR

# RESOURCES AND EVERYDAY CONFLICTS IN RURAL UKRAINE

## THEORIZING SOCIAL CHANGE

DEEMA KANEFF

UNIVERSITY OF PITTSBURGH PRESS

Published by the University of Pittsburgh Press, Pittsburgh, Pa., 15260

Manufactured in the United States of America
Printed on acid-free paper
10 9 8 7 6 5 4 3 2 1

Cataloging-in-Publication data is available from the Library of Congress

Hardcover: 978-0-8229-4877-3
Paperback: 978-0-8229-6773-6

Cover photos by Deema Kaneff
Cover design by Melissa Dias-Mandoly

Publisher: University of Pittsburgh Press, 7500 Thomas Blvd., 4th floor, Pittsburgh, PA 15260, United States, www.upittpress.org
EU Authorized Representative: Easy Access System Europe, Mustamäe tee 50, 10621 Tallinn, Estonia, gpsr.requests@easproject.com

To my parents

# CONTENTS

# ACKNOWLEDGMENTS

This book is very much a cooperative endeavor that could not have been completed without the support and intellectual inspiration from many people. Most importantly, I want to thank everyone in Brega, Ukraine. Without the villagers' willingness to accommodate me and include me in their community, this work would not have been written. I am particularly grateful to Valentina and her family for hosting me, as well as to Marusha, Luba, Tanya, Alyona, Kolyo, Misho, Olya and Vito, Zina and all their families for sharing their lives with me. There are many others in Brega, and from the surrounding district, who were also generous with their time. I am deeply grateful to them all. Viktoria Turchinskaya gave me a supportive and welcoming home during my trips to Odessa. I wish also to acknowledge Alexander Ivanovich Ganchev and Alexander Anatolyevich Prigarin at Odessa (the spelling commonly used at the time of my fieldwork and retained out of respect for my interlocutors) National University for their interest in my work and some very helpful discussions.

I feel fortunate to have received support from the Max Planck Institute for Social Anthropology (MPI) in Germany in different ways (intellectual, financial, and communal) over the years: from the initial fieldwork to the analysis and writing of the book. In particular, I am grateful to Chris Hann for the opportunities he has given me over three decades (including the possibility to work in Ukraine), for his counsel and friendship, as well as the practical assistance he provided while a director of the MPI. Chris Hann and James Carrier read early versions of the theoretical arguments, and their feedback provided me with the confidence to develop my ideas further. I remain appreciative for my continued access to the excellent facilities at the MPI in the final writing stages before completion, thanks to Marie-Claire Foblets, who has been extraordinarily gracious in welcoming me into her department during the precious summer months outside of the teaching semester. My eternal gratitude to her for showing interest in my work, for her encouragement and much valued company. I am also thankful to other colleagues/friends (all of whom have been associated with the MPI at one time or another) who have supported me throughout this long journey. Brian Donahoe always made time, listened patiently, and gave insightful feedback at various stages of the process. John Eidson, Kirsten Endres, Frances Pine, and Lale Yalçin Heckmann have all read parts of the work and provided me with thoughtful and helpful comments, in addition to much needed encouragement and precious friendship. My heartfelt thanks to all of you. Tetiana Bershak gave invaluable assistance through sourcing additional fieldwork materials that enriched the book. In the final few months of the long writing process, I participated in an informal writing group in my department at the University of Birmingham who motivated me to continue with the book while juggling the demands of teaching/administrative duties during the semester. The University of Birmingham also funded the trip to Ukraine in 2014, which allowed me to gather additional materials a decade after the initial fieldwork during the early 2000s.

I very much appreciate the helpful feedback from two anonymous readers, as well as the efforts of Peter Kracht and the editorial team (especially Kelly Lynn Thomas) at Pittsburgh University Press. I am especially grateful to Russian and East European Studies Series Editor Jonathan Harris, whose feedback undoubtedly helped improve this work. Rainer Hillebrand brought intellectual clarity to my ideas, and pushed my boundaries through long and engaging conversations. Thank you Rainer, for your generously given time, and most importantly, for your valued companionship over the course of many years. Yolanthe Daly has also given me unconditional friendship, and along with Rainer, has always been there for me. Finally, I am very thankful to my family. Unfortunately, my mother, Lillian, died in the final production stages of the book, and thus she never got to see the end result of the sacrifices she made (and for which I remain eternally grateful). Llyana and Stephen always took an interest in the project, in their own different and much appreciated ways. Sadly, my father passed away some years before the completion of this work. He has always been my guiding light and remains so.

# AUTHOR'S NOTES

## A NOTE ON LANGUAGE AND TRANSLITERATION/TRANSCRIPTION

In transcribing Bulgarian and Russian words, I have used the Library of Congress system without diacritical marks. Bregans were literate in Russian. Their everyday use of Bulgarian was only in spoken form (not written). Since my transliterations are of an unwritten language, and I am not a trained linguist, I did my best to replicate the language as I heard it. I did not appreciate, until I started the process, how much the spoken languages in Brega combined Bulgarian and Russian, so that the "pure" transliteration tables of the Library of Congress often seemed inadequate. I have tried my best to remain true to the languages as articulated.

While I appreciate that retaining the Russian spelling of personal names and geographical place names is no longer conventional in Ukraine, I have decided to do so to follow local practices and out of respect for the local people. This reflects not only the way the people I worked with inscribed and spoke these names (during the period of my fieldwork), but it is also an acknowledgment of local identity based on particular historical influences and a way to indicate local temporal and geopolitical views. All translations are my own unless otherwise indicated.

## A NOTE ON THE CURRENT WAR IN UKRAINE

When I first started working in Ukraine, the country was not at war with Russia. Indeed, the vast majority of the fieldwork carried out for this book was completed well before the onset of the war in 2014 and its escalation in 2022. During my last stay in Brega, toward the end of 2014, the annexation of Crimea and the onset of war in the east of the country were very much on people's minds. Thus, the early days of the war are part of the background, and mentioned where relevant (especially in chapter 5, on identity, the revaluation of this resource since Ukraine's independence and the tensions arising from this process). However, since then, sites within the study region have come under direct attack from Russia, and such a threat may well have modified local views or at least added new layers of complexity to old loyalties. Given that I have not been back to Ukraine, and thus not had firsthand access to local views since 2014 (although there has been some contact by other means), I cannot and do not claim that the opinions expressed in the book are a commentary on or reflect present-day local views of the war (nor is this an objective of the book). Furthermore, it cannot be assumed that the opinions voiced by villagers a decade or more ago are still current. Thus, I would caution the reader about coming to any conclusions concerning the contemporary situation in the region based on the ethnographic materials presented here.

Nevertheless, I believe that my book does provide valuable insights into the difficulties faced by an ethnic minority in Ukraine since the country gained independence in 1991, highlighting some of the exclusions the Bulgarian Ukrainians have faced based on language use and selective understandings of the past that have been, and continue to be, central to the nation-building project in the country. For a postwar democratic and diverse Ukraine, it is important that the experiences and views of all Ukrainians are heard and considered.

# RESOURCES AND EVERYDAY CONFLICTS IN RURAL UKRAINE

INTRODUCTION

# RESOURCES AND SOCIAL CHANGE

*Enterprise Land. Household Land. Water. Moral Authority. Identity.*

Resources are at the center of processes of social change. While this is true of any society in any given historical period, it is particularly relevant in the case of postsocialist Eurasia—including Ukraine—where reforms that amounted to nothing less than a radical transformation of social, political and economic life, took place not once, but twice in the last century: with the establishment of socialist states, and then decades later, with their demise and incorporation into the global capitalist economy. At both times, resources were important for anticipating and implementing social change: Centralized ownership and control of resources were crucial to engineering the socialist state; postsocialist reforms reversed many of these public/collective ownership arrangements, although there was no return to pre-Soviet arrangements. On both occasions, it was through the deliberate shifting of resources, through changes in their ownership/control/management and access that social transformation was orchestrated. The mobilization

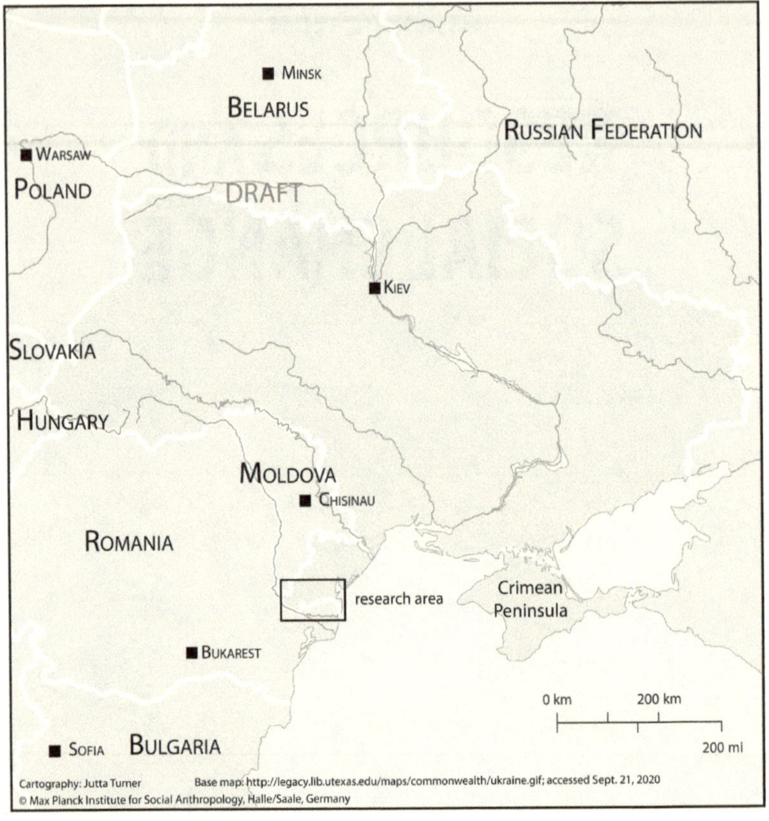


**FIGURE I.1.** Ukraine and research area.

of resources is at the center of any reform process. It is through the making of new resources and the unmaking and remaking of others that political economies are changed.

This book is a study of social change explored through the perspective of the revaluation of five resources (identified above in italics). Based on anthropological fieldwork in a rural village I call Brega, Odessa Oblast, Ukraine, the book explores tensions arising from various claims over resources, and the divisions (and sometimes alliances) that resulted from such events.

## REFORMING BREGA

The village that is at the heart of this book is in the southernmost part of the country. Ukraine is administratively divided into "oblasti" (provinces), which in turn are subdivided into "raiony"

**FIGURE I.2.** Southern Ukraine and the fieldwork region, located at the very southwestern end of Odessa Oblast.

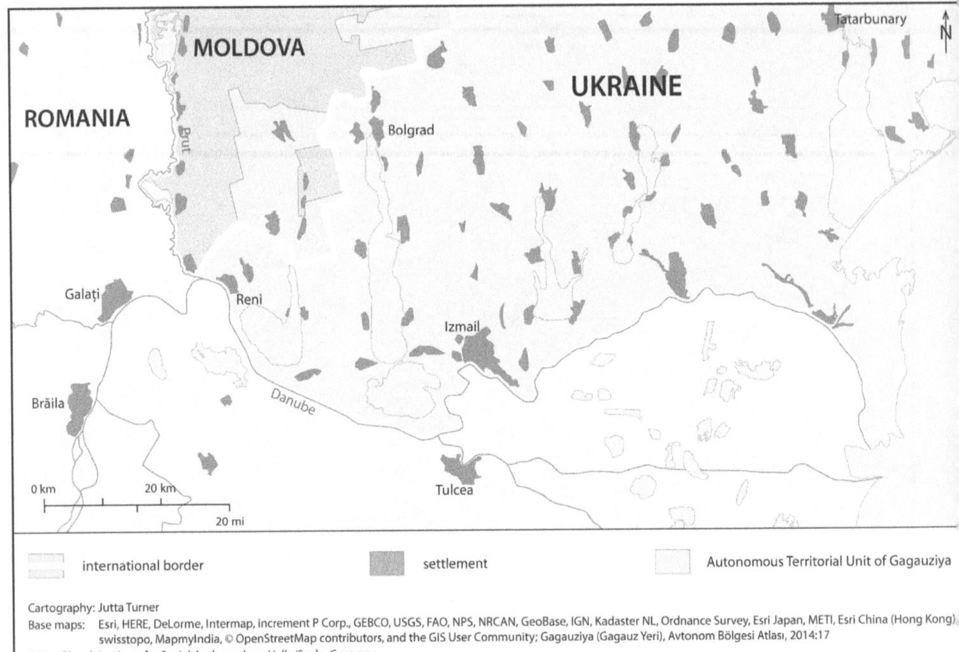


**FIGURE I.3.** Southwestern Odessa Oblast indicating the towns of Bolgrad, Reni and Izmail and all the settlements in the region.

(districts). For the sake of anonymity, I do not identify the specific administrative district in which Brega lies (see fig. I.1). When I speak of the "region," I am referring to several neighboring districts that constituted the southwesternmost part of the Odessa Oblast (see figs. I.2 and I.3). The rural lands in the territory tucked away at the southwesternmost part of the oblast, nestled between Moldova to the north and west, Romania to the south and the Black Sea to the east, were dominated neither by ethnic Ukrainians nor Russians. Indeed, there was no clear ethnic majority in this region that has always been culturally and linguistically diverse. Instead, it was several of Ukraine's nationally designated "minorities"—Bulgarians, Gagauzi and Moldovans—who predominated in the rural regions of the area, as they have for the past two centuries.

Records show that Brega was first settled in 1812 by 118 Bulgarian families.[1] The majority of Brega's 2,400 inhabitants identified themselves as ethnic Bulgarians (90 percent in 2014).[2] There were also Gagauzi (2 percent) and Moldovans (3 percent), while the rest claimed to be either Russian or Ukrainian (5 percent).[3] Neighboring villages were also relatively monoethnic—Moldovan, Gagauz or Bulgarian.[4] From the very beginning, their migration was intricately tied to the desire to escape Ottoman rule and settle within the Russian Empire, which offered them sanctuary. It points to a close and complicated relationship with Russia that continued (at least) into the first two decades of the twenty-first century: Bregans claimed their ancestry as ethnic Bulgarian while recognizing the important historical role Russia played in their past and present. It was a relationship evidenced through their bilingual and bicultural practices: Bulgarian was spoken within the village, and Russian was the lingua franca in the region and was used with "outsiders" and with other ethnic groups or in more formal settings. Since Ukrainian independence in 1991, an additional new layer of language skills has been required of the inhabitants. The Ukrainian language featured in all official government documentation (by law). I will say more about this identity in chapter 5. The important point for now is that the strong historical connections to Russia, which were expressed through the everyday linguistic and cultural practices of local inhabitants, gave a distinct flavor to the area. This orientation meant that this southwesternmost part of Odessa Oblast had more in common—at least politically—with Crimea or eastern parts of Ukraine than western areas of the country. At the same time, the region, especially the rural areas, was distinguished from the rest of the country—east and west—on the basis of the ethnic heritage of the inhabitants' cultural connections to present-day Bulgaria or Moldova, while the two nationally dominant ethnicities—Ukrainians and Russians—were minorities.

The particular ethnic and historical characteristics described above were notable distinguishing markers of this region. They were also important in understanding the making of the region's contemporary marginality from the rest of the country—a marginality based on linguistic and ethnic differences, as well as on the basis of divergent histories associated with such a heritage.

Such a marginality has been reinforced in a number of additional ways during the last three decades. Once a thriving economic center of the Soviet Union (Samokhvalov and Samokhvalov 2006), the area, after Ukrainian independence, was struggling economically, having lost much of the trading that once took place at the busy Soviet ports on the Danube River at both Reni and Izmail, which provided markets for agricultural produce from the region. Within Brega, the disestablishment of the former Soviet collectives led to high unemployment, and the agricultural enterprises that replaced the previous collectives employed only a very small fraction of the original workforce. This had significant impact on the village, as evidenced by the overall decline in population by 20 percent since 2000.[5] The region's economic marginality was reinforced by its peripheral geographic location. It is 300 km from the oblast capital of Odessa, which can only be reached by the one road that connects this southernmost end of the oblast to the provincial capital and the rest of the country. When I last traveled on this road, its condition was so poor, with such deep potholes, that the road was almost impassable by car in certain places. Schlegel (2016, 14–15) notes that in winter the road may be closed for days after heavy snowfall, cutting off the region from the rest of the country. More recent reports indicate that the EU was investing in improving this main artery road between the southwesternmost parts of the oblast and Odessa (de Waal and Jarabik 2018, 9). The borders with Romania (on the Danube River) and Moldova created additional barriers to trade, transportation, and communications.

Thus, the distinguishing features of the region in which Brega lies were in terms of ethnic makeup, geopolitical orientation, and history. Economic hardship may not have been a unique characteristic (since it is common in many regions of the country) but has played a role in adding to the isolation of the region and decline in population. In all ways, the area could be represented as marginal when compared to other parts of Ukraine.

Brega had another characteristic worth highlighting that made it quite different from neighboring villages in the region: Its leaders welcomed the restructuring of the agricultural system, and to this extent Brega was known locally as a "pro-reform" village. Driven by national laws and largely sponsored by western funding,[6] local leaders played a crucial role in how the reforms took shape on the ground (see also Allina-Pisano 2008, 12, 20). The fate of nationally driven and internationally sponsored reforms was ultimately determined locally. Allina-Pisano (2008), in her fascinating book on property rights in the Black Earth region of Ukraine and Russia, underlines how local state officials were crucial actors in land reform outcomes, their efforts strengthened by state decentralization policies. In the case of Brega, too, it was the local leadership who played the crucial role in shaping how the reforms were received and implemented. Brega officials from the collective farm were positively predisposed to the agricultural reforms and the main protagonists in pursuing reforms locally. Indeed, a former head of the agricultural collective told me that Brega, as the first village in the region to initiate the reforms by privatizing the sheep herd in 1991, was often presented by district officials as an example to other neighboring villages. I will say more about these agricultural reforms in chapter 1.

The village's pro-reform reputation was reinforced by the presence of the British government's development fund—known at the time as the "British Know How Fund"—which was active in Brega before my arrival and in the early years of my fieldwork.[7] Indeed, Brega was first brought to my attention as a possible fieldwork site by the Know How branch in Odessa. My ties to the Know How Fund were informal, through a British anthropologist working for the organization. She kindly introduced me to her Odessa colleagues, who in turn offered assistance by providing transport during my first trip to Ukraine, in order to find a suitable field site. Their help made it possible to visit a large number of villages (almost 50) over considerable distances in a relatively short period of time. On occasions when I had the opportunity to speak to the local officials in the villages I visited, I detected a lack of enthusiasm for my presence. It was only after I modified the way I presented myself, distancing myself from the British agency by expressing explicitly that I had no official affiliation to them, while at the same time playing up my ancestral connections to Bulgaria, that the reactions toward me warmed. Later, I learned that their suspicions of foreigners were grounded in the understandable assumption that "westerners" were there to enforce unpopular reforms. Not wishing to impose myself on a community that would be uncomfortable with my presence meant that I eventually settled in Brega (rather than another site closer to Odessa as I had originally planned), where I was welcomed by the proreform leadership.

When I speak of the reform process, I recognize that it is an umbrella term that incorporated a wide range of nationally-driven processes/policies, implicated a large number of resources and vast sets of institutions across different administrative levels. In the case of Ukraine, reforms were financially sponsored by foreign donors, the World Bank and EU,[8] and practically all dimensions of social life have been subject to reorganization at one time or another in the last three decades. Targets of reform include: the judicial system, the tax system, the banking sector, and the decentralization of various public administration institutions. Privatization of a vast range of assets and services—most recently affecting state-owned enterprises, healthcare, education, and pensions—has also been an integral part of the reforms. Such initiatives have gained momentum since the wave of civil protests in 2014, commonly referred to as "Euromaidan," when the country solidified its ties to the west.[9] Reforms have focused on six priority areas, one of which is the agricultural sector.[10] Land privatization, as a cornerstone of reforms across eastern Europe, was particularly important in the case of Ukraine because the country was a key agricultural producer in Soviet times and remained heavily dependent on its wealthy agricultural sector (Wegren 2002, 9). Further, land reforms have had the most direct impact on rural communities. Thus, they are of greatest relevance to this study.

Importantly, the impact of land reforms extended well beyond the immediate effects of the privatization of land and dismantling of agricultural collectives. Far more than the cooperatives and collectives in (other parts of) the former East Europe, in the former Soviet Union, collectives were "total social institutions" (Humphrey 1995, 7; also, Humphrey 1998, 450, 451–52, 487), which did more than just work the land. They provided housing for some of the workers, controlled the utilities, and contributed to the cultural and educational institutions of the village. The dismantling of the sovkhoz and kolkhoz over the course of many years had impact not only on landownership/management arrangements, but also on the related resources under their control—such as livestock, buildings, machinery, and housing. Many of the collectives' original services and utilities were also affected: water, provision of building materials, assistance to the school and kindergarten, library, and so on. While this book does not look at all of these in detail, it does highlight the disestablishment of the collectives and restructuring of the agricultural sector that went far beyond the material resource of collective land (discussed in chapter 1). The knock-on effect had implications for the resources of household plots and water, both of which are the focus of chapters 2 and 3, respectively. The attention to these material resources of land and water provides a way to explore changing relations within the community: between an emerging elite and ordinary villagers, within and between households, and between neighbors.

Beyond the wide range of material resources affected by the reforms, restructuring has also more indirectly, but just as surely, impacted on other areas of rural life. This was, again, especially true in the case of Ukraine, where in parallel to the reforms, a new nation-building project has also been underway (which has not been the case in many other postsocialist states). The search for a common national unifying identity, combined with the turning away from a secular socialist ideology, has put religion in the spotlight. The renovation and reopening of the village church, and the return of a Russian Orthodox priest after a thirty-year absence, resulted in growing tensions between the priest and the mayor as they and their respective institutions and followers—church and the village council—competed for local moral authority (the subject of chapter 4). At the same time, the unraveling of the USSR and foundation of a new independent Ukraine has led to a reappraisal of the position of ethnic minorities in the country, another indirect effect of the reforms on the local community (chapter 5). In both instances, we have nonmaterial resources—moral authority and identity—also as sites of contestation. I will say more about these, as well as the material resources of land and water below, and in the chapters that follow.

## CONCEPTUALIZING RESOURCES

The all-encompassing nature of the reforms in Brega (and indeed across the country and throughout the former Eurasian landmass) turns our attention to the theme of social change. Postsocialism and privatization have both featured prominently as analytical frameworks for understanding social change in the former socialist world. They provide two ways in which anthropologists and other social scientists have conceptualized transformation in such places. Many valuable insights have been generated through these terms, although they also have their limitations as explanatory frameworks. I begin by examining both concepts in order to later highlight some of the advantages of my approach.

### Analyzing Social Change in Former Socialist States

"Postsocialism" was an especially popular term used in the first couple of decades after 1989–1991,[11] although it has come under increasing scrutiny (e.g., Müller 2019). As an analytical tool, the term remains useful for the purposes of engaging with a broad field of comparison both on the basis of a shared and distinct form of political economy in the past and between cases that might not otherwise be considered together (Hann et al. 2002, 12).[12] This basis for comparison—which is both spatial and temporal—has enabled much fruitful work in considering together different former socialist states.

Spatially, the concept delineates one part of Europe from another on the grounds of shared political economy arrangements in history. Such a comparison can be useful, but it has also rightfully attracted criticism. One problem is that the spatial cordoning off of one part of Europe from the rest, that is, separating eastern Europe from other geographic regions, makes the term liable to privileging western discourses about particular territorial geographies and providing potential for western-oriented biases (Müller 2019, 541–43). Another problem is that the spatial segregation invites focus on differences between regions (for example, eastern from western Europe), which can mask important similarities. This latter point can be best highlighted if we compare the postsocialist term to another that can also be applied to analyze the reforms implemented after 1989–1991: neoliberalism. The latter provides a conceptual framework that enables a focus on the similarities of the reform process in eastern Europe with similar policies and processes enacted in many other places around the world (despite different starting positions). Socialist inheritance is played down, and possible similarities with other regions, rather than significant differences, are underlined. Yet, the emphasis on similarity presented by neoliberalism can distract attention away from potentially important "arenas of reflection and critique" that are offered by postsocialist studies (Rogers 2010, 14).

The temporal framework provided by the postsocialist concept is based on drawing a line between the socialist past and capitalist present. A straightforward reading of postsocialism understands transformation as a linear representation: "Post" denotes a concern with what happens after socialism. It also privileges one event in the past (the collapse of socialism) over and above others (Müller 2019, 538). One line of critique is based on this emphasis of rupture over continuity, which is seen to contribute to a delineation between eastern and western Europe and to create a temporal eastern European Other (Müller 2019, 541). In such an understanding, it is the "post" aspect of postsocialism that is given prominence. In all fairness, ethnographic approaches have shown that the term can also foreground continuity (Berdahl 2000, 3). Indeed, Hann reminds us that "strong threads of continuity mark even the most dramatic of social ruptures" (Hann et al. 2002, 5; Collier 2011, 22; Humphrey 1998, vii, viii). This latter perspective gives analytical preference to the "socialism" part of the postsocialism term, focusing on socialism's legacies, which often manifest themselves in particular types of social relations and lingering expectations of the state. Analytically, the postsocialism term can therefore offer a certain flexibility, depending on whether the emphasis in analysis is placed on the "post" or the "socialism" dimension: It can be used to highlight continuity or rupture. Such ambiguity may be an asset, but it can also introduce a lack of precision and confusion to an analysis.

Recent work suggests that the concept can also take on a wider range of spatial and temporal significances than it originally delineated, designating spaces outside those of the former socialist states and accommodating multiple temporal realities (e.g., Kaneff 2022; Chelcea 2023). While this addresses some of the noted problems and can thus satisfy those who find continued worth in the concept, the extended significance of the concept means that it remains a "broad church," with often vague and ambiguous usage.[13] In the end, comparison needs to be grounded in a situated and contextualized ethnography that at the same time must make use of a commonly agreed process. The problem as I see it, is that while postsocialist transformations focus on, "rearrangements, reconfigurations and recombinations" (Müller 2019, 537), these are free-floating processes to the extent that there is no agreement between scholars as to how these processes are defined—either emically or etically. As an analytical tool for the analysis of social change, postsocialism simply designates a broad spatial and temporal framework, but as such it is a "general label" (Hann 2006a, 5), rather than a precise device with clear analytical possibilities. This makes rigorous comparison difficult to achieve.

In sum, we have a term that is broad and vague, that allows us to consider a range of countries together but requires us to think about social change in terms of spatial and temporal dichotomies—west/east, socialist/postsocialist—that hinders the ability to provide a nuanced analysis and can reproduce undesirable political and ideologically loaded divisions.

"Privatization," a term associated often with the postsocialist literature, is an analytical concept that is of a different level of abstraction from postsocialism: It is less encompassing and divvies up the social world in yet another way—through the public–private dichotomy. This dichotomy is specifically applied with regard to the economic realm, to institutions, property, and services.

At the macro level at which Harvey (2005) describes the process, privatization is about the selling off of public assets—land, public utilities, social welfare services, public institutions of various forms—into private ownership. It is also about converting various forms of property rights held in a common/collective/state form into exclusively private property rights. Sometimes a transference of ownership does not actually take place; the handing over of control and management to private hands is sufficient and has similar consequences. In any case, privatization conceptualizes social change as taking place through the shifting of public assets into private ownership or control. Conceptualizing social change through privatization is useful as an indicator of a general trend and helpful at this level of analysis.

Privatization continues to be an important tool in how we talk about shifts in the ownership/management/control of particular assets. It remains one basic and recurring feature of neoliberal reforms (Dale and Fabry 2018, 237, 238; Cahill et al., 2018, xxix; Stenning et al. 2010; and others). This is particularly true in the case of the postsocialist world, given the starting point of state socialism where a far greater number of resources were governed by the principle of collective/state ownership, thus creating a far larger pool of potential targets for privatization (e.g., Verdery 2003, 5). The concept has been used to good advantage by anthropologists (see, for example: Abrahams 1996; Hann et al. 2003; Kideckel 1995; Verdery 2003). Ethnographic studies provide considerable detail in terms of the different forms that privatization can take (with respect to land this can be via restitution, the creation of new private properties, etc.) and their social impact. The greater detail of such studies also provides evidence that privatization may not require the shifting of resources from the public to private sector; sometimes it is a process that might shift resources from one form of public to another, such as agricultural collective control to municipal council control (as in the case of water that is discussed in chapter 3). In the same way that there are different forms of public ownership, there are also different forms of private ownership and many combinations in-between. Ethnographic studies give greater depth and nuance to the more macro level studies of privatization showing that privatization processes are complicated and by no means easy to subsume under the umbrella of public to private.

Yet, irrespective of whether the approach to privatization is macro level or achieved through providing greater contextual depth, insufficient attention is given to the critical examination of privatization as a concept, and the dichotomy on which it rests—public–private—which remains largely taken for granted.[14]

Privatization assumes, in its crudest delineations, a division of social space into public and private, a delineation that needs to be problematized. First, there is a lack of clarity of the public–private dichotomy on which understandings of privatization are founded. The dichotomy is muddied by the revolving door phenomenon, in which elites move freely between government and private sectors, and their interests as well as profit gains are unclear. The implementation of various neoliberal policies designed to reduce state control has also resulted in making less clear the distinction between public and private. For example, the outsourcing of state-owned assets (to private companies) and making use of other public–private partnerships in various combinations result in opaque arrangements which are often difficult to study because access to information, such as contractual arrangements between government and commercial companies, is kept private and not usually available in the public domain (not even under freedom of information requests).

It is not simply that the public–private dichotomy, on which understandings of privatization usually rest, is unclear and becoming increasingly murky. A second problem is that even when privatization is incorporated within national legal frameworks, local implementation is complex and can result in many variants and versions on the ground that look very different from the intended results. To take a specific example to highlight this point: Many anthropological studies have shown that the legal privatization of land in a formal sense (with the new individual owners holding land titles) reveals little about how land is actually worked, which is many cases remains in some joint or collective form, and land itself often still remains outside any commodity exchange circuit (e.g., Allina-Pisano 2008; Kaneff 1996; Verdery 2003). Legislating for privatization does not necessarily bring about independent, privately owned farming arrangements, nor does it guarantee land will acquire exchange value or become a commodity. It is from such ethnographic detail that we can problematize privatization and the public–private dichotomy on which it rests.[15]

My intention here is not to delve into great detail of critiques of either postsocialism or privatization—others have brought attention to both the problems and benefits in a far more comprehensive way than I can do here. My aim, through the brief discussion provided above, is to highlight that both terms make use of different ways of categorizing, in order to talk about social change. Postsocialism relies on creating a broad, sweeping distinction between two perceived forms of political economy—socialism and capitalism—and rests on a temporal and spatial East/West dichotomy. The other term, privatization, rests on a distinction of a lower analytical order, based on a division between public and private. Both concepts are useful tools for analysis that highlight important general trends and patterns. They enable comparison, but at the expense of important context specificities that are often vital for understanding the intricacies of processes of change.

What is needed is some means of analysis that can accommodate comparison but also take into account important ethnographic details. Macrolevel (privatization) studies, for example, cannot provide important contextual details. Ethnographically rich studies can, but the frameworks used, such as postsocialist and privatization, tend toward the dichotomization of social life—east/west, socialist/postsocialist, public–private—and rely on an abrupt way of demarcating the past from the present. A more useful approach would be one that does not rely on a history of rupture or on tools that are politically/ideologically grounded dichotomies. My approach, which focuses on the valuation/revaluation of resources through use-exchange-mobilization, addresses some of these concerns, in that it provides a context-specific, ethnographically grounded model that is relatively politically/ideologically free from geopolitical "East" or "West" associations. At the same time, it is fluid, presenting social change as a more smooth and continuous process, rather than one that is abrupt or dichotomous. In this way, comparison is a more rigorous tool that can be operationalized across time and space. In short, I am advocating moving from a less precise macro or meso level of analysis, offered by postsocialism and privatization, to a context-specific focus of concrete, ethnographically observed phenomena that has comparative applicability based on a study of resources and their valuation/revaluation.

I now develop resource valuation/revaluation as a mode of analysis that can shed light on processes of social change.

## Resources

Resources are essential building blocks of society. All societies need resources of a wide kind and have mechanisms for their allocation, although there is considerable variation in what is considered a resource, how it is controlled, managed, used, and exchanged. This makes it all the more surprising that so little attention has been given in anthropology to the conceptualization of resources. There are many studies that focus on particular *types* of resources—on land, water, oil and so on—although resource itself, as a concept, is relatively untheorized.[16] While there is a strong argument to be made for the development of a conceptualization of resources, the aim here is far more modest: to focus on resources as a means by which to examine processes of social change. This stems from a primary interest in the role of resources during times of political-economic reform. To this end, I focus on the revaluation of resources that takes place under conditions of transformation, such as the case of postsocialist Europe since 1989–1991, when incorporation into the capitalist world economy demanded a fundamental shift in the ownership of, and control over, a wide range of resources.

A general perusal of the literature points to a wide, indeed arguably infinite, range of phenomena that can potentially be resources: from forms of technology, skills, the past, the future, and all forms of knowledge (cultural, scientific) as well as labor (human and animal), to elements both organic (animals, insects) and inorganic (soil, water). Resources can be material or immaterial, natural or cultural, renewable and nonrenewable, finite or apparently limitless. All societies use resources, but the making of resources, and how they are allocated, managed, and controlled, is always specific to time and place, and dependent on different technologies operating within different political-economic milieus. What is a resource in a hunter-gatherer society may not be a resource in an agriculturally based society. Also, resources can be "different things to different people at the same time" (Richardson and Weszkalnys 2014, 16). For example, in some sites in post-socialist Europe, rural land has become an arena for contestation between different interest groups, such as between those developing rural areas as holiday or tourist locations, and others who use the same place for agricultural activities (e.g., Sikor et al. 2017). Further, resources are transformed over time. Some resources are exhausted—oil is a finite resource—or become replaced as new knowledge or technologies are developed (e.g., sustainable energies such as solar and wind energy are replacing nuclear energy and fossil fuels as countries make political decisions to turn away from non-sustainable and potentially toxic forms of energy). Some resources have a long lifetime and appear permanent (e.g., air, land), although they may be transformed over time (e.g., due to pollution or desertification). Others have short cycles in history: A material example would be the canal system in Britain, which had a relatively brief lifespan of approximately thirty years as a transport infrastructure, before the new technology of steam-driven train engines took its place.[17]

In summary, all manner of things can potentially be resources. At the same time, a wide range of agents at various levels of organizations are involved in the making of resources—from individuals, households, and kin groups to the largest of collectivities: rural communities, NGOs, transnational corporations, states, and even supranational organizations, such as the EU. One of the main challenges when trying to build a suitable conceptualization of resources is precisely the fact that the concept needs to be broad enough in order to incorporate just about everything in existence, while at the same time flexible enough to take into account any particular type of resource in any specific temporal and spatial context. The notion of resources lacks conceptual clarity because "It seems too inclusive at some times and too restrictive at others" (Uchibori 2011, 143).

My starting point is to consider material and immaterial resources together. In advocating such a position, I am returning to, and building on, a pre–World War II tradition. Zimmermann (1933, 24, 112) acknowledged and tried to account for a wide range of resources from the natural environment—inorganic (soil, climate) and organic (animals). Zimmermann (1933) also considered the social environment, which he divided into two orders: the first, tangible changes to the natural environment (such as tools, roads, churches, domesticated animals), the second, intangible cultural changes to the natural environment (such as knowledge and acquired skills). More recently, Uchibori (2011) and Ferry and Limbert (2008) have also taken the inquiry in this direction. In the case of the former, resources are separated into two main spheres: ecological (including nature, body, space, and subsistence) and symbolic (culture, knowledge, money, products), with the former providing the raw materials while the symbolic sphere attributes meaning to them (Uchibori 2011, 146). Unlike Zimmermann (1933) or Uchibori (2011), I view the social world as more than a filter for giving meaning to the ecological sphere, it is also a source for the creation and harnessing of resources.[18] Ferry and Limbert's (2008) understanding of resources also includes a wide range: from those more conventionally discussed (e.g., oil) to more immaterial forms, such as knowledge and historical documents. Yet, their conceptualization is largely focused on natural resources, while their discussion of immaterial resources is rather restricted, and seems in the end to reduce such resources to their material form.[19] Nevertheless, I share with both these latter studies an interest in moving a conceptualization of resources beyond materials designated as physical or material, and in so doing, advocate the value of considering material and nonmaterial together.

Such a position is at variance with most contemporary anthropological approaches to resources, which focus overwhelmingly on natural or material resources (Richardson and Weszkalnys 2014; Franquesa 2019).[20] The anthropological interest in infrastructure deserves a special mention as perhaps the most recent attempt to theorize material resources of a particular type—networks which enable exchanges of goods, people and ideas—such as roads, water systems or media structures. These provide an entry point into various processes of social life (Larkin 2013, 328). Interestingly, the anthropological study of infrastructure recognizes, from a very different perspective from my own on resources, the nonmaterial and ideational/imaginative aspects of material infrastructures, as well as the worth of such objects in analyzing processes of social change (Harvey and Knox 2015).[21] Nevertheless, the starting point of analysis remains grounded in the study of a physical phenomenon (Larkin 2013, 329).

Immaterial resources have not been ignored as much as confined to quite separate domains of the anthropological literature. So much of anthropology, across a range of theoretical approaches and research topics, could be seen as studies of immaterial resources that it is difficult to place such work within particular subfields of the discipline. Various approaches such as symbolic anthropology, or topics of research on intellectual and cultural property, the study of identity, ritual, and religion, among others, engage with immaterialities. Anything on the topic of the uses of culture could be about immaterial resources (even though the term "resource" is rarely used in such contexts[22]). For example, under particular circumstances, identity might be discussed as an immaterial resource belonging to a particular group, while traditional embroidery might be a material resource of this same ethnic group. Yet, identity is seldom or explicitly discussed as a resource.[23] Bourdieu's (1986) work on different forms of capital—social, cultural and economic (a list that has been extended by Bourdieu and others, see Neveu 2018, 21, 23)—is a good example of what, for now, I call immaterial resources.[24] It is from the juxtaposition between different resources—a conceptualization that exists at a level of abstraction higher than the consideration of either material or immaterial resources separately—that we can gain a further insight into the nature of resources. It provides a useful comparative position from which to enhance our conceptualization of resources. Such a position also allows us to take into account the many varied sites of struggle and tensions taking place in daily life in postsocialist contexts, which extend beyond material resources, but are also played out through contestations over immaterial resources. It is in considering such a diverse range of resources together, that we gain insights into the extent of social change following reforms.

## From "Sources" to (Social and Natural) "Resources"

People convert sources into resources. Human involvement is always implicated in the making of a resource, although the mode of intervention may vary. Resources are a result of an interdependency between "agents and environments" (Uchibori 2011, 144). The process of resource making involves transformation and human intervention (in many cases, exploitation might be a more appropriate term). Resources do not just exist out there, waiting to be discovered, they are made, unmade and remade through human effort, produced through the interplay of both mental and material practices (Franquesa 2019, 76). This characteristic is frequently applied to resources from the natural environment, but it works equally well for the social environment.

In their edited volume, Ferry and Limbert (2008, 84) identify the importance of human labor in the process of resource formation (see Franquesa 2019, 84). Citing both John Locke's classic work on the importance of human labor in the creation of property, and Karl Marx's refinement of the concept of labor "as appropriation," they argue that resources bring together the basic elements of nature and labor (Ferry and Limbert 2008, 8). Labor transforms something from its original, untouched state into a resource and is a necessary ingredient—along with a perceived use—in the production of resources. Labor can take different forms: Besides the traditional physical effort necessary in the harnessing of material resources, Ferry and Limbert (2008, 17n30) propose that the activity of discovering a new species—scientific work—or the "labor of documenting," or "preserving, archiving and manufacturing significant documents" can all be forms of labor. I concur and add that in the case of many immaterial resources, labor might even include the work of human thought. It was something Marx was well aware of when he wrote, "productive expenditure of human brains, nerves, and muscles" are all part of human labor (Marx 2015 [1887], 32). In all cases, it is human effort that is needed to transform a source into a resource: be this physical labor, the mental activity of human thought, or some combination thereof, including communication or forms of documentation (writing, etc.).

Human effort gives resources both a dynamic and also transformative quality, that is, resources transform and are transformed.[25] Such dynamism becomes clearer when we contrast resource with source. The beginning, the virgin state, is always the source, which "precedes . . . human activity" (Uchibori 2011, 143), while resource is the drawing of the source into the human world. Uchibori's (2011, 144) definition of resources as, "something that, being activated dynamically by human action, gives in its turn dynamic power to human life," emphasizes the interactive qualities associated with resources. Human activity both shapes and transforms resources, and in so doing, environments are transformed, new wants and needs evolve, and this in turn results in the making of new resources and the unmaking of others, as well as the shaping and reshaping of environments. Resources are, "always in flux and open-ended" (Richardson and Weszkalnys 2014, 16). Further, diverse human activity brings together the interaction of various resources, not in any linear form, but in a far more complicated manner, interweaving and creating various hierarchical dependencies in such a way so that "the entire structure of resource chains forms highly complex ones" (Uchibori 2011, 145; Zimmermann 1933, 9).[26]

As resources are created through human intervention, and something that we harness or mine from our surroundings, I see no reason why resources cannot also be considered to come from the socially constituted world that remains many orders removed from nature. In so doing, I am analytically separating the resource environment (a term I borrow from Richardson and Weszkalnys [2014]) into a natural and social one, recognizing, at the same time, that doing so comes with certain problems. The relationship between humans and environment is complicated and entangled; any attempt to make clear where the influence of the natural environment ends and a cultural one begins, and vice versa, is near impossible. Further, such nature-culture delineations are a legacy that reproduce a modernist dichotomy (Richardson and Weszkalnys 2014, 6; Franquesa 2019, 80).

Despite the recognized problems, there are important advantages in conceptualizing the resource environment as both social and natural. An exclusive focus on material resources does not give sufficient attention to factors of an immaterial or intangible kind, such as history, identity, or moral authority, all of which are potential resources under particular circumstances. If one wishes to add immaterial resources to the equation—as I do—then it becomes difficult to examine these resources together, without falling back into a terminology that includes nature-culture distinctions in some manifestation. Such a conceptualization may be less problematic than we think, as long as we do not lose sight of the fact that the nature-culture division is relational, and under constant negotiation and transformation, as "resource extraction generates a constant reworking of the boundaries" (Richardson and Weszkalnys 2014, 8).[27] Indeed, it makes perfect sense that a relational framework requires the consideration of both natural and social resources. It is, further, a dichotomy that has (arguably) widespread emic value. Any disadvantages in using such a terminology are outweighed by the advantage of being able to identify not only different sources (natural and social) from which resources arise, but more importantly, examine societal struggles over meaning and value more broadly, rather than only within the narrower confines of natural resources.

Social resources can be analytically distinguished from natural resources in terms of their respective sources. In the case of social resources, the source is also a product of human intervention, of human labor in some form. A social resource would be a resource that has a human (not physical) source; that is, its source is an element from the social world and a product of the interaction between two (or more) people. A natural resource necessitates engagement of humanity with the natural world and does not necessitate (although admittedly does usually involve) social connectedness with other humans. In theory, at least, the natural resource can be produced by only one person engaging in the physical world, while social resources are created out of the interaction between at least two people. At first glance, the idea of social sources appears to go against my earlier statement that sources precede human intervention. However, this is not so when we consider human sources are those aspects in the social world that remain unharnessed or unmined, as is also the case for natural resources. Social relationships, or ideas or knowledge that are harnessed for a purpose, become a resource. Sources from the human/symbolic world are harvested or mined as social resources. Thus, friendship is a source until it gains some utilitarian value when the friend migrates and becomes a useful contact and part of a network that can be exploited for accommodation or other assistance in the migratory course. The potential for the friendship to become a resource may always be there, although it will not always be harnessed. Information/data is a source until it is mined or harvested by Facebook and Google for particular purposes.[28] In other words, social resources—as is true of natural resources—are defined through both their requirement of human labor and their perceived use value. Social resources are any social source that is utilized (for a purpose); they are driven by human intentionality, interests, and appraisal.[29]

The terms "social" and "natural" resources serve as a reminder of the different sources from which resources can emerge—social or natural. "Material" and "immaterial," while useful in revealing something about the makeup of the resources, provides no definitive indication as to the resources' source (since natural/social resources can be material or immaterial—although more often than not, natural resources have a material form). Further, and more importantly, the distinction between natural and social resources becomes particularly useful when we examine the nature of social change in postsocialist contexts, for struggles take place over a wide range of resources. A focus exclusively on natural resources would not provide a sufficient picture of the total impact of reform policies on the community, nor would it shed light on particular forms of contestation and arenas for new power struggles, or on the way in which the communities are shaped and transformed by resources and their revaluation.

## THE USE AND EXCHANGE VALUE OF RESOURCES

Convertibility of a raw material, a source into a resource, presupposes a human "appraisal" (Zimmermann 1933, 3). Resources satisfy a desire, need, or want, and thus have a perceived use. Resources are therefore understood in the broad sense of "provisioning;" they fulfill the needs and wants of a wide set of actors across a wider range of collectivities, and in different political economies (Polanyi 1957, 248). Since the particular forms that wants and needs take are always culturally defined and specific to particular groups at particular locations in time and space, the use is seen as inextricably linked to the properties of the resource, that is, to the use to which the resource can be put. Thus, "The utility of a thing makes it a use value," and "use value becomes a reality only by use or consumption" (Marx 2015 [1887], 27). A resource can have use value without being part of any circuit of exchange. Indeed, all resources have use value independent of any potential or actual value they may have in terms of exchangeability.

Although some resources have only use value and lie outside any circuits of exchange, others also have value in some socially mediated form that enables comparison (partly derived from the labor needed to produce the resource) and conversion. In other words, they are tradable and have value as exchangeable items (Marx 2015 [1887], 34). There are various forms of exchange, which include market transactions or personal transfers. Anthropologists have highlighted that in any society, the circulation of items occurs through a range of distinct kinds of exchange (Davis 1992, 30). Circuits/spheres of exchange, where things perceived of equal value can be exchanged, are always embedded in wider political and cultural forces—including in property rights, legal regulations, religious sanctions and so on (Davis 1992, 44).[30] Capitalist market exchanges are seen as a dominant form of exchange in many places, where an ever-increasing number of objects are given value as commodities and made exchangeable through the universal standard of money. The use of money also makes more transparent the element of scarcity[31] in an exchange system, and in turn, scarcity creates the conditions for new forms of social tensions and conflicts, such as between buyers and sellers, or producers and users (Zimmermann 1933, 22). Thus, the introduction of money has a "revolutionary" impact on resource appraisal (on human needs and wants), revaluing resources and the environment (Zimmermann 1933, 22).

There are, of course, many other circuits of exchange that have been discussed by anthropologists. The classic work by Bohannan

(1955) revealed how three separate spheres of exchange operated in a hierarchical arrangement within Tiv society, before the introduction of general-purpose money eventually undermined the previous system. Work on the "economy of favours" points to another distinct form of nonmonetary exchange that has been observed across a wide range of postsocialist states (Ledeneva 1998; Henig and Makovicky 2017). An economy of favors is "a distinct mode of action which has economic consequences, without being fully explicable in terms of transactional cost-benefit analysis" (Henig and Makovicky 2017, 4). It relies on (personalized) socially-entrenched economic relations and creates social relatedness, while at the same time has economic implications (Henig and Makovicky 2017, 4). As a form of exchange, it operates outside a monetary system and cannot be explained by it.[32]

In short, resources have use value and many may also have exchange value. It is at this point, that the potential of "resources" as an analytical tool for understanding processes of social change becomes evident. I suggest that it is through tracking the movement of resources between systems of use and circuits of exchange that processes of social change can be identified and understood. That is, resource mobility can provide a useful way of talking about the effects of political-economic reforms. Before I develop this point further, I first need to say something about value.

Resources have value.[33] Indeed, value is intrinsic to all resources—through their (perceived) use and the labor by which they are created, and through their (capacity for) exchange.[34] In the previous section and above, I have identified the importance of "use" and "labor" (defined in the broadest sense) in the (re/un)making of resources. It is human appraisal (the denoting of something as having a use) and human effort (expending energy, both mental and physical) that transforms a source into a resource. To make explicit what is already implicit in the above discussion: A resource has intrinsic value through its (perceived) use and the work/energy invested in the (re/un)making of a resource. It is both of these—use and labor—that gives resources their "value." Value may also be gained through the resource's potential for exchange, although some resources remain outside any circuits of exchange (monetary or nonmonetary). Thus, the baseline is always use and labor; exchange may be present only as a latent possibility.

Revaluation occurs when there is a shift in the way a natural or social resource is utilized (through applied human effort) and/or in the way it is exchanged. That is, the mobilization of resources takes place through their reallocation, through new ownership arrangements, through new forms of control and new types of management. There are many reasons for the mobilization of resources, and countless catalysts that initiate resource revaluations, including: the development of new technologies, new environmental conditions, or the introduction of new laws and legislation. Here, my specific interest is in mobilizations introduced through the political-economic reforms often denoted as "postsocialist" (or "neoliberal") that were initiated across the former East Europe and the former USSR after 1989–1991. They resulted in the transformation of resources' values in terms of use and/or exchange. When I speak about the valuation/revaluation of resources, I am talking about their changing status (mobility), between systems of use and circuits of exchange.[35]

The shifting of resources between use and exchange values, or within systems of use or within circuits of exchange, was a crucial dimension of reforms initiated across the former socialist world. Many of the basic resources that in capitalist countries have both use and exchange value were, in socialist states, resources with use but little or no exchange value (at least not as monetary market exchanges). In the Soviet case, resources might have been exchanged as commodities in the market, but it was by no means the only or arguably the most important arena for exchange. *Blat*, or favors—through personal connections between family, friends, colleagues etc.—were often a vital and nonmonetary way of attaining goods and services (Ledeneva 1998). That is, while resources were embedded in a circuit of exchange, the form of exchange was an "economy of favours" (see Henig and Makovicky 2017), rather than, or sometimes alongside, a monetary form. The following chapters focus on the increased tensions and new divisions, as well as sometimes the creation of new solidarities, that are a consequence of resource revaluation. The movement of resources and their revaluation raises issues relating to ownership, access, control, and management that are core to understanding contemporary conflicts/solidarities. Here, I summarize the three underlying forms of resource revaluation that are the source of the tensions/

alliances detailed in the ethnographic chapters. See the Conclusion for a more general discussion that draws together the findings of the individual chapters.

First, the shifting of resources can take place within what I call "systems of use." Chapters 1 and 2 provide examples of this form of resource mobilization. "Systems of use" describe transfers within the same value category and denote different ways in which any particular resource can be utilized. Shifts within systems of use occur when resources lose their previous use and gain a new use, or the original use is modified or added to in some way, so that it takes on a different or modified use. The resource may move between different use values as a result of new labor activities (greater intensity or different types), new ownership, or control or management arrangements. This is essentially what happened in the case of enterprise (former collective) land (chapter 1) and household plots (chapter 2): The agricultural collectives were the main providers of household consumption goods (e.g., food) and services (e.g., domestic water); household plots were used far less extensively during (pre-Soviet and) Soviet times. Following decollectivization and land privatization, the new enterprises (that worked the former collective land) were no longer responsible for provisioning households. They dramatically reduced the variety of crops they grew and eliminated some other uses to which they had put the land (e.g., animal husbandry). At the same time, villagers became increasingly reliant on their own household plots as a source of food; that is, they were forced to make greater use of their household land. In both cases, the uses of the land have changed and appear inversely correlated: As one has reduced the variety of ways in which the land is used (former collective land), the other has broadened its land use activities (household land).

Second, resources can move from one exchange circuit to another. Both chapters 3 and 4 provide examples of such resource mobility. As in the previous instance, the shift in this case is also limited to mobility within the same value category: This time, the focus is on the shifts of movement between and within (monetary and nonmonetary) circuits of exchange. For example, the shift in value could be from a nonmonetary to a monetary circuit, as in the case of water (chapter 3). Or it could involve the resource being divided through the creation of two separate, nonmonetary exchange circuits operating in parallel, as in the case of moral authority (chapter 4). It could also be that a resource moves from a monetary to nonmonetary exchange (e.g., collectivised land [chapter 1], provided a salary to workers in Soviet times, but after the reforms, the newly formed enterprises offered no work and thus no monetary income for the vast majority). Many of the informal economy and sharing activities in the Soviet context were based on exchanges of a nonmonetary form (e.g., blat or barter). Some of these have more recently entered a monetary exchange circuit. One example is the case of household water (Chapter 3), where there has been a shift in value from a nonmonetary to a monetary circuit. The resource was free during Soviet times and had exchangeable value in several different nonmonetary circuits: as an entitlement received by workers from their agricultural collective; as part of an economy of favors that allowed some villagers to jump the queue and have water delivered faster through their connections to the collective delivery personnel; and through the sharing of water between neighboring households in times of need. The newly increased demand for water following land privatization, alongside the transferring of the control of the resource from the former collectives to the village council, which established a communal company to manage the resource, was a means to commodify water through the installation of meters and the charging of a fee to households for usage. This represented a long-term revaluation of the resource, from a nonmonetary to monetary form of exchange.

The immaterial (social) resource of moral authority (chapter 4) provides another example of how shifts in resource value can take place within the same category of exchange. In this case, the return of the priest to the village meant that the villagers' spiritual world had to be renegotiated to accommodate the reincorporation of religious practices alongside traditional customs. The resource was divided up between those who guided the practices and thus held moral authority: the priest as the religious leader, and village practitioners of traditions. With the reincorporation of the priest back into village life, and consequent division of the resource between religion and tradition, new forms of tensions emerged within the village as the priest and traditional practitioners (often sponsored by the mayor) vied for influence. The resolution was ultimately the sharing of the moral authority resource between leaders who offered villagers the opportunity to engage in distinct and often competing circuits of nonmonetary exchange that were based on a show of loyalty in return for (moral) guidance and other spiritual services. The revaluation of the resource in this example involved the division of moral authority through distinct nonmonetary exchanges that operated in parallel.

A third form of revaluation occurs when resources attain exchange value when previously they only had use value. Chapter 5 on identity provides an example of a resource that jumps value categories: a shift from use-only to also attaining exchange value. Such a movement is commonly associated with entry into a capitalist economy; for example, reform processes such as privatization have been important driving forces in giving monetary exchange value to resources that used to have only use value. However, while resources can gain a monetary exchange value (and thus become commodities), this need not be the case, and resources can also attain value through participation in a nonmonetary exchange circuit. Chapter 5 provides examples of both instances: The identity resource gained monetary exchange value in some situations and nonmonetary exchange value in others. In previous Soviet times, the resource had use value—Bregans' ethnicity was denoted in their passports as "Bulgarian," and this identification existed alongside their broader Soviet citizenship. In an independent Ukraine, identities have been revalued: Bregans' Bulgarian ethnicity was reworked as part of a designated Ukrainian "minority." Such a status did not create many exchange opportunities nationally, but it did provide exchange opportunities regionally and transnationally. Regional exchanges were based on villagers' connections to the Bessarabian[36] area and focused on marriage and (often) related trade activities. Transnational exchanges—based on Bregans' ancestral homeland of Bulgaria and long historical associations with Russia—existed through trading, migration, employment, and educational opportunities. For example, Bulgarians from the Republic of Bulgaria bought local handicrafts from (ethnic Bulgarian) Ukrainian villagers, apparently to display in museums in Bulgaria. Exchange opportunities through migration and work (labor for an income) have also been established. Bregans' identity as a Bulgarian minority in Ukraine is a revalued resource that has acquired exchange value both in a regional and transnational context.

In sum, the revaluation of resources takes place in three different possible ways. Some resources move within value categories: first, from one system of usage to another, or second, between circuits of exchange, such as from an economy of favors (nonmonetary) to a market economy (monetary). A third way is that resources can jump value categories, such as when resources with previously only use value are given exchange value (often but not necessarily associated with monetary exchanges in a market economy). Chapters 1 through 5 provide specific examples of the three forms of resource mobilizations/revaluations discussed above. They also look at the different types of conflicts and/or alliances that resulted from such revaluations: between use systems (chapters 1 and 2); between exchange circuits (chapters 3 and 4); and from use to exchange (chapter 5).

The above constitutes my theoretical framework of social change, which is founded on recognizing the importance of the mobilization and the revaluation of resources. However, as I have indicated above, there is another part to the analysis as the revaluation of resources has an impact on social relations. The effect of resource revaluation is a disruption of social relations: struggles over the ownership, control, and distribution of, and access to, resources. Resource mobility (whether within or between use and exchange) creates new sites of contestation, and these are manifested through the conflicts and tensions, as well as the new solidarities and alliances that characterize life. This provides the second part of my analytical framework: When resources shift in value and there is an associated change in their ownership, control, management, and so on, then the consequence is the rise of new tensions/conflicts and new solidarities/alliances.

It is through the mobilizations of resources that we can explore the impact on communities following reforms. I have not elaborated on the nature of the tensions and conflicts that accompany the revaluations of the resources discussed above—that is the focus of the ethnographic chapters to follow, and the brief chapter summary provided in the following section—but the effect of such movements is by no means harmonious. Shifts in how resources are re/valued, within and between use and exchange, are an arena for claims and counterclaims over ownership, access, and control, between different individuals and groups in the community and beyond. Such processes, in turn, are fundamental to understanding contemporary conflicts and tensions evident in the community. They are, in short, a means to understanding social change. These analytical points will become clearer in the chapters that follow.

## CHAPTER CONTENT

The book can be read in two different ways: as a monograph, or as a collection of individual essays. Read in totality, the book functions as a monograph, providing a picture of life in Brega during a period of particular upheaval during the important decades following the collapse of the USSR. The study focuses on the many tensions of rural life, within the community as well as between the village and the "outside," that have emerged as a result of contestations over a range of resources. At the same time, every empirical chapter is self-contained and can be read as a separate study. In this latter sense, the book is a collection of essays, each of which focuses on a different resource: enterprise land, household plots, water, moral authority, and identity. These resources provide an entry point for focusing on particular local relationships and the conflicts/alliances resulting from their valuation/revaluation: between "ordinary" villagers and agricultural leaders (enterprise land, chapter 1); between kin (household land, chapter 2); between neighbors (water, chapter 3); between the village priest and the rest of the community (moral authority, chapter 4); and between the village and "outsiders," regional, national and transnational (identity, chapter 5). Individual chapters provide an insight into new forms of community solidarity and the divisions arising from the revaluation of a particular resource as a result of the reforms. They acknowledge that resources are always embedded in, and expressions of, social relations, and a change in the ownership/control of resources results in the reconfiguration of these relations.

Each ethnographic chapter has two purposes. First, it gives focus to one resource and provides a detailed discussion of the nature of the particular revaluation following political-economic reforms: how it is an example of the shift from one use to another; or of one type of exchange to another; or of jumping categories between use and exchange. This analytical discussion is taken up again at the end of each chapter. The second purpose of each chapter is to focus on the way in which relationships in the community (and beyond) have been impacted and disrupted by the particular resource revaluation under discussion. The primary ethnographic material revolves around the different tensions and/or alliances that have arisen as a result of resource revaluation.

Chapter 1 is the first of five ethnographic chapters and provides an example of how a resource can shift from one use to another. Its focus is on the changing value of enterprise—former kolkhozes and sovkhozes—land from one use to another, and the social frictions that were bound up with this process. More specifically, the revaluation of the land involved a contraction in usage: from having a wide range of uses to a more restricted provisioning of the household. During Soviet times, the land maintained households in three main ways, providing: subsidized crops (foodstuffs for consumption); a range of entitlements and services (school breakfasts for the children; water for domestic consumption etc.); and salaries. The latter enabled villagers to engage in Soviet markets and consumption. All these uses were based on an exchange that depended on villagers being employed by the collectives. However, the foodstuffs and services were a limited exchange: one-off transactions exclusively used to provision the household. It was only the salaries that provided an opportunity to engage in an exchange (monetary) circuit. In contemporary times, the land's use value was dramatically reduced: Households were no longer provisioned through subsidized foods and services, and the vast majority had also lost their work and with it any access to a salary. Instead, as landowners, villagers rented out their land to the four men who led the new agricultural enterprises. In return, villagers received a rent that was paid in kind: grain. In the vast majority of cases, the rent was used entirely to maintain the household. It was only the lessees who had access to any of the profits from the land, and therefore any opportunities to engage in monetary exchange circuits. All profits were concentrated in the hands of the lessees, while the majority of landowners struggled to make ends meet. Thus, with the revaluation of the land, new divisions crystallized between landowners and lessees. It was essentially a story of rising inequalities and discord, based on the relationship between those who leased and had control over the land (as well as unprecedented opportunities for profits), and the landowners, who received a set nonmonetary rent that barely provisioned the household and excluded them from any opportunities to engage in the market, while at the same time depriving them of control over the land and how it was used. The division was a consequence of the land's revaluation, its decreasing use value for the majority in the community.

In chapter 2, the focus remains on the resource of land, but the interest is on household plots. Much as in the case of enterprise land, the resource of household plots is also an example of how a resource can shift from one system of use to another. However, in this case use value has increased as support in the form of employment and foodstuffs from the new agricultural enterprises has declined. Correspondingly, the importance of household land (a term I use interchangeably with "plots") has changed dramatically: from having a minimal and supplementary role in the maintenance of the family and household economy during Soviet times (when the collectives provided most of the villagers' consumption needs), to taking on the central role as main provisor in contemporary times. This process of the revaluation of household land from one use to another impacted household relations: It contributed to an increasing importance of, and reliance on, kin whose responsibilities in household production increased along with the greater burden of activities. I suggest that internally—within households—such an increased range of activities reinforced, if not expanded, family divisions based on age and gender. Externally, mutual assistance between kin from different households ensured the reproduction of the household and its members. Households relied on other households for additional help, especially when they engaged in the production of cash crops (the only source of income for many). In the process, households of "close" kin were strengthened, while links to other households made up of more "distant" kin were weakened. The engagement in cash crop production, which demanded reciprocal labor exchanges between households, was the basis of new solidarities that operated alongside age and gender divisions within households. Such new alliances and divisions were a consequence of the household land's new and increased use value.

The increasing importance of household land also resulted in the rising need for water. In chapter 3, the focus is on water as a resource that has been revalued: from being exchanged in a few nonmonetary exchange circuits to a commodity in a monetary exchange circuit. In Soviet times, water for households was free and not in great demand, as most of the villagers' personal food consumption needs were supplied by subsidized produce from the agricultural collectives. The new significance given to water since the disestablishment of the agricultural collectives was a result of households' growing reliance on their plots for the cultivation of crops, at the same time as store-bought foodstuffs became too expensive in what had developed into a cash-poor community with high unemployment. At the same time, national water reforms decentralized control of the resource and encouraged its private management. The chapter focuses on water as it was transferred from the control of the former collectives to the village council, and the challenges faced by the communal company established to manage the resource and transform water into a commodity for which villagers had to pay. The resultant growing animosities and divisions between neighboring households centered on nontransparent local price arrangements, as well as differential access to water, as neighbors competed for the precious resource.

Chapter 4, on moral authority, is the first of two chapters that focuses on an immaterial (social) resource. It provides another example (alongside water) of a resource that has shifted between two forms of exchange. In this case, the resource was divided into two separately operating, nonmonetary exchange circuits. With the restoration of the village church and return of a priest to the village, new sites of contestation arose between figures who possessed moral authority, that is, those who played a prominent role in the spirituality of villagers. The community's spiritual world was split along the lines of formal religion (the Orthodox Church and the priest as its representative) and traditional Bulgarian practices (sponsored by the mayor, village council, and the rest of the village). Villagers were unwilling to denounce—as the priest demanded—their traditional "pagan" practices that were integral to their everyday life and local identity. Thus, the resource of moral authority became the focal point of competition: The mayor and priest—as representatives of the respective institutions of tradition and religion—vied for moral authority and influence in the community. This competition took place through villagers' attendance of, and displays of support for, religious and traditional events, in return for services that provided (moral) guidance, spiritual healing and community solidarity. The distinct exchange circuits operated by those with moral authority provided an uneasy arrangement that reinserted the priest back into village life (albeit in a restricted capacity), while enabling the continued practice of traditions. Moral authority was transformed into a shared resource between the priest and mayor, although the sharing was a division that granted the priest only limited influence in the community.

The final ethnographic chapter (chapter 5) gives central attention to identity. It provides an example of a social resource that jumped categories from having use value to one that has now also acquired exchange value (monetary as well as nonmonetary). Located in an ethnically mixed region, the village of Brega, with its overwhelmingly Bulgarian population, finds itself at the margins of the new nation state as part of a designated "minority." While the Ukrainian constitution guarantees the rights of minority groups, the pursuit for national unity based on only one state language (Ukrainian), and a history based on a selected past, provided little scope for the active inclusion of citizens who did not share these linguistic/historical attributes. As a consequence, a Bregan identity had little exchange value in the national arena. At the same time, villagers' multilayered identity (as bilingual speakers with close connections to several ethnic groups and nation-states) presented various regional and transnational exchange opportunities. Bregans shared a migratory past with other inhabitants in the region, that entailed an alliance to Russia against their historical enemy the Ottomans. This presented opportunities for exchange through marriage, which in turn led to new trading possibilities. Regional trading and bartering also occurred through other forms of relatedness—between kin, acquaintances and so on. Villagers also had considerable opportunities for transnational connections with the Republic of Bulgaria, as well as with Russia—the community had long and close historical and cultural associations to both in different ways. Through their transnational ties, alliances were created via trading, migration, and economic exchanges, some of which held monetary advantages, some of which had nonmonetary exchange value. Such an identity presented few national advantages for the "minority"—instead, it was a potential source of marginalization and tensions. However, from a regional and transnational perspective, the identity resource provided considerable potential for exchanges that created new (or built on previously established) solidarities.

In the Conclusion, I return to a more general discussion of resources, drawing attention to how the particular conflicts and alliances of my ethnographic case provides the basis for a theory of social change. A focus on resource revaluation gives ethnographic substance to macro and meso studies that present the reforms as a specific form of capitalist expansion. If we explore the changes in terms of the mobility of resources, we see the greater intricacies that are masked by postsocialist and privatization approaches. Resource revaluations provide a more nuanced way to talk about the social upheaval that is manifested in different locations around the world, as a result of similar (neoliberal) processes. I conclude by emphasizing the greater relevance offered by this study: While the revaluation of resources is particularly important in contemporary (rural) Ukraine, a result of the deliberate drive to reconfigure a wide range of resources in alignment with ongoing reform goals, it is by no means limited to this part of the world. The struggles over resource valuation/revaluation, the (re/un)making of resources, as well as the tensions, new alliances and inequalities generated as a result, are evident across communities in postsocialist Eurasia and beyond, as resources take on new value and meaning in the global capitalist economy.

## IN THE FIELD

When I first traveled to Ukraine in June 2000 for a month to explore possible fieldwork sites, my original intention was to study property relations.[37] It was from an initial position of an interest in "land" (that originated with my earlier work in Bulgaria), that I decided to extend my study to include different types of properties. In part, this was a consequence of what was happening on the ground; Soviet collectives were far more ubiquitous, and thus their dismantling had far greater impact than their counterparts in other rural communities across socialist Europe. I soon realized that various material properties need to be considered alongside nonmaterial forms, as sites of contestation extended well beyond the bounds of the former. Over the years, I gradually came to the conclusion that in a study of social change, a focus on "properties" could be more fruitfully conceptualized, and comparatively explored, as different types of "resources" (Kaneff 2021a).

My search for a suitable village on the basis of ethnicity—I visited almost 50 Bulgarian villages in the Odessa Oblast—was for the purely practical reason relating to my own language skills as a fluent speaker of the Bulgarian language. Some two centuries after the initial migration of Bulgarians to the region, the minority retain strong linguistic and cultural connections to their ancestral homeland. This made the area an attractive choice for a fieldwork site. I conversed with villagers in Bulgarian and on the odd occasions, when necessary, in Russian (although my comprehension skills in Russian always remained stronger than my oral skills).[38] In an area so ethnically diverse, a knowledge of Moldovan/Romanian and Gagauz would have been an added bonus in order to communicate with natives from neighboring villages in their own insider languages. There were not many situations that demanded this approach, as my focus of study was very much rooted in Brega (and migration and other community ties took me to the district townships and Odessa more often than to neighboring villages). However, one such event was when I attended a wedding in a nearby Moldovan village (the bride was from Brega—see chapter 5). At this celebration, I conversed using the same language as all other guests, the lingua franca, Russian. The occasion never arose when I needed Ukrainian, as it was not spoken or used in this part of the country (my limited comprehension skills of the state language were thus sufficient for the situation).

I returned to Ukraine in October of the same year to begin my fieldwork. During the following years (2000–2004) I completed over a year's fieldwork in total that covered every month of the year.[39] A decade was to pass between this primary fieldwork and my next trip to Brega in 2014. In between (and after 2014), I kept in touch mainly through phone calls, although occasionally also by post (the region was not connected to internet, and did not have reliable mobile phone coverage until relatively recently). Carrying out the year plus of fieldwork over some years had advantages: helping to develop relationships of trust as villagers witnessed my long-term commitment to the community through my regular return trips. It also gave me the benefit of seeing how things changed over longer periods of time. It is important to add, while the last fieldtrip provided me with an opportunity to hear village views on the war that had erupted in the east of the country, I have not carried out fieldwork since the escalation of the war in 2022, and thus cannot make any claims to know the present views from the region. Thus, this study stops short of 2021. Nevertheless, the long-term ethnography over a two-decade period provides insights into a Ukrainian minority's experiences and challenges since the country's independence (see chapter 5). This in turn offers the reader a background appreciation of what can be understood as one long-term cause of the present war.I do not make any claims or conclusions relating to the war beyond this.

Given my previous work in Bulgaria, I could not help but make comparisons. At least in terms of agricultural production, the two regions were similar: both areas are lowlands influenced by the Danube River (with my Bulgarian site to the south of the river, and the Brega one to the north), known for their fertile soils and undulating landscape that are conducive to horticulture—fruit and vegetables—as well as viticulture and the growing of various grains. However, here the comparison ends. Brega is located on a lake's edge, which while providing a source of fresh fish, made the village—much like the rest of the region that is pervaded by large lakes and smaller waterways—swampy and attractive to mosquitos. The climate, characterized by temperature extremes, had a severity that I have not experienced elsewhere. Summer nights were so humid and stifling that I sometimes had to force myself to inhale and exhale, applying conscious effort to a breathing process that is normally automatic. At the other extreme, the winters felt extra cold because of the dampness, a feeling compounded by the lack of sufficient indoor heating (Some mornings there was ice on the inside of our windows!). The household where I lived was not one of the wealthier ones, neither in labor or monetary terms, and much like most other houses, had only running cold water from the one tap in the room where we ate our meals. There were no bathroom or clothes washing facilities (this was done in large tubs filled with buckets of water we carried by hand from the water storage tank). I bought an electric kettle, which made boiling a liter of water easier, and this was the only means of obtaining warm water for bathing over the cold winter months. A very small number of

**FIGURE I.4.** View of Brega with the Russian Orthodox Church and school (large white building to the right of the church) prominent. In the foreground are the grape vines in a household plot. All photos were taken by the author unless otherwise noted.

better-off households—usually those who had men with plumbing and carpentry skills—had their own bathrooms, but this was not the norm. In short, conditions were hard, much harder than those I had experienced in rural Bulgaria.

The situation had improved when I returned in 2014, by which time my host's end of the village had been connected to the gas infrastructure, allowing households who could afford it (many took out bank loans) to construct bathrooms and indoor toilets. To my dismay, there was still no canalization, which meant that all human waste, and worse still, chemicals from the various detergents and shampoos used, were washed directly into the soil, into a pit in front of the house.

In Brega, I lived with Valentina. Her house was conveniently located on Ulitsa Lenina, a long street (of 110 houses) that was also the address of the village council building, the former kolkhoz headquarters—now home to the new agricultural enterprises' administrators—one of the village shops, the library, and the kindergarten. These facilities were found approximately halfway along the street, while the school and the church were located behind the council building, on an adjoining road that ran perpendicular to Lenina. One could hardly refer to this arrangement as a "center," because although located within proximity of each other, the buildings are not arranged in any orderly fashion around a common square.

When I first met her in 2000, Valentina, a single parent, lived with her teenage daughter soon to start her tertiary level studies, and her elderly mother and father. By 2014, she was living alone; both her parents had died (her father just before I returned to the village in 2001). Her daughter, now grown up and with a family of her own, worked as an accountant, having married an ethnic Russian Ukrainian living in a village some 70 km north. Valentina's household became "my family," and I remain indebted to them for their many kindnesses and different forms of assistance during the time I spent with them. Valentina's extended family—aunts, uncles, and cousins—also took me into their homes and lives, sharing special occasions (birthdays, weddings, Easter etc.) and everyday trials and triumphs. Through them, I gained important insights into household economies and kinship relations, the workings of the agricultural enterprises and the impact of land reforms on families.

For the first decade or so of our acquaintance, Valentina (a librarian by training) was employed in the village council, as secretary to the village mayor. In this capacity, she introduced me to those who worked in the village council. This constituted another circle of contacts and was an important source of data. Council administrators and accountants, the librarian and the official in charge of local land privatization reforms all became part of my close circle of contacts. My regular presence at the village council also gave me access to the mayor (there were four different ones spanning the two decades of my research in the village). I spent many days at the village council and was able to copy vast amounts of information from the census materials, obtaining statistical information about the village from the late 1940s onward (all copied by hand, as there was no other technology available). Hanging around the council was a good way of keeping updated on the main events in the village; people with complaints regularly attended in the hope of speaking to the mayor or other council workers. I sat in on meetings of the village council (when permitted), which were normally attended by the small circle of local officials, namely: the mayor, the heads of the agricultural enterprises, the school director, the doctor, and when necessary, the priest. The village council was also a source of my social life—the council women regularly held banquets (everyone contributing food and drink) during their lunch hour at the office in celebration of their respective birthdays or other significant occasions. Sometimes, we met at their homes.

My neighborhood was another important location of social engagement and source of information. Village households consisted of houses located close to the street, set on large rectangle-shaped blocks of land that extended away from the street (see chapter 2). The houses were hidden behind high walls, usually not visible from the street. Next door to us on the one side were Marusha, a kolkhoz worker before becoming unemployed following the disestablishment of the collective, and her husband, who managed to hold onto his job in the present-day agricultural enterprise that villagers still refer to as the sovkhoz (as I do). The middle-aged couple, both of whom were distant relatives of Valentina's through different genealogical lines, were already grandparents, and their younger son and his wife also lived with them. Across the road, Luba, a kindergarten teacher, lived with her husband, who worked at the sovkhoz. By 2014, their two teenage children had grown and married out of the village. I saw Marusha and Luba on a daily basis. Summer evenings, we gathered on the street to pass time and talk, sitting on wooden benches built into the external wall of the household enclosure. Often, others from the neighborhood walking past would join us for a while before continuing on their way. When it became too cold to meet outside on the street, there would be almost daily visits to each other's homes. I kept track of what was happening in the neighborhood in this way, as well as gathering information from a large number of villagers, all of whom worked in their own household plots, and a few of whom also still had jobs in the agricultural enterprises. Conversations covered a wide range of topics that concerned them, from commentaries on national politics and international affairs, to more local concerns relating to the latest news from the agricultural enterprises.

Soon after I first moved to Brega, I sought out a Russian teacher from the school for private classes to augment those I already had before arriving. Lessons with Tanya—held on a weekly basis at her home—allowed me to establish friendships at the other end of the village. This was important, because unlike most other villages in the district that had had either a sovkhoz or kolkhoz, Brega had both. My close friendship with Tanya gave me access to information about the kolkhoz end of the village (Valentina lived within the former administrative jurisdiction of the sovkhoz, although the boundary with the kolkhoz was just one hundred or so meters further along our street, in the direction of the "center," which was itself within kolkhoz territory). Tanya was a committed church attendee (following the death of her father) and a teacher at the school. Through her, I gained access to both institutions. Tanya's agricultural land was worked in cooperation with that of other schoolteachers, and through her, I therefore also obtained information about a "social sphere" form of land arrangement (Luba belonged to another such cooperative and was another good source on this type of farming—see chapter 1). Tanya happened to live across the road from one of the private farmers with whom I also developed a close friendship.

With a population of approximately 2,400 and area of approximately two and a half square km (1,000 houses with an average of 0.25 ha), the village was too large for me to get to know everyone. However, the connections I developed over time covered a good sample from the community, from the village leaders to ordinary citizens, and included access to every type of agricultural land institution, from the agricultural enterprises to the small cooperatives, from those few individuals registered as individual private farmers to householders working their plots. My connections extended to both the sovkhoz and kolkhoz ends of the village, as well as to all main institutions: the agricultural enterprises, the village council, the school, the kindergarten, and the church. Through village contacts, I also had access to the district capital where a number of villagers held prominent positions—in government and in the cultural center. I relied on a variety of data gathering methods: primarily participant observation, but also semi-structured interviews (used especially with agricultural enterprise officials and other village officials whom I did not know so well). I collected statistical materials going back to the late 1940s that were held in the village council, local histories written by villagers and writings/research on the region from a number of academics at Odessa National University (as it was known at the time of my fieldwork) as well as scholarly (and other) publications from the Bulgarian Cultural Center in Odessa. Media sources, especially regional newspapers, were an additional source for local news, as our TV connections were unreliable, and thus rarely used.

It is perhaps a platitude to state that this book has been a long time in the making. Yet, the lengthy period of gestation brings with it a strength and added worth—the benefit of two decades of research, during which I have been able to track changes in the community and thereby develop my ideas about resource revaluation and social change.

CHAPTER 1

# ENTERPRISE LAND

## NEW AGRICULTURAL ELITE AND LANDOWNERS

The case of enterprise land—that is, land worked by the agricultural collectives in former Soviet times—is presented as an example of a resource that has shifted from one form of use value to another. The revaluation involves a shift from having a wide range of uses for village households to a much reduced and limited use.

In Soviet times, the collectivized land was useful in maintaining the household in three crucial ways: through the production of goods—fruits, vegetables, animal husbandry (meat and dairy products)—for household consumption; through services provided to households (e.g., domestic water deliveries); and through the salaries employees received. All three were a form of exchange: Employees gave their labor to the collective and received goods, services, and salaries in return. However, the former two, goods and services, were exchanges of a very limited nature—one-off, non-tradeable and nontransferable transactions—and used directly to sustain the household. As they were used for provisioning the households, I attribute their value as overwhelmingly of "use" rather than "exchange" value.[1] Only one of the three entitlements provided potential for entering an exchange circuit: The salaries that all employees received that allowed villagers to engage in Soviet consumption and markets.[2]

The implementation of reforms to privatize the land resulted in the revaluation of the resource, leading to changes in ownership, control, and management. The establishment of the new agricultural enterprises, which replaced the collectives, created a new arrangement whereby a small number of lessees rented the land from the new landowners (that included essentially all villagers). In the course of a few years, the enterprises reduced the breadth of their production, provisioning households through a much more limited number of products (primarily grain) given as rent. This exchange (land for rent) did not present any further ongoing transaction opportunities; rent was used purely to maintain the household. Soviet services were also no longer provided by the agricultural organizations but were transferred to the responsibility of the village council or completely closed down. Further, it was only a very small number of villagers, lessees and those still employed by the new agricultural enterprises, for whom the land provided any potential for engagement in the market, made possible through the profit/salaries received. This new arrangement, whereby only a small number of villagers benefitted from exchange opportunities from the land, whilst for the vast majority the land had limited use value, was a source of new conflicts and divisions in the community. At the heart of the problem were disagreements about the rent paid; discord was evident between the lessees themselves, as well as between the landowners and lessees. These tensions are explored later in the chapter.

The revaluation of land was initiated by national legislation to privatize the resource. As with so many of the different reforms in Ukraine, land privatization has been a long and drawn-out process. It was first initiated in 1991, and since then, there have been various amendments and decrees at the national level to resuscitate the momentum, a process that continues to the present day.[3] Hurdles and delays over the years have been attributed to various factors, including resistance from conservative political forces from within national parliament itself, as well as bureaucratic resistance at various other levels of government administration (Wegren 2002, 21–22, 33). Faced also with concerns to its national sovereignty, political reforms have often been prioritized above economic restructuring, and this divergence in priorities continues to split political agendas and slow down the reform process (Jarabik and de Waal 2018, 1, 5). Land reform is still ongoing. The undeveloped agricultural land market is seen as part of the "unfinished" business of agricultural land privatization and pivotal in the building of "a new Ukraine modern state" (Ukraine Reform Conference 2018, 2).[4] For the duration of the period covered in this book, the land market has remained an elusive goal, as witnessed by a moratorium on agricultural land sales introduced in 2001 as a temporary measure that continued for the following twenty years.[5]

It is hard to convey the deep impact of land reforms on the rural communities, which went well beyond the immediate effects of the privatization of land and dismantling of agricultural collectives. In the former Soviet Union, collectives were "total social institutions" (Humphrey 1995, 7; 1998, 450, 451–52, 487) that maintained the whole community in many ways beyond offering work: They provided housing for some of the workers, controlled the utilities, and contributed important support to the school, kindergarten, libraries, and cultural house among other institutions. The dismantling of the sovkhoz and kolkhoz over the course of years thus had impact not only directly on the villagers through the loss of employment, but also less directly through other related resources that were controlled or owned by the collectives: livestock, buildings, machinery, and housing. Many of the collectives' original services and utilities were also affected: water, provision of building materials, assistance to the school and kindergarten, library and so on. In Brega, the effects of land privatization were most immediately felt when workers began to be laid off from the unraveling agricultural collectives in the late 1990s, almost a decade after the reforms were implemented nationally. The impact of the reforms was compounded after the legal establishment of the new village agricultural enterprises in 2000, which during the course of a few years disengaged from providing foodstuffs to households and transferred some services to the village council while closing down other services (e.g., the communal baths). The process of divorcing the working of the former collective lands from the rest of the community took years and was a painful and difficult period for many villagers.

Before summarizing the arguments that follow, I need to first clarify the particular land that constitutes the resource discussed in this chapter. Since its settlement in the early 1800s, Brega's general spatial layout has not changed significantly. The village itself, one side of which fronts on the shore of a lake, is composed of approximately 900 single-story houses built on plots of land that vary in size (usually between 0.18 hectares and 0.5 hectares). Historically, these household lands have not been the main site of production in the village. It was the arable lands surrounding the village's built-up area, that were collectivized during Soviet times and subseequently privatized after the disestablishment of the Soviet Union (although still worked by large organizations), that were the main site of village agricultural production throughout its history.[6] It is also these vast lands, amounting to approximately 7,500 hectares (pasture and arable land), which are the focus of this chapter. (Household land is the focus of chapter 2.)

In the following section on the history of Brega land, I sketch the changing land arrangements over time: from pre-Soviet and Soviet times (when everyone labored on the land, and the land had use value including access to the market through salaries for all), to contemporary times in which the land still has use value for everyone—but in a much reduced and transformed form—and exchange value only for a very small minority, those who work and/or lease the land.

In the first of the two sections that follow the history section, my focus is on the tensions within the agricultural elite based on differences between the four men who initially leased the former kolkhoz land and led the newly established agricultural enterprises. The enterprises paid the village landowners an annual rent for the lease of the land. In the early 2000s, soon after the enterprises were legally established, one of the four enterprise leaders tried to introduce an element of competition by offering a higher rental payment than the leaders of the other three enterprises. This introduced an element of rivalry between the leaders. In the end, the leader who tried to offer a more generous rent went bankrupt, and the three others continued paying the same lower rate. While this may not have served villagers' interests in their longer-term pursuit of a higher payment, it aligned with community views that their agricultural leaders should work as one, and their desire for equality.

The penultimate section focuses on divisions/alliances between leaders and ordinary villagers (the landowners). The ongoing tensions in this relationship were also founded on the amount of rent given, which landowners felt was too low. Over the years, their resentment strengthened as they witnessed the increasing wealth of the lessees who reaped all the profits from working the land. In Brega, the source of the antagonisms was the exclusion of most of the local population from access to the market economy (due to lack of salaried work and thus cash), while their leaders were able to afford a luxurious lifestyle through unprecedented profits from the land. The fact that the leaders held exclusive control over the land and determined how it was used, thus excluding the landowners, was another point of antagonism.

In summary, with the revaluation of the land, new conflicts and inequalities have emerged in the community: between an emerging elite (the lessees) who control, work, and profit from the land, and the vast majority, who despite being the landowners, are excluded from working the land, have no control over their land nor access to the profits from it. The revaluation of the resource and the tensions arising from such a revaluation are points I return to at the end of the chapter.

## A HISTORY OF BREGA LAND IN PRE-SOVIET TIMES

Seeking to expand its empire through the settlement of friendly Christian populations in the newly won lands that had been under Ottoman rule, Russia welcomed the first Buglarian migrants who established Brega.[7] Letters dating from 1816, from Russian officials representing Tsar Alexander I, provide evidence that the settlers were enticed by land tax exemptions and by formal release from having to serve in the Russian army. A locally written history (Mavrov and Bratkov 1967, 7) notes that the 118 Bulgarian families who established the settlement were granted 6,619 hectares of land. Elderly villagers to whom I spoke reinforced claims made in the literature that all original settlers were allocated an equal amount of land. Cultivated crops in the early years included wheat, barley, oats, millet, beans, and a variety of vegetables; there also was cattle and sheep breeding. By the mid-1800s, viticulture had become well established. These agricultural activities remain central today.

Despite the starting point of equal land blocks, over time, inheritance served to create a more unequal land distribution. Memories from a few elderly villagers confirmed that pre–World War II (i.e., pre-Soviet times), a poor household might only own 2–3 hectares, which was not enough for survival. Poorer householders were thus compelled to work the lands of richer families—those with 60–70 hectares—in order to make ends meet, paying 50 percent of the harvest as rent to the wealthy landowner.

Although privately owned, the land was held as a communal resource,[8] and until 1936 was worked in rotation. This meant that all households were allocated land in different fields surrounding the village on an annual basis. According to archival materials from the early 1900s, it was a communal committee that determined land issues, including which particular blocks of land a villager received every year and in which field. The system of sowing and harvesting, as well as determining where crops would be planted, was also decided communally. My elderly neighbor, Diado Shiro,[9] described how the system worked. He gave his father, who had owned 60 hectares of land, as an example: "Every year, everyone in the village received different allotments of land. So, they'd give my father 5–6 hectares in one place in order to grow corn, 5–6 in another place in order to grow wheat, and so on, up to the total of 60 hectares. My father had plots in different places. The following year, he still had the 60 hectares, but the plots were in other places." Diado Shiro believed the system to be fair, because it meant that from year to year, everyone would have both good and bad land. A previous head of the sovkhoz highlighted the environmental and agricultural advantages of such a rotation system: "You shouldn't sow the same crops in the same place every year, so people changed fields every year." The exception to this rotation system was family vineyards, which remained in the same plot year after year. It was only after 1936, while the territory was under Romanian control, that this system of rotation was abandoned. "An engineer came," Diado Shiro recalled, "and measured up the land." From that time on, householders were assigned and worked the same land plot This was a period, the former head of the collective recalls, when "there was a lot of buying and selling of land." The implication being that in the decade leading up to entry into the Soviet Union, inequalities were exacerbated even further between those with very little or no land and large landholders.

The first agricultural collective was formed soon after the region's inclusion in the Soviet Union toward the end of World War II. Unlike most villages, Brega ended up with both a kolkhoz—made up from the property of the people—and a sovkhoz, which was established on unclaimed land that became government owned and administered. My host's elderly mother, Baba Mina,[10] who was among the first employees in the kolkhoz (established in 1945), confirmed that it was made up from the collected property—land, horses and other animals, and so on—of the villagers who wanted to join. According to the memories of another elderly pensioner, a second kolkhoz was formed in 1947, made up of wealthier villagers who were the last to join and did not want to be in the same cooperative as the poorer ones who had established the earlier collective. Eventually, in 1950, these two collectives were merged under the name "New Life." This kolkhoz continued until 1995, with a land area of 4,273 hectares (Institut Istorii 1978). While much of the early information relating to this period was destroyed in two (suspiciously convenient) fires in 1947 and 1950, the memories of villagers to whom I spoke concur in a number of ways. It is clear that from the very beginning, kolkhoz workers received payment only in kind, in the form of bread, and in the following years, they were given an increasingly larger range of products: wheat, corn, oil, cabbages etc. Payment was based on "trudodeń/trudodni," or workday/workdays, the norm of how much a worker should do in a day (Humphrey 1998, 86). It was only in later years, from the mid-1960s (as elderly villagers recalled), when the kolkhoz was fully established, that this system was phased out, and workers were paid both in kind and through a cash wage (rubles). It was at this time that another payment system, "cheloveko dni" was introduced. This involved produce being sold rather than given to workers, although at a heavily subsidized rate (e.g., see Humphrey 1998, 219). Villagers' accounts confirm that the salaries were more than sufficient to cover their needs. This combined system of payment continued throughout the Soviet period and continues today for the small number still employed in the contemporary enterprises.

The land that was claimed by the government for a sovkhoz had never been in private ownership, nor was it ever previously cultivated, although some of it had been used as pastureland. The land, not always of the best quality and located on hilly terrain, was difficult to farm. It was also far away from the village, and thus hard to access due to a lack of transport. The land, which amounted to approximately 3,000 hectares, constituted the basis of the second village collective, a sovkhoz, formed in 1948 and named after the district.[11] The sovkhoz, as a government-owned and administered organization, was privileged to the extent that it received state resources: machines, technology, fertilizers and chemicals.[12] The working of the more challenging sovkhoz land was therefore made easier; the kolkhoz did not have access to such equipment in the early years.

From its establishment, the sovkhoz paid only a cash wage to its workers. Thus, from the earliest Soviet days, there was a division of sorts within the village based on whether a villager worked in the sovkhoz and was paid only in money, or in the kolkhoz where members were paid a combination of money and in kind. Sovkhoz/kolkhoz delineations had more than just economic implications: Often, living arrangements were structured on the basis of whether one worked in the sovkhoz or kolkhoz. When moving house—for example, because of marriage—the person would usually swap workplaces, as was the case of Baba Mina. She grew up in the kolkhoz end of the village, and worked in the kolkhoz for seven years, from 1945 until her marriage in 1952, when she moved to live with her husband who worked as a driver for the sovkhoz. At this time, she transferred from working for the kolkhoz to the sovkhoz, where she remained until her retirement in the mid-1970s. Generally, it was where you lived that determined which institution you worked for, simply for reasons of convenience: It reduced commuting distances in a village that spans a few kilometers, meaning that most would have to travel by foot some distance before reaching even the closest fields on the village outskirts.

Sovkhoz or kolkhoz membership also determined pension and land entitlements. The woman I lived with, Valentina, explained that until 1991, a worker's specialization was recorded in the *kho-*

**FIGURE 1.1.** Former kolkhoz headquarters, subsequently the headquarters of the three enterprises that eventually evolved out of the former kolkhoz.

*ziaistvennaia kniga*, the owners/workers book in Russian), which identified where the person worked and the nature of the work, whether the person worked in the fields, was a tractorist, a vet, and so on. Occupation and workplace determined from whom the worker would receive a pension, and how much household land someone was entitled to receive (0.15 hectares for sovkhoz workers, 0.25 hectares for kolkhoz workers). After 1991, when these books were transferred to the council and the collectives were formally dissolved, an individual's affiliation to either the kolkhoz or sovkhoz was no longer recorded.[13] Nevertheless, local identities continued being influenced by the sovkhoz-kolkhoz village split and villagers often referred to the period as "in the time when there were two khoziaistva."[14] Landowners in the former sovkhoz continued to see themselves as belonging to the sovkhoz, and they still referred to it as such. Former kolkhoz landowners spoke of the kolkhoz when discussing issues at the community level that affected them all. When issues relating to internal affairs between the enterprises (former kolkhoz land) were at hand, then they identified themselves with the particular organization to which they now belonged, by using the leader's name. For example, Valentina asked another villager, "Who are you with, Prodonov? [*Ti pri kogo si, Prodonov?*]" "No, Petur," he replied, thus indicating his membership in the enterprise Avant Garde that is led by Petur.[15]

By the 1970s, the kolkhoz had caught up with the sovkhoz in terms of technology. Archival documents from the village council from 1983 show the similarities between the two organizations, in terms of number of workers and forms of agricultural production. The kolkhoz had 1,650 workers; there were 1,655 in the sovkhoz. Each of the collectives had its own cow, pig, poultry, and sheep farms. They also had vast vegetable gardens irrigated from water from the lake, plus their own respective machine stations, tractor and field brigades, and so on. They both ran kindergartens and even communal baths and saunas for their dairy workers. Both grew similar crops and looked after a wide range of animals. Salaries were reportedly higher in the sovkhoz, and their workers were also entitled to higher pensions once they retired at the age of 50 years. However, the kolkhoz's additional in-kind payment, and rights to slightly larger household plots of land, were compensation, and meant that all villagers got a similar overall amount, although in different (monetary and nonmonetary) forms. Irrespective of whether they belonged to the sovkhoz or kolkhoz, villagers relied on the collectives for the vast majority of their food consumption needs (Household plots were used primarily for storing grains for animal feed for their animals and the occasional cultivation of fruit trees, see chapter 2).

There are two main points to highlight from this very brief history of the land: First, all villagers were involved in working the main agricultural land. Whether the land was owned privately and rotated annually, as in the pre-Soviet period, or whether the land was run by a socialist collective, as in Soviet times, everyone was involved in cultivating the land, or else in an occupation that supported the production activities of the collectives as "social sphere" workers (i.e., schoolteachers, health workers, etc.). Second, everyone had a say, directly or indirectly, in decisions involving the land: in what was grown and where and when. This was achieved through different arrangements in the two different periods: The rotation system of pre-Soviet times was run by a communal com-

**TABLE 1.1. NEW OWNERS OF THE FORMER COLLECTIVE LANDS**

| THOSE ENTITLED TO LAND | AMOUNT OF LAND |
|---|---|
| Kolkhoz workers | 3.34 ha |
| Sovkhoz workers | 4.1 ha |
| Social-sphere workers | 0.5 ha (initially), later up to 1 ha |
| Families (i.e., 2 adults and their children under age 18) | 0.5 ha (initially), later up to 2 ha |
| Private farmers | Various: from 3 ha to 118 ha |

*Note*: The table shows the groups of people granted land and the theoretical amount of land entitlement. Apart from the land, all other collective assets were also privatized: the buildings, animals, machinery, and so on. My focus here is only on land.

mittee (as far as I could ascertain, members were elected on a regular basis); the Soviet collective system was run by brigades with their expert agriculturalists and workers who discussed and ratified decisions at regular meetings and at annual general meetings attended by all employees.

Following land privatization in 1991, these labor and management arrangements changed dramatically.

## POST-SOVIET LAND PRIVATIZATION

In Brega, the sovkhoz and kolkhoz no longer exist, at least not as legal bodies. Privatization transferred ownership of the land to individual householders, and the land was worked in various individual and group arrangements: enterprises, households, social sphere workers, and private farmers. The sovkhoz was transformed into one enterprise;[16] the kolkhoz was transformed from an initial five to the current three enterprises. Almost everyone in the village was a landowner on the basis of being a member of a family and/or on the basis of where one worked during Soviet times (see table 1.1).

All villagers were allocated land on the basis of their previous work in either the sovkhoz or kolkhoz, thus acknowledging the past bond between land and labor.[17] To be eligible for land, a collective employee needed to have been working in the kolkhoz/sovkhoz at a particular cutoff date in May 1995 (irrespective of how long the person had worked).[18] Kolkhoz members were all given equal shares—land "certificates" as they were called—amounting to 3.34 hectares; sovkhoz members were given more to compensate for the poorer quality of the land, amounting to 4.10 hectares.[19] These theoretically equal plots actually varied between individuals once they finally received their land titles, since land, even within any one particular enterprise, was not of equal quality. Thus, people allocated a plot in a poorer field may have slightly larger plots, while those who received land in the better fields may have smaller ones.[20]

The kolkhoz was reformed into five enterprises (later reduced to three); the sovkhoz reformed into one enterprise some years later. All the villagers, as landowners, became affiliated with one of these new enterprises. The land was leased, and owners were paid an annual rent in the form of grain (usually wheat, corn, and some additional amounts of sunflower seeds). Over the course of a decade, the enterprises dismantled the vegetable gardens, fruit orchards and animal farms, and also relinquished control of all their additional services (control of the water was transferred to the council, as were the libraries; other services, such as the sauna and communal baths, were shut down). Table 1.2, which provides the vital statistics of the five agricultural enterprises, summarizes the number of members and workers belonging to the enterprises.[21] Two of the enterprises were short-lived: The service cooperative was dismantled in 2003,[22] and the fourth enterprise, "Zorya," went bankrupt in 2004, its members and land divided up between the three remaining former kolkhoz enterprises. The former sovkhoz, now carrying the same name that it originally had, but with a changed legal status, has remained stable throughout the period, except for the huge cutback in workers between 2003 and 2014. Such cutbacks were made earlier in the case of the former kolkhoz enterprises: From approximately 900 workers in 2000, their joint workforce was reduced to approximately 150 in 2003, and 67 in 2014. The total number of enterprise workers (sovkhoz and the other surviving three) was 101 in 2014. For comparison, the total number of workers in the kolkhoz and sovkhoz in 1983 was 3,305. These dramatic figures speak for themselves as to the level of disruption experienced: Over 90 percent of the original collective workforce was left unemployed, and most have not had full-time salaried work since.

**TABLE 1.2. ENTERPRISE STATISTICS**

| NAME OF ENTERPRISE AND ITS LEADER | NUMBER OF MEMBERS: 2000/2003/2014 | NUMBER OF WORKERS: 2000/2003/2014 | AREA WORKED, IN HA:[a] 2000/2003/2014 |
|---|---|---|---|
| Avant Gard (formerly kolkhoz land)—led by Petur and then Tzyankov | 176/179/260 | 22/48/22 | 440/610/1,000 |
| Budjak (formerly kolkhoz land)—led by Prodonov | 196/196/201 | 15/NA/19 | 631/675/600 (and 200 that was rented out for viticulture) |
| Dudza (formerly kolkhoz land)—led by Valero | 196/198/225 | NA/NA/26 | 585/648/800 |
| Zorya (formerly kolkhoz land)—led by Ponte | 294/293/NA | NA/40/NA | 859/985/NA |
| Raionski (formerly sovkhoz land)—led by Fedor | 713/660/640 | 250/230/34 | 3,497/2,350 plus 2,336 pasture[b]/2,758 plus 2336 ha pasture |

*Notes*: I am aware that some of these land figures do not add up, but they are the official figures provided to me by the respective accountants of each enterprise. I attribute any discrepancies to different uses some land might have had during different years. Humphrey (1998, 199) was correct to remind us of the multitude of figures available, often given by different officials within the same collective, and the difficulty of working out which are the most accurate.

a. This was worked land and did not include pasture land. The sovkhoz possessed as much pasture as worked land.

b. The local official of the Land Resources Committee provided another figure for the land worked: 2,954 ha.

As a consequence of job losses, household plots have taken on a new and vital significance (chapter 2). National law entitled all families to receive up to two hectares of land, although in every village the amount of land allocated was different, depending on the available reserve. In Brega, the norm for household plots granted to families—defined as a husband, wife, and their children under 18 years—was initially 0.5 hectares. In later years, families could apply for more land up to the full entitlement of two hectares. While I refer to this land as the "household plot," some of the land lies outside of the built-up village area, since many families did not have their full half hectare entitlement surrounding their houses. The additional amount necessary to make up the plot to 0.5 hectares was allocated from land outside the village set aside specifically for this purpose.

While the former collective lands, as enterprises, were still entwined with household economies, the nature of this relationship changed dramatically. Households were dependent on enterprise land in two ways: One was through the rent families received from their land worked by the enterprises. The payment was in kind (grain) and used to feed the household: The grain was milled for bread and also used for animal feed. This exchange of land for nonmonetary rent was part of the reason for a cash-starved local economy.[23] Rent varied in quality and in terms of what was given from year to year, but was restricted to a small selection of grain and seed crops.[24] The rent was used to reproduce the household, and did not usually provide any opportunities for making money or engaging in a market economy, except in the relatively exceptional cases where households had a few land titles (through inheritance), in which case excess grain could be sold for cash or used to raise an extra pig or two for sale. The second way in which households and enterprises were linked was via the *delianki* arrangement (see chapter 2). Villagers had the option to take on a parcel of land from the enterprises, "renting" a specific area of planted vines (or onions, pre-2005). They were responsible for carrying out the labor-intensive tasks involved in production, while the enterprises performed the heavy mechanized work. After the harvest, the household received the profits after paying a "fee"—amounting to a certain proportion of the yield—to the enterprise. This enabled those households with sufficient labor to farm additional land and sell the produce for cash. This was the only way households could gain cash via enterprise land. However, it was not an option available to households who did not have the workers to enter into such labor-intensive activities—a situation that included an increasing number of households—as younger, unemployed family members emigrated to urban locations in search of work. The vast majority of Brega's population survived on the rent that they received from the land they owned in the enterprise(s), as well as the working of their own household plots.

This arrangement between households and enterprises was founded on the fact that the agricultural organizations were no longer obligated to provision individual households. According to the head of the sovkhoz (speaking at the village annual general meeting in 2003), the enterprises "should only be concerned with one task: to make bread," that is, to focus on the production of grains that provided the staple food. Such a refocusing of their activities reduced the range of crops under production, as the enterprises no longer cultivated fruit/vegetables, and their animal husbandry activities were almost eliminated, restricted to the sole purpose of partial payment of their workers' salaries.[25] The freeing of enterprises from having to provision households took place in parallel with the transferring of a wide range of their additional former Soviet responsibilities and resources to the village council, dismantling their role as "total social institutions" (Clarke, cited in Humphrey 1998, 452). From running all the main village services, including supplying water to households, providing housing for some workers and supporting the school and libraries, the enterprises gradually scaled down their activities, and their main remaining function was to cultivate grain crops for market.[26] In short, enterprises have disengaged entirely from household provisioning, as well as given up most of their wider community engagement in services that kept the village running (a responsibility transferred to the village council).

By far the largest and most important players in terms of (former) collective land were the four enterprises that together worked most of the village's land (approximately 85 percent of the total). However, there were two other groups of landowners who deserve a brief mention in order to complete the picture.

The first group consisted of the relatively small number of villagers who had not worked in the agricultural collectives, social sphere workers. They were also entitled to land, although of a lesser amount. The "social sphere" groups (following village terminology) included schoolteachers, medical workers, those employed by the village council and in the water irrigation station (that once supplied water to the sovkhoz and kolkhoz)—in other words, those professions that supported the agricultural collectives but were not considered part of them. Most of these workers, having received their titles, worked the land jointly in groups that varied in size from eight to twenty-four members. For example, Tanya, a teacher at the school, joined a group made up of fifteen of her work colleagues. During the first year or two, tensions emerged within the group, as some members took a greater interest and a more active role than others. This led to accusations that they all reaped the benefits, while only a few did all the work (for no extra remuneration). By 2014, many of the groups still operated, but had split into smaller groups of two to four title holders. Others had totally abandoned their land and let it go fallow, something made possible once the payment of government salaries became more regular and stabilized after 2005. It confirmed what Tanya told me in 2001, "If salaries were decent, we wouldn't need land."

The second group comprised private farmers (*chastnie fermeri*). It is difficult to ascertain their numbers, because some farming arrangements remain informal, despite growing pressure on them to formalize and thus pay the appropriate taxes. Legally registered private farmers in Brega rose from two in 2000, to ten in 2003, while in 2014, this number dropped down to four. They worked anything from 3 to 118 hectares of land. While the farmers were relatively successful in the mid-2000s, in more recent years, they appeared to be struggling or at least downsizing: They reduced the amount of land that they worked, as well as the variety of activities in which they were involved. In the two cases that I knew particularly well, the farmers found themselves in an increasingly precarious position: in debt, with no possibility of government support, disillusioned and struggling to pay their taxes.[27] The rent they paid the owners of the land was in kind, but unlike the enterprises, it was far more generous: up to 20 percent of the harvest.

Before turning to focus on the new divisions arising from the re-

**FIGURE 1.2.** Receiving annual rent from the enterprises—the weighing and collection of grain.

valuation of the land, I conclude this overview of the history of Brega land arrangements by highlighting two points. First, during Soviet times, villagers worked the land as employees of the collective and received a salary in return (which allowed them to buy consumables and engage in the Soviet market), as well as a wide range of foodstuffs and services that sustained villagers' households in multiple ways. After 1991, this relationship between the former collective land and its workers was dramatically transformed. Ex-employees of the collectives became landowners, but their unemployed status signified their alienation from the land in the sense that they were no longer involved in its cultivation. Instead, their land was leased, and they received a "rental" payment in kind. This arrangement has transformed their overall relationship to the resource. Former collective land still had use value, but the way in which it was useful was transformed: It was useful in a much more restricted way, only providing the very basic grains for household survival. It was still a use that had an exchange dimension (ownership rights were converted into rent), but this exchange

**FIGURE 1.3.** Receiving annual rent from the enterprises—the collection of grain.

was a one-off transaction that did not create opportunities to engage in an exchange circuit, as the grain was used to sustain the family and maintain the household. The land provided no further uses—no services or other foodstuffs were given to households. Further, the vast majority did not receive any monetary income, as they were not employed by the enterprises. The revaluation of the land has gone from the land having a wide range of uses for all households, to having a much more restricted use value. Access to a monetary income was only an option for a very small number of village inhabitants, namely, those who still worked at the agricultural enterprises, and especially those three enterprise leaders who leased the (former kolkhoz) land.

There is a second way in which the new arrangements represented a transformation of villagers' relationship to the land: the issue of who had determination over the resource. In pre-Soviet times villagers had, by all accounts, little emotional attachment to any particular land plots outside the village, as they worked different blocks every year in a rotation system. Nevertheless, via the communal committee, everyone had a say in the way land was rotated and worked (what crop was grown and where). Similarly, during Soviet times, local determination over the land was shared through the brigades of the collective that had direct control over the land, as well as through the regular and annual meetings of the collectives that kept employees informed and involved. While the land was under different ownership, control and management arrangements in the three periods I have discussed, in each period except the present one, there was some form of communal/community involvement in determining the use of the land (including in pre-Soviet times when the land was also privately owned). The contemporary period (post 1991) was the first time in the village's history that so few people had complete determination over the land, while the majority had no input into how the land was worked.

To summarize: Post-Soviet reform has meant that the land has reverted to private ownership, and in the process, everyone was granted an equal amount (something that was seen as a fair arrangement). Everyone leased their land to one of the four enterprises, and in return received an annual rent in the form of grain. Thus, the land still had use value, though vastly reduced from previous times in the sense of the range of services and provisions given, and this use still involved an exchange that was a one-off transaction. However, unlike Soviet times, the land no longer provided possibilities of a monetary income for the vast majority. Further, the new lease arrangements meant that most did not labor on the land or have a say about how it was cultivated.

The revaluation of the resource and consequent tensions over who had control of the land and the amount of rent paid were evident within the agricultural leadership themselves, as well as between the leadership and ordinary villagers (the landowners). It is these divisions that are the focus of the rest of this chapter.

## DIVISIONS BETWEEN BREGA ENTERPRISE LEADERS

One night, sitting with my neighbors on the street and relaxing after a long day's work, Luba (who lives across the street from us and works at the kindergarten) recited an old Russian fairytale of the crab, lion, and frog. The three were given the task of moving a bale of hay. They tied themselves to the bale, and all moved in their accustomed way: The crab tried to crawl sideways into its hole, the lion ran forward, the frog hopped into the pond, and the bale of hay did not move at all, because they pulled in different directions. It is exactly the same with the "cooperatives" at present, Luba concluded, providing the moral of her story: All the leaders are "pulling in different directions, toward his own hole, his own place, his own interests, and no one is moving the hay. It's not getting us anywhere, and nothing gets done."

During the early years in Brega, I was told repeatedly by villagers, "We have too many leaders in this village," and the "village needs to be one, not split up into different agricultural organizations." This contemporary problem was seen to have a historical source that originated in the Soviet period, when the village had both a sovkhoz and kolkhoz, "which split the village in two and sometimes means leaders acted against each other." Having two collectives necessitated an extra village agricultural leader, as well as a third Communist Party branch (i.e., one in the sovkhoz, one in the kolkhoz and the third, the council). Bregans observed that other villages "have only one agricultural leader and things get done. Here they are all against each other and nothing happens."[28] This problem was exacerbated by the post-1991 land reforms, at which time the total number of leaders more than doubled: from three (the mayor and head of each collective) to seven (the mayor, the head of the former sovkhoz and during the early reform years, the five leaders of the [former kolkhoz] enterprises that eventually dwindled to the current three).

From a very different perspective, the village agricultural leaders also complained about the excessive number of leaders. They felt that everything would operate more smoothly without one of their counterparts, namely, the head of the fourth agricultural enterprise—Ponte. As Petur, the former head of the kolkhoz and the senior leader of the three agricultural enterprises told me in 2003: "The three cooperatives . . . work together, but with the fourth enterprise there are difficulties. . . . We can't work normally with him [the leader of the fourth enterprise]." The demise of Ponte's enterprise and its eventual bankruptcy is a particularly useful event on which to focus, because while it happened some time ago (in 2003–2004), the incident highlights how divisions within the leadership arose from different understandings of the new rental arrangements: whether the exchange of land for rent should be based on a competitive or noncompetitive form. It also sheds light on the current makeup of agricultural institutions in the village.[29]

Petur explained that the kolkhoz was first divided into four, because this was a "natural" division based on the water irrigation system that was already in place, which also aligned with former kolkhoz brigade divisions. (The fifth enterprise was the service cooperative that was eventually disbanded. The machinery it controlled was divided up between the other enterprises.) The four enterprises were legally registered in their present form at the end of 1999, and when I started living in Brega in 2000, Ponte was already being mentioned by Petur as "a problem," although the crisis only came to a head a few years later.

The division between the leaders manifested along a few lines. First, unlike the other three enterprise leaders, who all had tertiary degrees from Odessa in agriculture and had worked subsequently as specialists in the village kolkhoz, Ponte's tertiary degree was in economics, and he had never worked in the village. Instead, he had been employed by collectives in other villages in the district. At the time of his leadership of the fourth enterprise in Brega, he was also a politician, one of the four elected deputies representing the village at the district council.[30]

Second, if educational qualifications and work experience were one source of potential difference, then so were the different personalities and leadership styles of Petur and Ponte. Ponte spoke well on public occasions, making lots of alluring promises (which, it turned out, he often could not keep). The wife of a private farmer told me that Ponte was a popular choice among the people, because "he had promised the workers that they'd keep their jobs and so they voted him for leader." Tanya, a schoolteacher, confirmed that Ponte was a popular figure who seemed principled, and at the beginning attracted members who did not like Petur (indicating that from the earliest years one was seen as an alternative to the other). Ponte had a small band of loyal followers who worked for him and supported him, but as the months passed and Ponte made more mistakes, loyalty to him also started to wane. In 2003, a private famer, Mishol, told me that Ponte did not have good skills as an agriculturalist, and yet accepted advice from no one. Petur was of the same opinion and told me in 2001: Ponte was ambitious but "doesn't understand the issues." Ponte was even criticized for his management style by his own deputy (Nikolai), who told me that he never spoke directly to his workers, leaving the deputy to do this, while Ponte spent his days going to Odessa or Izmail, seeking additional loans from banks. Nor did Ponte listen to advice from his accountant, who eventually resigned in 2003 precisely because Ponte refused to take her advice, although he was clearly sinking the enterprise deeper and deeper into debt: "I tell him it is not possible what he wants to do, there is no money, but he won't listen." His stubborn and obstinate character was also frequently noted by his deputy, who once politely described him as "edlichen" (one of a kind): "Ponte does his own thinking and doesn't do what the other leaders do and that is why he is in so much trouble." Ponte characterized himself to me the same year as someone who was "independent," worked alone and "didn't bow to Petur."

Petur, on the other hand, although of a similar age and also with a tertiary education—as an agronomist with a specialization in viticulture—had a very different leadership style. He was better connected within the Brega agricultural scene because he had always worked in his native village, having held the position of head of the kolkhoz since 1986. Petur was derided as "negramoten" (illiterate) and "rude" by Ponte, and he did come across as a more down-to-earth leader, who often spoke gruffly, frequently lost his temper, and used some colorful and often inappropriate language. People would also note, in making a character assessment of Petur, that despite his quick temper, he would eventually calm down, and then he would be helpful. Mishol told me once, when we were discussing the two men, that Petur was far more trustworthy than Ponte. "Petur helps, he might have a 'bad' character, get angry and lose his temper, but when he gets over it, he'll listen and help. Ponte talks '*krasivo* [beautifully],' and people are taken in by this. Ponte promises a lot but doesn't deliver." Petur was also seen as a good agronomist and more experienced than Ponte when it came to agricultural affairs. Petur was well liked by his workers, and unlike Ponte, had a hands-on approach, communicating with his workers directly on a daily basis.

While Ponte worked independently, the other three enterprise leaders stuck together. In 2001, Petur described the activities that the three enterprises performed in unison: they bought fuel and their seed supply together (he explained it was cheaper to do so); they helped each other in technological operations and shared/exchanged information and advice; they gave the same rent to their members at the same time;[31] and even sold all their produce together. In short, as Petur told me, "We act like (one) *khoziaistvo*," and so use less resources and save money. However, they did sow and harvest their lands individually. They also had separate accountants. The three leaders met every morning in the old kolkhoz headquarters building, where they shared one large office that also housed their accountants. Here, they agreed what they would be doing on that day—under Petur's guidance. Notably, the relationship between the three leaders was not equal, to the extent that Petur, as the former head of the kolkhoz, was always the senior partner of the three. Sometimes he was referred to as "the General," denoting his authority over the other two leaders. The other two (who were younger than Petur by more than a decade) looked to Petur to lead, followed his advice, and from all signs, were apparently very willing to grant him the senior position. One of the workers in Petur's enterprise told me: "The three cooperative leaders help each other; there are absolutely no problems between them. They are almost 'as one/*za edno*.' There are no arguments, and they listen to Petur. . . . Petur is the senior partner."

This working "as one" was visually reinforced following their successful sale of organic grain to the UK in 2002–2003 (a market connection initiated through the UK government's Know How Fund). With the profits from the sale, they each bought a jeep for work, and they all bought exactly the same model and exactly the same color: a Lada Niva in burgundy. While the internal dynamics might have been hierarchical—as Ponte's wife said in a somewhat derisive way, "the two are like puppies around Petur and they do as they are told"—they worked together and portrayed a united front. Over the years, the dynamics did not change between the three enterprises, which continued to operate together at least for the first two decades after their establishment (and possibly more). There were minor variations in rent given, although these were minimal: perhaps one would give 100 kilograms of sunflower seeds, while the other an extra 100 kilograms of corn instead, for example. The personality and leadership style differences described in this section somewhat explain the tensions between the three enterprises

**FIGURE 1.4.** Ponte's worker out in the field, sowing.

(led by Petur working together with the other two) on the one side, and Ponte, on the other.

Beyond the different leadership styles, and Ponte's unwillingness to work with the others, it was the giving of rent that became a particularly significant source of division. In those early years, Ponte gave significantly more rent than the other enterprises. This drew commentary in the village, and some considered withdrawing their land from the other enterprises in order to join Ponte's. It also enhanced his popularity with the villagers and satisfied his own members.

However, when Ponte gave more rent, it also put him at loggerheads with the other three leaders. Petur and the other two had deliberately decided to give the same amount of rent to their land title holders. As Petur told me in 2001: "The three cooperatives think it's better not to cause friction between the people by giving different amounts of rent. So, we give the same rent to everyone, so people won't say, 'He gets more than us,' so we won't offend or upset the people." Then he went on: "But the fourth cooperative doesn't see it like this. He [Ponte] gave more rent initially, but now he is left with none, not even enough grain for sowing for next year, while we decided to give our rent gradually. Initially we gave 600 kilograms, but we'll give again another few hundred kilograms later" (this did not eventuate). In this same season, Ponte gave one ton to the landowners in his enterprise, which was as much as the private farmers gave and almost twice the quantity given by the other enterprises in that year or any other.

From what I could ascertain, Ponte was only able to give more rent because he was not paying his debts, and was taking out new loans to cover the shortfall.[32] From all the accounts provided by ordinary villagers (which also correlated with what Petur told me on another occasion) Ponte did well the first and second year, and in the second year he gave more wheat (rent) than the other three. Then, in the third year, he could not afford to pay his electricity bill, and after he continued to refuse to pay his bill to the fifth cooperative (for machinery used), the other three enterprise heads got together with the fifth cooperative to cut off his water supply. With no water, Ponte was unable to irrigate his crops, and as a consequence he had poor harvests the following year. This was the source of a huge scandal between the leaders. While I was not privy to the details, it undoubtedly compounded Ponte's financial difficulties in the period before his enterprise was declared bankrupt. On another occasion, when Ponte owed a sum that he refused to pay, Petur reportedly went to the fields where Ponte kept his enterprise's cows, loaded up 10, and sold them to the slaughterhouse in order to pay off the debt. In both cases, Petur and the others took action against Ponte to force him to pay his debts. These acts only angered Ponte more and made him dig in his heels further. It was what Ponte's deputy had in mind when he said that the other leaders "get in his way," "interfere in the running of his cooperative [*te mu mushaiat*]," and generally went out of their way to make life difficult for him.

In offering more rent, Ponte became an obstacle by creating a situation of competition that went against the arrangement of the other three leaders who established a noncompetitive exchange relationship among themselves and with their landowners (by giving the same rent). Ponte's actions set up a rivalry between them, and "Petur," I was told by Sasho (an unregistered private farmer who used to work in the kolkhoz as its chief engineer and thus knew Petur well), "does not like competition!" It was a view in line with how Ponte viewed the situation. A couple of times in the last months before he went bankrupt, Ponte told me, "Petur is a 'star khoziain' [an old owner/master] who doesn't allow competition," emphasizing that Petur operated in the old ways of former times in which this type of competition was not encouraged. Workers in the other three enterprises, however, supported their bosses' position, and were clear that they saw Ponte's competitive activities as a sign of arrogance and superiority. One mechanist said of Ponte: "He holds himself above us, wants to be better," underlining the need for equality between the leaders. This ideological position was also in alignment with general village expectations; villagers wanted their leaders to work as one and maintain equality between everyone.

All leaders saw themselves as pro-reform. However, Ponte's attempt to introduce a competitive dimension indicated a very different way of understanding the particular nature of the relationship, both among the enterprises and between the enterprises and landowners. For all the leaders except Ponte, the new relationship was not to be a competitive one that divided the leaders or enterprises. They did not vie for economic advantage among themselves. Working together brought them economic benefits, such as saving on costs (e.g., bulk buying fuel, sharing machinery, etc.). They also sold their products as one on the market for the same price, maintaining a unified front and equal economic relations. The leaders did not encourage competition in the relationship between themselves and the landowners, as evidenced in the same rent that they paid to their respective members. They recognized that giving a different rent would only incite local discontent and increase divisions within the village (not to mention put one leader in competition with the others). Thus, in their model of reform, there was no room for competition internally between themselves or with the landowners, nor was any external competition encouraged, as evidenced through the sale of all produce to the same buyer. They eliminated any potential competition by working together, buying necessary materials together, selling harvests together and by giving the same rent.

Ponte's activities introduced an element of internal village competition. By providing a rent that was higher than the other leaders,' he was acting against the agreement made between the other three, and also potentially undermining it. It was a provocative act. However, in the end, because his attempts at competition through the giving of more rent were only achievable through taking on greater debt—as well as not paying off the local debts he had inherited—his actions were unsustainable. Petur (and the others), unwilling to tolerate competition, especially when this took place alongside the accumulation of raising debts through nonpayment of local water and electricity bills, took the matter into their own hands (such as selling Ponte's cows to pay off some of his debts). In the end, Petur's deeply rooted connections within the village, his stronger control over resources and access to them, the full support he had from the other agricultural leaders, plus his greater success as an agriculturalist, visible for all to see in the better crops growing in the fields, placed him in the victorious position.[33]

Ponte "resigned"—the enterprise was declared bankrupt—in early 2004, and he has not worked in the village since. Although his wife still lived in their Brega house after the bankruptcy, Ponte was away most of the year working a wealthy man's lands (according to Ponte, "a politician in Kiev who owns a lot of land") in eastern Ukraine, close to the war frontier.[34] When he did return temporarily for visits, he kept a low profile and stayed at home. Memories are long, and to this day, some of his workers have not received any form of salary or compensation for their work.[35] Ponte did not repay these debts, despite being legally responsible for them. At the time of his resignation, district officials scrambled to find someone to replace him and take over the running of the enterprise, but were unsuccessful, as no one was willing to take on the high level of debt he/she would inherit. At the end of the season, the land in Ponte's enterprise was divided up equally between the other three enterprises, giving them a greater number of members. The three enterprises continued to work together closely, the two remaining men with Petur's successor, following Petur's retirement in 2007.

Arrangements were not based on internal competition. Ponte, the only leader who tried to work competitively, offering a higher rent to landowners, was ultimately ousted. His exit from the local scene signified the end of any deep divisions within the agricultural leadership, and eliminated any competition in terms of rent, a situation that continued into the following decade and beyond. Nevertheless, the amount of rent remained a source of discontent between the two distinct interest groups that emerged in the village, the lessees and landowners, and these were the source of ongoing divisions.

## DIVISIONS BETWEEN ENTERPRISE LEADERS AND VILLAGE LANDOWNERS

Following the departure of Ponte from the local scene, the criticism of "too many leaders" was heard far less often. The status quo in the village returned to something similar to Soviet times, at least in the sense that the main division was between a united sovkhoz and a united kolkhoz, as there were no longer internal divisions between the leaders of the (former kolkhoz) enterprises. The overall picture was complicated a little by the existence of private farming activities and groups of social sphere workers, although these other actors were small in number and had little political clout in the community. Villagers approved of the three enterprise leaders working together. Marusha, my neighbor, told me: "Brega is the only village to have broken up its kolkhoz, other villages have kept one organization . . . but at least our leaders stick together." In a discussion between Marusha and another two neighbors on the eve of Ponte quitting, the women agreed, "It's better if he gives up," and one of the neighbors added, "Yes, there's too many *khozaistva* here. Now at least there'll be one less." Few seemed to share Ponte's view of the need for any internal competition and were satisfied that Petur and the others worked as one.

There were some ways in which the joint—noncompetitive—operations of the enterprises suited ordinary members and worked in their favor. In 2014, Marusha described to me the rent situation. In speaking about the "troika," as she had begun calling the three remaining (former kolkhoz) enterprise leaders, she said: "They give the same rent. They agree among themselves what to give. They realize that they need to give the same rent, because if one gives less, then people start leaving the cooperative." The situation was much as it had been a decade earlier, following Ponte's exit from the local agricultural scene. She went on to indicate the positive implications of this "same rent" approach for others in the village by comparing it to the sovkhoz: "The sovkhoz too has learned to give as much as the [other] cooperatives. People started pulling out their land last year, because the sovkhoz was not giving as much as the cooperatives. And so now, this year, the sovkhoz is giving as much as the cooperatives—a little less, but not a significant amount less."[36] From the perspective of those with land titles in the former sovkhoz, the "same rent" approach worked to their advantage, putting pressure on the head of the sovkhoz enterprise to equal the rent given by the other agricultural leaders.

However, the united leadership arrangement that advantaged ordinary enterprise landowners in some ways, also served to disadvantage them in other ways. The biggest cause for concern was once again associated with the question of rent. Villagers may have approved being given the same rent, but the low amount of this payment was an ongoing source of discord. Villagers often expressed dissatisfaction with the rent they received and frequently felt that they were being shortchanged. On one such occasion in 2004, a woman from further down our street passed by while Marusha, Luba, and I were sitting outside enjoying the pale winter sun. She announced to us, "They [as the leaders were commonly referred to] are asking people to sign that we've received 600 kilograms of corn." "What?" asked Marusha incredulously. "There's no way those four rows could be more than 100–150 kilograms." "Well," retorted the other woman, "that is what they are claiming." Luba said thoughtfully: "Petur knows what he is doing. He is, after all, the old leader" (referring to the fact that he led the kolkhoz pre-reform days). Marusha agreed, "Yes, Petur is the most cunning [*khitur*] of them all," and added, "He tries not to upset the people by giving them 'something,' but ultimately he looks after his own interests." She then went on to summarize what they had received in rent that year: "So far, we have received 10 kilograms of sugar, four rows of corn and he has promised oil. And with this, Petur thinks he will have accounted himself to the people," referring to the fact that all enterprise leaders had to balance their accounts and show that they had paid their due rent per land certificate, thereby fulfilling their obligations in the eyes of the law.

For his part, when I raised the issue with Petur a couple of months later, he told me in a tone that barely concealed his frustration and annoyance, "We [the enterprise] planted the corn, harvested it, and stored it in the granary. '*Normalni* [rational/reasonable]' people went and took their corn from the granary and received their 600 kilogram entitlement. '*Nenormalni* [irrational, unreasonable]' people said they'd pick it themselves. They did this because they wanted the bottom part of the corn [the corn stalks] for animal feed. And now these people are unhappy because they say they didn't receive the full 600 kilograms." From Petur's perspective, he was being helpful in allowing people to access extra animal feed, and if someone wanted to collect the corn from the fields, then the risk was theirs, as there was no precise way to gauge how much they would harvest from the allocated rows. In an attempt to establish his reasonableness, Petur added that the "cooperatives" had plowed the villagers' household land (the extra plots outside the village), and in this way given the people a little extra help. This assistance was not recorded in the books nor was the cost passed on to enterprise members. Nevertheless, villagers were often not certain if they had received their full entitlement and remained suspicious that enterprise leaders were trying to cheat them out of rent. Similarly, those still working for the enterprises found themselves between a rock and a hard place, fully aware that what they were being offered in goods in lieu of a salary was set at an expensive rate (calculated in terms of the market prices) and meant a loss for them. At the same time, uncertain as to whether things would get better, they felt compelled to accept the unfavorable deal. To hold out for something else might mean they lost out altogether and received nothing.[37]

Besides often feeling shortchanged in terms of rent received, villagers also expressed dissatisfaction that so much of the profit from their lands stayed with the leaders. Over the course of a few years, I heard multiple expressions of dissatisfaction. "Once there was one leader who stole, now there are five to steal," I was told by a former mechanic from the kolkhoz in 2000. "Everyone grabs for themselves. What we need is a leader who thinks about us all," an elderly neighbor speaking about the enterprise leaders told me in 2003. The same point—that enterprise leaders were stealing from the people—was repeatedly expressed across the community, from schoolteachers to former collective workers and private farmers. Sasho told me in 2004: "Petur and the others are cheating the people. He is using our land . . . piling up a capital, while giving 'nothing' in rent. They [the enterprise leaders] are siphoning off the profits—and there are profits—but the cooperative members never see any of this and get nothing out of it. The leaders are piling up capital for themselves at the expense of villagers whose land they use." He provided more details as to how this was happening. He calculated that after taking out all the costs for working the land, the enterprise had a net harvest of approximately 9 tons of grain per land title, and of this he received from the sovkhoz 500 kilograms in rent. I asked him, "So where does the rest go?" "Aha!" he responded, "a good question. I ask myself the same question. There is only one answer." I countered, saying, "Surely you'd see something, yet no one here drives an expensive car or has a fancy house." Sasho replied, "They wouldn't be so silly or obvious about it. They probably have a bank account somewhere, or even in a few places, where they are piling up money." His wife Aksana, a teacher at the school, nodded in agreement. "It might not be obvious from their houses here," she told me, "but their children have nice houses in Izmail and Odessa, and undoubtedly, they have bank accounts where profits are accumulating." Sasho also pointed out that there was no reinvestment in the cooperatives—no new tractors being bought, etc.—so it was not as if the profits were being put back into the land. "Clearly, the money stays with a few." His opinion was echoed by a large number of other villagers. Nadia, a pensioner who owned land in the sovkhoz enterprise, provided a similar calculation. She said, "I get 500 kilograms in rent per certificate. We have two certificates—one each with my husband. What is 500 kilograms? What can I say . . . [she is momentarily lost for words] . . . the leader has no conscience and no shame. Work it out: Together we have two certificates, which amount to eight hectares of land, so together we receive one ton of wheat. But the year before last, which was a good year, they got at least 16 tons from the same eight hectares. Is that proper?"

There were numerous indications that there was some truth to these allegations against the leadership. A worker of the former service cooperative who had some insider knowledge told me that Prodonov, the head of the Budjak enterprise, had bought a BMW and kept it hidden in his cousin's garage. I suggested that this was perhaps only rumor. "No," the worker responded, "people have seen it, although he tries to keep it hidden. Everyone steals and fills their pockets. They take what they can . . . and then they will leave." Tanya, the schoolteacher, said on another occasion, "It's OK if they worked for this money, but they are cooperative employees. How could they be buying BMWs while there is nothing for the others in the cooperative?" Such views had changed little a decade later, in 2014, although the leaders' wealth was more visible. Marusha told me the leaders "have set themselves up alright and live well—just look at the cars they drive," and nodded to farther down the street, where outside the kolkhoz headquarters, a range of the latest model Lada jeeps and four-wheel drives were parked alongside a few western cars. At this time, also, villagers were commenting on the wedding of the daughter of one of the enterprise leaders. The wedding reportedly cost 60,000 UAH. Marusha's husband, Kolyo, thought this was "Impossible!" He could not imagine that a wedding could cost so much. His wife shrugged her shoulders and said with alcohol and the venue costs, it was quite possible. It was this rising and visible inequality—between the agricultural leaders who were obviously gaining in wealth, while many ordinary landowners were just making ends meet—that increased tensions and was at the root of accusations of stealing aimed at the enterprise leaders.

Indeed, whereas the lessees had "excessive" access to profits, the vast majority in the village, the lessors, had very little cash or opportunity to engage in the market at all. Operating in a largely cashless economy was an unwelcome aspect of the first decades after Ukrainian independence and this posed a perceptible contrast to their lives during USSR times. The worth of the land as having only use value for the vast majority was reflected in the way villagers talked about their property. They did not say they wanted land because they needed money, they said they wanted land because they needed *zimka* [wheat] or bread. Therefore, land = rent = zimka/bread, and thus the survival of the household. Rent in kind gave householders grains with which to feed animals (meat for the household), and once milled, it provided the household staple, bread. Payment in kind was used far more often in village exchanges than money.[38] Produce from the land lay outside of any monetary exchange circuit and was an alternative to it for most of the rural population. Landowners were given little choice in this matter: Unemployed, and with agricultural skills that were no longer required, they survived through self-sufficiency and remained largely excluded from engagement in the market economy.[39] A handful of villagers found casual or seasonal labor in one of the enterprises, but there were few opportunities for regular work/income. Only once the workers reached pensionable age, which in some cases meant waiting a couple of decades or more, did they have access to regular cash.

In short, with no access to cash from their land (when once they received salaries from it), villagers were largely excluded from engaging in the market economy. The rent they received from their land was so low that it barely sustained the household. At the same time, they saw the growing wealth of the enterprise leaders, who were evidently able to engage in market consumption of the most luxurious kind. To add insult to injury, the leaders' profits were made from the land that was owned by the ordinary villagers.

What most villagers did not realize was that they did not belong to a cooperative, although this is how they constantly referred to the organization. Petur also referred to the enterprise as a "cooperative," although recognizing, "In legal terms, the organizations are not cooperatives at all—if we understand by this organizations jointly owned and run by all members—but actually 'enterprises,' where a large number of people lease their land for which they are paid a rent, although the lessees gain all the profits. In Brega we call it a 'cooperative,' but in Bulgaria [I imagine he used Bulgaria as a comparison, as he viewed me as from there], this would not be a cooperative, but an 'enterprise.'" Speaking a year later in 2004, he acknowledged that this arrangement was not ideal: "We made a mistake: the fact that the ownership is collective, but the running is not." Clearly, it complicated the situation, and he would have preferred not to have the inconvenience of so many owners (Indeed, some villagers speculated that when the leaders accumulated sufficient capital and the land market opened up, the leaders would buy up the land.[40])

The enterprise leaders, the lessees, were not required to account for themselves or discuss their decisions with landowners. They were, they told me, only answerable to their accountants. There was no legal requirement to hold annual meetings with the ordinary membership, nor was there any legal requirement for them to share the profits.[41] There was a legal minimum rent that leaders were expected to pay annually to the landowners, but that was the extent of the obligation. In the contracts, it was stated that every year the enterprise needed to give 1.5 percent of the value of the certificate (i.e., the assessed value of the land) as rent to the land holder (As there was no established land market, the value of the land remained unchanged). The rent varied from year to year, because the it was calculated in terms of the market value of the particular produce given as rent. As long as the basic rent was paid, ordinary members had no rights over the remaining profits. Lessees had only one legal responsibility to the landowners: to pay the annual rent. From a legal point of view, there was no stealing, and the fact that all the profits remained with the leaders was also within the acceptable legal framework. While the former sovkhoz was slower in changing its status, it eventually also adopted the same legal structures, which meant that all agricultural organizations in the village were of the same legal type. (In other villages, there were other types of organizations, some closer to what we would recognize as true cooperatives.)

Petur claimed that in 2000 they had held three general meetings, and that at these meetings the new status of the institutions was made clear. It might have been clear to Petur, but not to the vast majority of villagers. Marusha described these same meetings to me (in 2001), emphasizing that everyone wanted one cooperative, but there had never been a proper vote on the issue, and she accused the leaders of making an informal agreement among themselves without consulting the people.[42] Marusha added that ever since the meetings in 2000, all decisions taken concerning the land—such as sowing, etc.—were not done through consultation with the people: "*They* just make the decisions among themselves, and *they* don't tell the people anything." Of course, it was from this time that the four enterprises were officially created, and thus there was no further legal obligation to consult with the landowners in how the land was used. Nor was there any legal obligation to hold annual general meetings at which people were kept informed or could voice their opinions/concerns. Once taking an active interest in collective land and involved in its cultivation, after the establishment of the enterprises villagers (as land owners) felt alienated and marginalized.[43] While I was not in Brega at the time of the 2000 meetings, and thus relied on what others told me, the tensions were still palpable a year later. Petur believed he acted honestly and openly in the creation of the new legal enterprise; ordinary members were of a very different opinion.

Protests from landowners were futile. Before the land titles were finalized and distributed, in the early 2000s, when there was only a technical ownership of land via certificates or land shares, it was relatively easy for villagers to move between enterprises. Doing so served as a suitable form of protest. For example, many moved into Ponte's enterprise because they did not want to be in Petur's. When Ponte's enterprise started performing badly, many moved back to the troika. However, once the land titles were handed out and villagers were allocated a designated plot of land rather than a technical share, it became much harder, nearly impossible, to shift between enterprises since the plots were relatively small and leaders were unwilling to take on an extra plot in another field. Additionally, the fact that leaders gave the same rent and acted as one made shifting enterprises a pointless exercise. The one bargaining chip that the landowners had had, withdrawing their land from a particular enterprise, was removed once the land titles were distributed and the troika worked as one. The leaders were also not obliged to listen to the complaints and concerns of the villagers.[44] As Sasho astutely noted: "The leaders don't care what people think. They do what they want. They just aren't interested in what happens or what people think. And why should they?" Marusha reinforced this point of view: "You can't complain or do a thing. If you go to Petur to complain about anything, then his answer these days is dismissive: 'If you don't like it, take your land and go.'" Her husband explained why this was not realistic: "With no technology or machines, it is not possible to work your own land. And the costs: such as fuel, seeds, planting, and fertilizer are too high. It is hardly worth it for four hectares."[45]

While ordinary villagers had little influence over the lessees, the agricultural workers in the enterprises did have some moral leverage. For example, in 2004, one of the three enterprises charged a higher fee than the others. The fee was associated with the cash crop of onions that was planted by the enterprises and contracted out to willing villagers who carried out the more labor-intensive work. The latter paid a fee to the enterprises and kept the rest of the proceeds. The harvested onions in enterprise Budjak, led by Prodonov, were particularly small, yet he had increased his "norm" (meaning the fee individual households were charged by the enterprise for the planting and watering of the onions) above that of the other two enterprises. The former required that all his members pay 180 UAH per *delianka* (usually paid in kind), while Petur and Valero's (who led enterprise Dudza) price was 140. There was a meeting between Prodonov and his enterprise workers, and what ensued (as reported to me) was a very "noisy" meeting that was so unpleasant Prodonov stayed home for a week, claiming he was sick. At the meeting, he apparently justified the extra costs because the water was particularly expensive for their enterprise. This made his workers even angrier, because the previous year, which had been a drought year, the government had subsidized the water, yet Prodonov had not taken account of these subsidies. Such a unified demonstration against their leader was a rare event, provoked precisely because one leader tried to implement a charge that was higher than those of the other two leaders, an equally unusual occurrence. However, unlike ordinary landowners, protests expressed by the workers did have some impact, although the outcome remained the same: The fee stayed higher in Prodonov's enterprise that year.

Ordinary villagers were trapped. Working their land was not viable, and they remained dependent on the rent, as a matter of survival, but had no opportunities for social mobility or consumer engagement in a market economy. It was a situation that led to their relative powerlessness: They had no say in how their land was used, nor any recourse to protest. In principle, lessees could offer help of various kinds, but they were under no legal obligation to do so. Landowner dissatisfaction concerned two issues: First, villagers had no regular salary/income. At the same time, they watched their agricultural leaders siphon off all the profits (from their land), with all the benefits this gave the leaders in terms of having access to money and ability to engage in a commodity market. This was one major tension: The agricultural elite (the leaders of the enterprises) accumulated unprecedented wealth and engaged in a market economy from which ordinary villagers were excluded. It created a new form of inequality in the village between those who had access to the market and those who did not.[46]

The second tension concerned the issue of who had influence over the land. Everyone was a landowner, but only the three lessees had any determination over the resource. The leaders took the risks, and they also pocketed all the profits. Never before in Brega's history had such exclusive authority over the land been given to so few people. In both pre-Soviet and Soviet times, the land was presided over by the community (in different ways). However, following the 1991 reforms, the resource was, for the first time, taken out of control of the community. The way in which the leaders and enterprises were talked about reveals the new relations that were seen to characterize Brega. In 2014, Marusha told me, "They are now all separate kingdoms," highlighting the perceived hierarchical structure of the enterprises and the exclusive power held by their leaders.

## THE CHANGING USE VALUE OF ENTERPRISE LAND AND NEW AGRICULTURAL ELITE

Land is a resource that is at the center of post-Soviet rural divisions. Problems arising from the long and drawn-out process of land privatization in Ukraine are well documented.[47] Research from other locations in the country have shown that land privatization has not improved efficiency, nor has it been successful in creating a class of independent property owners (Allina-Pisano 2008, 57).[48] Macro perspectives of land privatization have concluded that there is continuity between the farming arrangements of today and those of previous times (Mamonova 2015, 617; Nikulin 2011). My Brega case does indicate some continuities, such as in terms of leadership. However, a focus on the revaluation of land reveals a far more complicated and nuanced story. It underlines the dramatic changes to the way in which the resource has been revalued, and the accompanying new divisions arising in the community resulting from changes in ownership, control, and management.

New enterprise land arrangements led to a contemporary shift in value: For the majority of villagers, land had retained its use value in provisioning the households, but in a far narrower way than in Soviet times. The agricultural enterprises were no longer the main household providers through a wide range of foodstuffs and services. Their focus was solely on the cultivation of grains for the market. The rent had use value for the majority of households who required it for their survival. It did not present any additional exchange opportunities, but was a one-off, non-tradable transaction (land for rent). This then was a notable shift: from Soviet times when collectives supplied their workers and households with a wide range of foodstuffs and services for the maintenance of the household, to a restricted provisioning of the household that was largely limited to grain. One consequence for villagers was that they had to significantly expand and increase production on their household land (see chapter 2).

During Soviet times, the land also provided opportunities for engagement in markets through salaries received from the collectives. The enterprises established almost three decades ago provided no monetary exchange opportunities. Some villagers, such as those who owned a surplus of land titles through inheritance, could convert additional grain into money, feeding an extra pig or two for sale, and in this way could receive a small additional income. For those who worked in the enterprises and received a wage, that is, the odd 101 from a population of 2,400, former collective land also had some monetary exchange value, even though in-kind payments constituted at least part of their salaries. However, it was primarily the three men who leased the (former kolkhoz) land from the landowners,[49] who received the profits and reaped the benefits. For them, the produce from the land had (potentially) huge exchange opportunities, through the hundreds of tons of annual grain sales that remained in their hands and from which they profited. The risks were theirs, but so were the spoils. This elite group of three had far greater access and possibilities to engage in the market than they had in previous times as part of the kolkhoz leadership. While hidden BMWs in garages might have been rumors, there was enough evidence to indicate that the lessees had done well for themselves. The value of former collective lands has shifted from providing everyone with an opportunity to engage in monetary exchange through receiving salaries, to having monetary exchange value only for a very tiny minority: the elite leadership of the enterprises, and to a much lesser degree, their workers.

Thus, at the most general level, the shift in land revaluation for the majority of the villagers was from the land having a wide range of uses through provisioning the household via the services, goods and salaries (the latter also presented opportunities to enter monetary exchange circuits), to the more recent situation where land had a much reduced and limited usage (and provided little opportunity for engagement in monetary exchange circuits). There were only an exclusive few who had access to the profits from the land. (Land itself remained outside of any monetary exchange system or form of commodification, for the period discussed here.)

This contemporary situation differed from the past (Soviet and pre-Soviet times) in terms of who had control over, access to, and profited from the land (or more precisely, its produce). It constituted a basis for new community fractures: between a tiny minority (the three lessees) who were involved in the control of the land and profited from it, and the vast majority (of landowners) for whom the land was purely a source of agricultural produce that enabled the maintenance of the household. Such discord emerged despite the lack of internal competition between the village enterprises, a situation that operated to the financial benefit of the local leadership while also satisfying the moral demands for equality within the community. Divisions in the rural community most likely always existed; however, the particular form they took after the establishment of the enterprises was unprecedented. These new divisions were a consequence of two principal factors: first, the disproportionate amount of profit that was being concentrated in the hands of such a small number of local people; and second, the degree of control over the use of the land that was being concentrated in the hands of those who worked the land, which was, again, far fewer hands than ever before.

Villagers commented with some resentment on the visible and growing inequalities between themselves and the agricultural leaders, who were seen as increasing their personal wealth. They also commented on their own exclusion from the land in the sense that they no longer had a say or any control in how the land was used and what happened to it (despite it being owned by them). It was not only ordinary village landowners—such as Marusha—who emphasized the inequalities through the way they spoke about the enterprises as "kingdoms." When I visited Zina in 2014 (a former economist in the village kolkhoz, who had become an official in the district capital by 2000), she was clearly disillusioned with how the reforms had unfolded. In earlier years, she had worked with Petur in her native Brega to help bring about local reforms. However, a decade later she had changed her opinion, blaming Petur for "fragmenting" the kolkhoz, while insisting her intention was not to break up the kolkhoz, but simply initiate a reform so that it could work more efficiently. It was clear that over time she had become dissatisfied with how the breakup of the collective had been implemented. She told me, "Nothing has changed in ten years. The three cooperatives operate as they have always done, each leader is like a 'little king,' and they don't do anything. The original idea didn't work; that is, we didn't create small organizations all under an umbrella association. It did not work because each leader wanted to control his own organization, and in it they are like tsars. They don't consult with the people or have annual meetings. Cooperative leaders are like kings, and nothing has changed [from a decade earlier]." Her choice of words, referring back to pre-Soviet "feudal" times, was not coincidental. It reflected a view of the contemporary enterprise arrangement as both regressive and excluding.

## CHAPTER 2

# HOUSEHOLD LAND

## NEW FAMILY DIVISIONS AND ALLIANCES

Household land is another example of a resource that has shifted from one form of use value to another. The resource has become more important since the land privatization reforms, with its rising prominence observed across the former socialist world after 1989-91 in a range of urban and rural contexts (e.g., Pine 2002; Meurs 2002; Yalcin-Heckmann 2010). This is equally true in Ukraine where the expansion of the use of household land is notable since decollectivization. Household land in Brega has moved from having a supplementary role in the maintenance of the family, to central to the family's survival. In this respect, the region under discussion here is similar to other parts of Ukraine, where an increasing dependence of subsistence farming on household land has also been noted (e.g., Mamonova 2015, 614).

At the same time as household land gained importance, household economies remained intertwined with the operations of the agricultural enterprises. However, the nature of this relationship has been dramatically transformed, as the new agricultural enterprises, unlike predecessor collective organizations, were no longer a source of guaranteed labor or income, nor did they provide a wide range of subsidized foodstuffs and services. The agricultural enterprises did, however, continue to play a vital role in the survival and self-sufficiency of the households: through the payment of rent that supplied households with grains for their staple food (bread), and through the opportunities they provided for households to be involved in cash crop production (such as grapevines).

Household land is presently under private ownership rather than being held in "permanent use" as it was during Soviet times. Following numerous amendments and decrees after 1991, the concept of "permanent use" [*postoianno polzvane*] was gradually phased out.[1] Laws passed in 2005 guaranteed full ownership rights to householders over their plots. This meant that the land could be exchanged through monetary and nonmonetary transactions: It could be bought and sold, as well as inherited.[2] By far, the most common form of transaction was inheritance, although gifting also occurred.[3] As noted in the previous chapter, every family in Brega was entitled to own 0.25 hectares of land surrounding the house, and up to another 1.75 in the fields outside the village (which was also categorized as "household land"), a full entitlement of two hectares. If there was more land surrounding the house, the family was given proportionately less additional land in the fields. Privatization provided villagers with access to more household land than in previous times.[4] Yet, in practice, few claimed the full entitlement. By 2014, many had given up working their household land located in the fields, preferring to focus all their production efforts on the land surrounding their houses.[5] Thus, although villagers had access to more household land than in Soviet times, most have not taken advantage of this opportunity. Having potentially more household land did not explain the new expanded reliance on the land, or the new intensity with which it was cultivated. The importance of household land can only be explained through the knock-on effect that the privatization of collectivized land has had, leading to the decline in use value of former collective land (chapter 1) and corresponding increasing use value of household land.

The term "khoziaistvo" has come into common usage, appropriately capturing the change in circumstances, as livelihoods became less directly involved in the operations of the new enterprises, and more directly reliant on household land. It reflected the transformation of relations within and between households and the former collective lands. In Brega, khoziaistvo was applied to a variety of contexts: It could refer to individual households, to larger institutions such as the agricultural enterprises or private farms, to the whole village[6] or even sometimes the economy of the whole country (all can be a khoziaistvo). However, in every instance, private ownership was a precondition. As Petur, the head of one of the agricultural enterprises, told me: "Until you get private ownership [*chastni sobstvennost'*], you can't have a khoziaistvo." Zina, an economist at the former collective who had been promoted to working in the district capital and was a lead reformer, reiterated the point: "The privatization of land makes everyone into a 'khoziain.'" [7] A khoziaistvo was an economic unit; more precisely, it can be conceptualized as a separate (but not necessarily independent) unit of economic production. The household provided a good example, as it continued to depend on the agricultural enterprises despite operating like a separate economic unit. Thus, when applied to a village household, it was not just the house, or the land surrounding the house, but as Valentina once told me, it included the complete package—the house and people who lived in it, the land around the house, and the animals. Our household constituted one khoziaistvo, our next-door neighbors—Marusha and Kolyo—constituted another khoziaistvo, and so on. The head of the khoziaistvo was a position (usually) shared between the senior couple (husband and wife)—the "khoziain/khoziaika" respectively—although, if the senior male was away (or after his death), it was his surviving wife, the "khoziaika," who becomes the sole head. In most of the families I knew, the role of running the household was shared between the senior couple, each with his/her respective duties and responsibilities.

As noted above, the transformation of the household and its family members from agricultural collective employees into members of a khoziaistva did not sever the link with the land located outside of the village: households still relied on former collectivized land, as they had always done, although the relationship between the household and enterprises took a very different form. The greater importance of household land, as a khoziaistvo, represented a change in the value of the resource: from being little used and relatively insignificant, the land became crucially important and central to the survival of the household. In the process, household relations were transformed. Internally, new divisions emerged between generations and genders, harking back to divisions more commonly associated with pre-Soviet days. Externally, households developed new alliances with other households: enabling villagers—who were left without work after decollectivization—to engage in additional activities that expanded the household economy and introduced possibilities for income from cash crops. These household divisions and alliances are the focus of the chapter.

In the following section, I provide a brief history of household plots, detailing their changing and increasing use over time. I also provide a general background discussion on the types of activities in which present-day householders engaged. In the next two sections, I focus on the impact on relations—within and between households—resulting from the revaluation of household land use. In the first of these two sections, the focus is on the consequences of the revaluation for internal household relations. Without salaries or employment, all family members became involved in household production. One activity that has been revived is the baking of bread at home, as households could not afford to buy their bread at the shop as they once did during Soviet times. Through this example, I show how there has been a renewed division of traditional family relations in terms of generation and gender. In the second of these sections, my focus is on the impact of the revaluation of land in terms of relations between households. It is through labor exchanges of primarily a nonmonetary form, via newly rejuvenated labor relations with kin and *kum*[8] from other households, that households were able to engage in cash crop production (growing onions and vines) on enterprise land. New alliances were formed between households through labor exchanges that enabled the expansion of the household economy. Land revaluation has resulted, in short, in changes in social relations *within and between* households: in the renewal of internal traditional household divisions and in reinforcing external solidarities, respectively. This is a topic I return to at the end of this chapter, where I discuss the changing use value of household land, and the types of divisions and alliances created in the process.

## A BRIEF HISTORY OF HOUSEHOLD LAND FROM PLOTS INTO KHOZIAISTVA

The history of household land (or household plots, I use the terms interchangeably), considered from when the village was first settled some 200 years ago to the present, was one of its growing importance from the perspective of the survival of the family. Based on the memories of elderly villagers, some of whom could recall pre-Soviet (i.e., pre–World War II) days, household land was not used for growing anything: The land simply contained a few fruit trees, housed the animals (perhaps a cow and horse in the case of wealthier households, and more commonly pigs, sheep and poultry) and any equipment, such as a stone mill (that separated the grain from its husks) for the preparation of animal food. It was also a storage site for animal feed (grains) that lay exposed to the elements since there were no storage barns. All crops—grains, vegetables, and the vines—were grown in the fields surrounding the village and only brought home once harvested. Baba Mina (my host Valentina's elderly mother) painted a poignant image, when she described the household land in pre-Soviet days as a "wild space," where chickens were given free range to scratch around. Her elder sister recalled there was nothing in the household plot "except grass," as all food was grown in the lands outside the village.

It was only after the main lands owned by families that surrounded the village were incorporated into the Soviet collectives that villagers began to make slightly greater use of household plots. More specifically, a proportion of the land was planted with rows of vines sufficient for the production of wine for domestic consumption. The vines were established, at least in the case of our home, and Marusha's next door, in 1956, when the household vineyards located outside the village were taken over by the collectives. It was in these early years, after the loss of the main lands outside of the village, that householders also started planting a small quantity of various vegetables—just enough for immediate fresh consumption. However, the vast quantities of fruit and vegetables required for winter preserves were provided by the agricultural collectives, which villagers could buy at very cheap prices (or sometimes help themselves to, with or without official permission). As Tanya's (a teacher at the school) elderly mother said, "In Soviet times, we had everything in terms of food, and it all came from the kolkhoz: tomatoes, capsicum, aubergines, meat, bread, fruit . . . and they sold everything cheaply." She continued, "In those days, we didn't grow many vegetables in our gardens, and there was no need to . . . because we could get everything at a very low cost from the kolkhoz." On another occasion, Marusha explained: "We had salaries and could buy everything we needed at very cheap prices, so there was no need to grow our own food." Tanya also added that because they bought most of their produce, they had a lot less work on the household land, and therefore also more leisure time.

The kolkhoz and sovkhoz were also the source of fresh meat for many villagers. As Marusha pointed out, in those times, "you couldn't keep so many animals at home, because you got less grain from the collectives—100–200 kilograms at the most. If you wanted more, you had to buy it, which," she added on reflection, "you could, because in those times, you got salaries" (alluding to the fact that for many years after 1991, households were cash-starved). She added, "We've never been without a pig; every year we've had one." However, in terms of the raising of animals, comparison with village statistics from 1986 reveal the extent to which household production has risen. In 1986, only 450 houses (i.e., less than 50 percent of all houses—which numbered 962 in total) looked after a pig; in 2003, approximately 70 percent of the households had at least one pig, and a decade or so later almost every household had at least one pig (if not more). The number of houses with cows has also increased significantly (only 10 cows were privately owned in 1986, which was about 1 percent of the households; some three decades later it was about 10 percent of all households). While the total number of houses with poultry remained consistent with Soviet times, chickens used to be bought already hatched from the collectives. Marusha said she would get 100 or so every year from the sovkhoz. After the establishment of the agricultural enterprises, every household took its own eggs to a private villager who had installed an incubator and charged for the service. Everyone also used to buy their bread at the kolkhoz shop. No one baked at home, contrary to the situation before 1944 and again since 1991.

Thus, despite having lost access to the main productive lands outside the village during collectivization, this land continued, through new social arrangements, to provide for most of the villagers' consumption needs. The use of household land increased marginally, due to the sowing of some rows of vines for the making of wine sufficient to satisfy household requirements. There was also a limited variety of vegetable and fruits grown in the household plots, just enough for immediate fresh consumption during the summer. Overall, household plots remained relatively unimportant in terms of the provisioning of the household, similar to the situation in pre-Soviet days. It was the collectives that were the main provisioners of the household, and the latter were dependent on the former.[9]

It is only since the collapse of the Soviet Union and Ukrainian independence that household land has become of central importance to families. Indeed, for the first time in living memory, and from what I can ascertain, for the first time since the settlement of the village 200 years ago, household land has become the main source of produce for families. No longer able to rely on the large-scale production of food from Soviet collectives, the land surrounding each house began to be worked intensively in order to produce all the vegetables, fruit and meat required for the needs of the household. This land's rising importance, and its central role in the survival of families, was a feature of recent times.

Contemporary household production focused on the cultivation of grapevines and the growing of a wide variety of vegetables: peppers, tomatoes, cucumbers, onions, garlic, aubergines, radishes, carrots, beans, potatoes, cabbage, beetroot, pumpkin, and different types of marrows and berries (usually raspberries and strawberries). At the end of the yard farthest from the street and the water supply, rows of corn for animal fodder were also grown. Access to water restricted the cultivation of vegetables, especially those that required particularly large quantities. Water accessibility also restricted where these crops were sown in the yard (especially for those whose land extended uphill from the street, meaning that water had to be transported by some means). The yard often also had a small number of fruit trees: apple, apricot, cherry, and plum.

Most households raised various animals for meat, wool, milk, and/or cheese. While the vegetables and fruit grown on the household plots were almost always purely for household consumption, animals were sometimes also looked after as a means of making extra cash. The circumstances of the household dictated what was necessary, how many and what kind of animals were raised. The average number of poultry raised was thirty-five birds per household. The keeping of rabbits and goats was rare (less than 1 percent of all households). My household, which lacked a male for most of the time I lived there—Valentina's father died in 2000—kept approximately thirty to forty chickens (for eggs and meat), fifteen geese, one pig, and four sheep with usually as many lambs. The sheep were given into the care of professional shepherds over the summer months, who would herd, milk and shear them. This service was paid for, and in return, we received the milk (which was then made into cheese at home), wool and meat. Whatever was not needed was left with the shepherd in lieu of his payment.[10] Some of the lambs were sold for cash. Most of these activities were phased out following Valentina's daughter's marriage. Marusha's household, with its greater number of mouths to feed, and also higher number of laborers (including two men), usually kept three pigs, eighty or so chickens, as well as geese, turkeys, and ducks, and twice as many sheep and lambs as our household. They also had a donkey (some households owned a horse) used for transport, as well as a motorbike with sidecar (also for transport purposes). Some households kept a cow or two, with the extra milk/cheese that could be sold to other villagers providing an additional source of cash. Normally, if households needed extra cash, pigs and sheep were raised for sale, but this depended on having enough corn and wheat to feed the animals. This, in turn, depended on receiving annual rent payments from the agricultural enterprises, which consisted of different quantities and combinations of wheat, sunflower seeds, corn, etc. Those with sufficient cash could buy extra animal feed, but many households were not in a position to do this. Households with more land titles received more rent from the agricultural enterprises, since payments were given on the basis of number of land titles owned. Grains, important as the main source of animal feed, plus wheat for the household's bread, were stored in sacks in the attic. Many households also had their own small mills to grind the grain coarsely for animal consumption, although the finely milled flour needed for making bread was taken to the (privately owned) village mill. Cats, always thin and hungry looking, were kept to protect the attic and cellars free of mice and rats; most households also owned at least one dog, chained up by the street entrance, for security and to serve the function of a doorbell.

There were additional ways for households to make a bit of cash on the side. After Valentina's father died, the grapes from the vines in our household plot were no longer made into wine for household consumption as they had been over the previous decades but harvested and sold for cash to private buyers from outside the village in search of grapes to make their own wine. The lake on which the village was located provided some households with another source of income, as a number of men would fish on a casual basis, selling fresh fish to other villagers.[11] A few houses in the village kept bees and sold honey; those with larger numbers of sheep, or a cow, sold milk or cheese; those with high numbers of poultry might sell their unneeded eggs, and so on.

Household khoziaistva were dynamic and their situations fluctuated, expanding and contracting over time according to the needs and number of their members.[12] Its changing composition determined its different needs and practices. Thus, if a family was faced with the cost of paying for a child's tertiary education or upcoming wedding, more pigs were raised and sold, or an extra *delianka* of vines was looked after.[13] When the household declined in size—such as in the case of Valentina, who lived alone following the death of both her parents, while her married daughter lived in a village closer to Odessa—she no longer kept sheep. She had one pig only because her daughter and son-in-law appreciated the extra meat and came back regularly on weekends to help with the various tasks related to its raising, such as collecting the rent from the agricultural enterprise that provided feed for the animal. In other words, household expansion and contraction followed the life cycle of families and their life courses, as well as being determined by wider political-economy factors that placed greater demands on households.

Every house had a cellar where the large number of meat, vegetable, and fruit preserves (that were consumed in the winter

**FIGURE 2.1.** Marusha in her cellar, stocked well for the winter.

months) were stored. Fresh eggs, apples, pears, grapes, potatoes, onions, and garlic were also stowed in the cellars, where the low and constant temperature meant that such produce could survive many months, especially when packed in straw. For hardworking and organized households like Marusha's, cellars were a library of neatly cataloged jars arranged on the shelves according to contents and year of production (since some remained from the previous year or two). Jars of pickled cucumbers, tomatoes, carrots, fruit compotes, jams, preserved meats, and stews were all neatly arranged, ready for consumption during the winter.

A household khoziaistvo also relied on: the rent received from the family's land that was worked by the agricultural enterprises or private farmers (rent was paid in grain used for animal feed; wheat that provided the source of household bread, corn for animal feed, sunflower seeds for oil, etc.); the salaries of those still lucky enough to have either full-time employment[14]—agricultural enterprises paid in cash and in kind—or, as in the case of Marusha, the occasional payments received from casual seasonal work such as pruning vines for the agricultural enterprise; and pensioners' salaries, which were particularly welcome, because they brought in the only reliable and regular source of cash for many households.[15]

However, pensions were so low that they often did not cover the household's entire need for cash, so additional earnings through various household activities were important and necessary.[16]

The above offers a flavor of the wide range of activities in which contemporary household khoziaistva were engaged. From a long-term historical perspective, the ongoing dependency between household land and land surrounding the village (land currently worked by the enterprises) is notable. One can identify a direct correlation between the two lands: From the earliest days, when it was the land outside that was the sole site for production while household land was just left "wild," a situation that continued during Soviet times, to contemporary times when land outside the village, now privatized, was focused primarily on the production of large grain crops and viticulture, leaving families to intensively farm their household land. While there has always been a strong interdependency between land outside the village and household land, the nature of this relationship (and the use and exchange value of both) has changed significantly. The point worth emphasizing is that since 1991, the privatization of former collective land had a knock-on effect of massive unemployment which combined with the withdrawal of the new agricultural enterprises in provisioning households, significantly increased the use value of household plots. Household production was radically transformed: The range of what was produced was extended, while the quantity produced has increased. The greater range of produce and an increased intensity of cultivation points to the new and growing importance of household plots—their revaluation from lesser to greater use. Such a revaluation also had, in turn, repercussions in terms of changing social relations: relations within the household as well as between different households.

## WHEAT/BREAD AND INTERNAL HOUSEHOLD DIVISIONS

Wheat and bread were the basis of the household khoziaistvo. Villagers often expressed the importance of both. Katya, a neighbor and sovkhoz accountant, in conversation with neighbors while sitting next to one ton of onions being cleaned in preparation for sale (2003) underlined the importance of both wheat and bread: "Wheat is very important; and bread is the most important of all! . . . We can do without these [pointing to the onions, the cash crop], we can do without everything else, but not without bread. Bread is the foundation [*baza*] for everything."

As the staple crop/food, the importance of wheat/bread was evident across all domains of social life. For the household economy, wheat was an important crop, if not the most important one. Reworked as bread, it was the basic food that accompanied all meals. Wheat provided, to quote an elderly baba, "bread for us and food for the animals." The household economy relied so much on wheat that when it was in deficit there were dire consequences, as became clear in 2003—a particularly dry year—with the lack of rain threatening the agricultural enterprises' wheat crops. At a gathering of neighbors on the street one night in May, Katya expressed her concern, "The way this season is going, there'll be nothing. We'll be eating corn; there'll be no wheat." (Corn was normally reserved for animal fodder.) People nodded somberly, then Marusha added that the lack of wheat would also mean that next year's meat would be expensive (many households were already slaughtering their animals, as they had insufficient feed), so "those who can feed animals this year will do well."[17] Thus, the lack of wheat had direct impact not only on villagers' supply of the staple food, bread, but across the household economy: how many animals could be supported, how much meat they would be eating the following year (given inevitable price raises) and possibly how much money the household could earn if they were in a position to sell surplus meat.

Wheat, like bread, played a significant role not only in the sustenance of daily life, but also in most life cycle rituals and religious services, including weddings and commemorating deceased relatives.[18] Every special occasion demanded the cooking of particular breads with different shapes, forms, and decorations. Further, all funeral processions filed past the village mill. Depending on the deceased's alliances and also his/her home location, the procession may or may not have passed the church or the council building. However, as Marusha told me, "No matter how out of the way it is, all funerals pass the mill."[19]

In short, ritually and economically, wheat and bread were central to the household khoziaistvo. This was as true in Soviet times as it was after 1991.[20] I discuss the all-important wheat-flour-bread nexus as a way to examine the impact of the revaluation of household land on household relations. One effect was that householder duties increased significantly as waged work options disappeared and the cultivation of household land increased in terms of the range and intensity of activities. Also, men's and women's responsibilities became more burdensome in different and complementary ways: Tasks were delineated on the basis of gender.

In Soviet times, the agricultural collectives were responsible for all parts of the process: Wheat was grown by the collectives, it was milled into flour by the collectives and bread was sold to the villagers by the collective bakeries (both sovkhoz and kolkhoz had their own bakeries). All workers of the collectives were involved, directly or indirectly, in the process of transforming wheat into bread, from its cultivation to buying and eating the finished product.

Since the establishment of the enterprises, the link between villagers and the wheat-bread nexus has been severed. As noted in chapter 1, only a small minority worked the enterprise land and were directly involved in the production of wheat. While most villagers were no longer involved in the production process, they nevertheless still took a keen interest in the process as observers. Wheat remained a topic of frequent discussion, and villagers often commented on the progress of the wheat in the fields. One night in 2003, Katya reported to a gathering of neighbors on the street, that the wheat in the seventh field (Ponte's) was very good. This was worthy of comment, because in that year, which was a drought year, the wheat crops were not doing well. Conversations often also focused on wheat prices, who was selling and the quality of the wheat. This was of particular interest to those villagers who did not receive enough wheat from their rental entitlements and needed to buy additional supplies. Marusha reported that her sister had said that the wheat sold at the mill was very good quality, unlike that for sale at the shop owned by the local businessman (Angelovski).

While most villagers were no longer participants in the production of wheat, they were more directly (personally) engaged in the conversion of wheat to flour and bread, which were no longer activities in which the agricultural enterprises were involved. It was householders who were obliged to collect the wheat from the enterprises, organize its milling into flour and bake bread. Further, these activities had a gender aspect: Men were responsible for working the wheat into flour; women were responsible for working the flour into bread.

Men collected the heavy sacks of grain from the enterprise when the annual payment of rent was handed out and transported it home for storage. They also had the responsibility of hauling the sacks to the local private mill to be ground into flour (for bread) for human consumption. The poorer quality wheat they milled at home more coarsely for animal feed. Men tendered and slaughtered the larger animals (pigs and sheep) raised in the khoziaistvo. Concern for looking after animals, including food preparation, had always been their task, but during Soviet times, this responsibility was minimal, given the smaller number of (larger) animals raised by the household. Accordingly, households did not receive so much grain from the collectives, nor was it needed, as daily bread and meat were mostly produced by the kolkhoz/sovkhoz and sold to the householders.[21] Thus, the men were not as engaged as they were in more recent times with milling the flour for the household bread or for animals.

Once wheat was milled into flour, women took over the process. Similar to the case for men, women's work options were largely restricted to household production.[22] Their responsibilities and tasks at home have increased, and the making of bread was one of the most significant activities, alongside tending to the smaller animals (poultry), growing vegetables/fruit and making the winter preserves.

Unlike the Soviet period, when bread was very cheap and everyone bought their ready-made loaves at the bakery, since the early 1990s and the breakup of the USSR, villagers have not been able to afford to buy bread.[23] Baking at home was a significant change in householders' lives, as evidenced in the frequent reminiscing of village women. In the first months after arriving in Brega, while sharing lunch with the council women, I was told how baking bread was something new because they no longer had the money to buy bread.[24] On another occasion, Marusha and Katya recalled how between the early 1970s and early 1990s, they never baked bread at home. The only time they worked with dough was on special, ritual (religious or other) occasions, such as when they would make the sweet breads for Easter and pita bread for wedding ceremonies. Bread, it was explained to me, was cheap. So cheap that sometimes they would buy bread to feed their animals! It was easier and cheaper than feeding the animals corn. Plus, there was no deficit in cash, as they all received decent salaries. Marusha explained that bread was only 20 *kopeiki* a loaf, whereas a decent monthly salary was between 80 and 100 UAH. So, if both spouses in the household worked, you would receive 180 UAH/month, and "on that you lived very well." Katya added, "You could even put money in your savings account."

In summary: The expansion of household activities has reorganized internal relations in terms of gender, as evidenced through the division of tasks relating to wheat-bread production. Gender roles were strengthened through the additional self-provisioning activities taken on by households. These divisions were, if not overcome, at least reduced during Soviet times through employment in the collective where household relations—between male and female—were equalized through the appropriation of tasks by collectives and the receiving of salaries that gave everyone "equal" access to flour/bread. Gender demarcations between men and women in the household became more prominent after the leveling device of salaries was no longer available. The task of turning wheat into bread has been "domesticated" in a particular way with gender divisions incorporated into the process. With the elimination of waged agricultural work on former collectives, it was not only that many of the provisioning tasks were transferred to the responsibility of individual households, but in the process, traditional gender hierarchies gained new saliency.[25]

Hierarchies of power manifested through age (generation) between the younger and older members of the households have also become more pertinent. This was evident in the baking of bread. It was the senior women who were entrusted with the highly important activity of baking. In this way, as I suggest below, senior women were reasserting their responsibility for the reproduction of the household, and in the process, their own position of authority within it.

Senior women took an active interest in the flour: They commented on its quality, as this was relevant to their own activities, the working of the flour into dough and bread. "Khubav," or "nice [in the sense of good]" flour, was partly defined in terms of color—it needs to be white; black or darker-colored flour was seen as bad flour. “Good” flour was also partly defined in terms of texture: It should be fine. Fine white flour was seen as a sign that the bread would rise sufficiently. On one occasion, while lunching at Marusha’s house, she cut us some bread, and Valentina commented that it was “krasiv,” or “beautiful.” Marusha proudly turned the loaf around so we could see more clearly its texture inside and agreed with us it was good. Bread was described as krasiv and khubav when it was light and high, in other words, well risen, and it broke in a particular way, separating in lengths—a sign of good quality. These features, I was told, related to the type and quality of the wheat and to the milling process. It was commonly thought, too, that flour, much like wine, improved with age. It was said that wheat needed to be stored for a few months before being milled into flour, otherwise it was no good for bread making—the dough from such flour was too runny. Baba Mina noted that her three-year-old flour had become even better than in the original year that it was milled. An observation confirmed by Marusha, who said, “They say if you keep flour, every year it becomes better.” Quantities of “nice/good” flour, therefore, were put aside for future years in order to ensure that there would be sufficient amounts for special occasions (as there was no guarantee about the quality of wheat from year to year).[26]

Undoubtedly, the return to baking bread at home represented extra work for women, and often they spoke wistfully of how they used to be able to afford to buy bread. Yet, at the same time, I rarely heard them complain of the extra burden (perhaps in part because many had had no waged labor for over two decades, and the increased household demands were thus not experienced as burdensome as might be the case if they also had full-time employment alongside such domestic duties). It was clear that the women took a genuine interest in the art of bread making. Meeting on the street, after a long day of physical work, women talked about how their bread had turned out. Most baked at least once a week and commented on the process. They discussed the quality of the flour and critically assessed their own efforts: The oven was too hot, which made the outer crust too hard; a crust that was cracked indicated that the dough was not kneaded sufficiently; there were debates about which type of fat to use—whether it was better to use pig fat or sunflower oil, and so on. Conversations and exchanges of information about bread were at the same time a public account of their household responsibilities.

Such conversations about wheat, flour and bread point to the new role in the household of senior women, who dominated the latter part of the process as bread makers. More than gender, contemporary bread making reinforced traditional age hierarchies between women from the same household (men never baked). Memories as to who baked the bread in pre-Soviet times confirm that it was the senior/elderly woman, often referred to as "bulkata," that is, "the bride."[27] Patriarchal arrangements that brought daughters-in-law to live in the husband's households meant that eventually the bride became the senior woman of the household. The important point is that it was the woman in charge of the social and biological reproduction of the household, bulkata, the daughter-in-law, who also baked the bread. Never totally absent, these age hierarchies were less evident or relevant during Soviet times, when the majority of villagers worked for the collectives, received a salary and were less burdened with tasks that sustained the family, such as baking bread. Household hierarchies were negated through waged labor that helped equalize the relationship between different generations of women in the household by enabling the daily staple to be bought and by the meals provided by the kolkhoz and sovkhoz canteens. Only special-occasion bread was baked at home. In other words, waged labor removed central tasks relating to the production and reproduction of the household. The tasks were transferred to the collectives. The result was less hierarchical or pronounced age-based household relations.[28]

In contemporary times, as in pre-Soviet days, it was again the senior woman who had the responsibility of making the bread. Baba Mina, who baked in our household, declared that the reason she had the bread making task was because her daughter, Valentina, was too busy working. Yet, in many other cases, where the younger women did not have waged work, such as in Marusha's household, it was still the senior woman who had the responsibility of bread making. Women seemed reticent to explicitly discuss such task allocations. When I asked Marusha why she makes the bread and not her daughter-in-law, Sonia, she responded awkwardly, "So far, Sonia hasn't baked bread [and added as a justification], in any case, what else do I have to do?" A laughable question, as Marusha was the hardest working person in her household, responsible for garden cultivation, cooking meals, making the winter preserves and looking after her grandchildren. I was hard-pressed to find one case of a younger woman who had the responsibility of baking the household bread, and no one in our little group of women sitting outside one evening could think of a case in the village. When I pushed Marusha about whether the woman who made the bread in the household was the head, she smiled and said, "Well, that is not true anymore. . . . Traditionally, it was the senior woman who baked the bread, but now we are more equal." Marusha's point is well-taken: Perhaps, relative to pre-Soviet times, there is more equality in household relations, but with respect to Soviet times, I suggest, there is less. Age hierarchies have returned in response to the new household tasks carried out at home.[29] Given the high importance of bread across a range of domains of social life, the senior woman's new role as bread maker reinforced and gave her renewed authority in the household.

Authority attained through the position of bread maker indicated responsibility well beyond this one activity. Bread making was a sign of the senior woman's overall commanding position in the running of the household and her influence in making decisions relating to the entire khoziaistvo. Such authority was evident on a daily basis. In our household, despite being middle-aged in her fifties and tertiary educated, Valentina always deferred to her mother's authority. She made no decision concerning the running of the khoziaistvo without consulting her mother. Without Baba Mina's authorization, Valentina would not buy the extra wheat from their agricultural enterprise that she knew was necessary for animal feed or organize the sunflower seed to be turned into oil. When she delayed performing her tasks—such as organizing for the pig to be castrated—she was admonished by her mother for neglecting her duties. Similarly, in Marusha's household, despite the presence of a senior male figure (her husband), I witnessed Marusha's commanding position on many occasions. Marusha and her husband jointly ran the household, but with a tendency to drink too much in the evenings, Kolyo often submissively gave in to Marusha's word, prepared to trust her decision-making capacities. Marusha's daughter-in-law (who played no part in baking the bread) helped around the house and was often allocated tasks by

**FIGURE 2.2.** Baba Mina baking special-occasion bread.

Marusha. In short, along with making bread came authority in the household; it was a signifier of responsibility and internal household power. Responsible for the provisioning of the household in its staple food, a senior woman had powers far beyond that provided simply on the basis of her role as bread maker. It was a sign of authority and wider household powers in the decision-making and running of the khoziaistvo.

When the senior woman became too frail and no longer had the strength to make the bread, she passed on the task to the next woman in terms of seniority. This process was done in stages. First, the successor was given the task for everyday bread making, while the elder woman continued making bread for special—ritual—occasions. Only later, when she felt the younger woman was competent and well trained in her bread making skills, did the elderly woman hand over this task to the next woman in seniority. This was the case with seventy-year-old Katya, who told me in 2014 that she no longer did the baking of bread, a responsibility taken on by her fifty-three-year-old daughter-in-law. Katya explained that she herself baked full time until two years earlier, then in the previous year, she only baked the special occasion bread, leaving her daughter-in-law to bake the everyday bread. Since 2014, she has not baked at all, giving up the all-important task of the special occasion bread baking, too. It was a symbolic, as much as a practical, handing over of decision-making and running of the household to the younger woman.

It made little difference that by 2014 some households had bought bread machines. Luba, our neighbor from across the road, no longer made bread by hand; she used her machine, and was very pleased with the results. Luba told us how all machines were different and turned out different types of bread in terms of shape and appearance. Her machine made bread in a round shape and 30 cm high. Other machines made rectangle shaped loaves, and so on. Bought for her by her godchild (*krustnitsa*), she was so happy with the bread made by the machine that when she first got it, some three years earlier (in 2011), she took a loaf to the kindergarten where she worked to show the women. According to Luba, when the other women saw how nice the bread was, a colleague went and bought the same machine. Not all machines, Luba cautioned, made good bread. Indeed, one colleague stopped using her own machine because it did not make good bread—it remained white on top even though it was cooked inside. Other women, such as Marusha, continued to make bread by hand. Aksana, (a schoolteacher) refused to use a bread machine, because "I don't like the idea of it." However, the use of these machines did not greatly change conversations; the women still took an active interest in the outcome of the bread and the quality of the flour, regardless of whether the bread was made by machine or by hand. Nor did the use of bread machines change power hierarchies in the household: It was still the senior women who owned and worked the machines that made the staple food. Despite new technologies, the process was still individualized, and authority over the process remained in the control of the senior woman, who continued to assert her authority as an expert through shared conversations and the cooking process.

The revaluation of land and changing land arrangements of the past decades have shifted the important activities once performed by the collectives into the household domain. The example discussed here was the fundamentally important wheat-bread nexus, which after Soviet times lay outside of the domain of the new agricultural enterprises (except for the production of wheat that involved only a small minority of the village) and came under the new responsibilities of each village household. This greater burden on households, and the personal involvement of families in the production of flour and the baking of bread, has revived traditional (pre-Soviet) gender and generation divisions within the household, providing a clearer demarcation of roles between women and men, and (re)introducing hierarchies of authority on the basis of age.

## ONIONS, VINES, AND EXTERNAL HOUSEHOLD ALLIANCES

I once commented to Sasho, a former engineer in the kolkhoz and now an unregistered private farmer,[30] it is commonly said that it is best to keep work separate from family and friends, as this can put these relationships at risk. He laughed and said, "Here, it's the opposite: You should *only* work with family and friends." His comment resonated with what I witnessed in Brega: Household khoziaistva relied mainly on labor from kin and kum.[31] Other social relationships—such as those with neighbors or work colleagues, who were also close in many other respects—were almost never called upon to contribute to activities relating to household production. In this section, I look at two cash crops—onions and vines—both of which necessitated the help of additional labor from outside the household, in order to explore the way in which relations between households have changed as a result of the revaluation of household land. It was onions in the years immediately after 1991, and grapes, especially after 2005, that provided households with cash.

Onions were grown by both the kolkhoz and sovkhoz since 1988, according to recollections from Marusha and Katya. Both collectives encouraged villagers to look after a "delianka" of onions. In the years after 1991, this arrangement was continued by the agricultural enterprises (the successors to the collectives) who were responsible for planting, watering, hoeing, spraying and digging the onions. Householders would perform the more labor-intensive tasks—the incessant weeding between the long rows of onions, and after the onions were dug out, there was the back-breaking work of scouring the earth for the "gold," putting them into piles in order to dry, and then days later, loading them onto trailers (provided by the collectives/agricultural enterprises) to deliver home. In the final stage, once home, every single onion was cleaned by hand, its outer peel removed, and its stem cut. Clearly, the cultivation of onions involved a lot of intensive labor at various stages of the process that also necessitated cooperation between the large agricultural organizations and individual households. The joint effort was recognized in the sharing of profits. Part of the proceeds was returned to the collectives/enterprises as a fee for their contribution; the payment could be made either in cash or a proportion of the total crop (which varied from year to year, depending on the yield). In 2000, Valentina paid 100 kg of onions to her agricultural enterprise, from an estimated one ton harvest.

Onions were the pride and joy of villagers. The way onions were spoken about left no room for doubt as to how much this crop meant to them. Katya, having just had her two tons of onions delivered in front of her home in 2001, while we (Marusha, Valentina, and I) watched on, exclaimed: "But how beautiful they are and they shine like gold! [*No kakva krasota, i bleshtiat kakto zlato*]." Onions may not have had as much symbolic worth across the vast range of domains of social life as wheat/bread, but their importance as a currency, as "gold," was not to be underestimated.[32] Villagers

**FIGURE 2.3.** Marusha, her two sisters, and mother (furthest to the right) cleaning the onions after harvest.

were clear about the importance of the crop in the years after 1991: Onions provided the only source of cash income for many, if not most, households. Marusha, permanently unemployed since she lost her job with the disestablishment of the collective, told me (in 2004): "Thank goodness for the onions and grapes, otherwise we would have no cash at all." Onions, as one of the few cash crops, was a means for villagers to engage in the cash economy. Marusha reminisced that while profits were not very high when the onions were sold to the government in the early 1990s, what they got "was a lot for those times." A number of villagers (including Valentina) told me that their children could not have studied if not for the onions. The profits from onions also enabled the buying of consumer goods: Marusha's household bought a TV from the profits from onions in the early 2000s. Galya, the wife of the sovkhoz vet, and a nurse who was forced to retire early when the village hospital closed, aptly summarized the situation: "Onions have been the hope of the people—they have been the only source of cash and supported them through these difficult times."

The arrangements between the agricultural organizations and

households concerning onions did not change dramatically after 1991, except that a private market for the onions developed: They were sold to private buyers and the price negotiated, rather than being sold to the government for a set price. As Marusha recalled, it was in 1992 for the kolkhoz, and 1993 for the sovkhoz that the crops could be sold, for the first time, to private buyers. Buyers ranged from small traders from surrounding villages (including from Moldova), who swapped sacks of apples for onions, to large lorries from northern Ukraine that would either trade (1 kg of potatoes for 1.5 kg of onions) or buy the onions for cash.[33] There was also one trader in the village who made significant profits from buying onions in the village for 30 kop/kg and selling them in other parts of Ukraine where they had contacts for 1.30 UAH/kg.

The concern with profits grew at the same time as villagers' need for cash increased, following the loss of employment with the rise of the agricultural enterprises. However, after 2004, involvement in the cash crop started winding down.[34] One hurdle was the increasingly unreliable market for the onions. In the early years, buyers were easily found, as there was a constant demand from nearby Moldova. However, by the time I arrived in 2000, villagers were already expressing their concern over a declining market. Bregans were aware that Moldovans came, bought the onions relatively cheaply, and then sold them in Moldova for high profits, approximately three times higher than the price that they had received. Despite occasional expressions of anger at being taken advantage of in this way, this source of buyers was missed once it started drying up, as border restrictions between the two now independent nations came increasingly into force. At the same time, petrol costs rose sharply, which made transporting the crops to Ukrainian markets farther north expensive and unprofitable, plus there was rising competition from other parts of the country. All these factors made the onions in this very peripheral part of Ukraine uncompetitive. The situation wavered: Some years, the price was high, and buyers were easily found—such as in 2003, when the drought meant onions were scarcer and their price was high. In this year, lorries drove straight to the fields and bought the onions before they were even transported home for cleaning. More often the price was low and the market unreliable. The following year, in 2004, uncertainty dominated. As Valentina said:

"We work them, they are beautiful, we take them out . . . and then can't sell them." "Yes," agreed Marusha, and posed the rhetorical questions: "Who will take them? Who will buy them this year?" It was for this reason that the onions were not only described as "beautiful," but also sometimes as "nashata muka," that is, "our torment/agony." The difficulties of finding buyers and the low price eventually reduced the production of this cash crop. All the work and effort, with no guarantee the onions could be sold, put an end to their torment. The outcome was sealed after the enterprises' irrigation equipment was stolen—onions require significant quantities of water at particular times—and with no means to replace this equipment, the enterprises had little choice but to stop their involvement in onion production.

As it became more difficult to find a market for onions, villagers turned to the only other cash crop, grapes. This was also not a new market and, while the market for grapes had run parallel to onions, it outlasted them. It was in 1990 that the collectives set up a similar arrangement for vines to that established for onions a couple of years earlier. It was in that year that Marusha (along with many other villagers) committed herself to looking after a certain number of rows of vines from the kolkhoz (that were planted by the collectives and on collective land). She has looked after the same rows (delianki) ever since, and the arrangement between households and agricultural enterprises has changed little since the first years: The enterprises carried out the heavy work relating to the vines, such as the plowing and spraying, while households performed the lighter work, the digging, pruning and harvesting. It was the latter—the harvesting—that required extra labor beyond most households' capacities since the grapes had to be picked and sold within a matter of a few days. Unlike onions, they did not keep well. Much as with onions, the villagers paid a "norm," a "fee" to the collectives (and then later to the agricultural enterprises), which was part of the harvested grapes. The fee varied, depending on whether it was a good or bad year.[35]

Household involvement in collective vines began as a consequence of Gorbachev's directive to uproot vines across the USSR in an attempt to combat alcoholism. The head of the agricultural enterprise, Petur, told me that the kolkhoz "gave" (i.e., placed in "permanent usage") 156 hectares of vines as "delianki" to the

**FIGURE 2.4.** Picking the grapes in Valentina's household plot (the house can be seen in the background) with help from her cousins.

people in 1990, thus saving the grapevines from destruction, following government directives that they uproot the collective vineyards. The kolkhoz had a total of 415 hectares of vines at that time, and all were uprooted but for the 156 hectares that were "given to the people." He noted, regretfully, that they could have saved a higher proportion of the plants had more villagers taken on more of the vines. While the collectives were legally compelled to uproot their vines (except for those they could "transfer" to the villagers' keeping), there was no such legal pressures on the vines on household land. However, here too, householders uprooted part of their crop. For example, Tanya told me that their household plot produced approximately three tons of grapes a year, far more than they could consume as wine. While not legally forced to uproot their vines, her household did get rid of half of the plants, because there was nowhere to sell the grapes—the state market was gone. As she said, "What would we do with three tons of grapes? There was nowhere to sell them."

Over the past two decades, state financial support has reversed this situation, aiming to develop the viticulture market again. This was part of the reason, if not the main one, that vines have continued to provide a stable and reliable source of household income (as opposed to onions).[36] In addition, villagers were aware that grapes provided a more reliable income than selling animals (fed on the grain provided as rent). Further, since vines were usually productive over many decades, they were seen as a potential source of long-term income. Vines were also attractive because one could use them to get loans. Sasho, the unregistered private farmer, "mortgaged" his family's household vines in order to obtain necessary machinery parts for his combine harvester. When the grapes were harvested, he gave them to the company from which he had received the machine parts. In short, vines were seen as a good form of long-term investment due to the longevity of the plants' productivity and ability to provide rental and loan options.

Grapes also had an assured local market. Since 1990, and at least until 2014, villagers sold their grapes to the winery in the district capital. While the price of onions varied from year to year (from 30 kop to over 1 UAH), and the market became increasingly unreliable and distant, the price of grapes has remained relatively constant, at 80 kop/kg or above. Vines were an attractive cash crop because the market for them provided a relatively steady and good price—even though there was some fluctuation from year to year, and different types of grapes brought different prices. Private buyers (small-scale) also bought into this market: In 2014, there were a number of individuals who knocked on doors inquiring of the householder if they wished to sell their grapes (such individuals were usually from nearby townships and wanted to make wine for their private consumption). In most cases, private buyers bought grapes from household plots, rather than from the larger quantities of grapes being looked after by villagers under rent from the agricultural enterprises. The price was good, and villagers were receiving up to 1.40 UAH/kg. Sellers who did not make wine for household consumption, or those with too much for their own consumption, were therefore well placed to earn from such sales, although the quantity sold was not particularly large (compared to the harvest from the agricultural enterprises' delianki).

Grapes had special importance in the household khoziaistvo.

Much like onions, the extra cash from grapes was sufficient to allow the carrying out of large household projects that would not be ordinarily affordable. Valentina said that the earnings received from the sale of household grapes paid off a loan she had taken for the installation of gas pipelines to the house in 2010. As in the case of bread (and unlike onions), grapes in the form of wine were also important across a range of spheres of social life, being symbolically important in various life cycle rituals, in religious services and when hosting guests at home. Most households relied on their grapes, not only for income, but also for wine for private consumption. The importance of household grapes in the annual village life cycle became particularly clear when Valentina, in her role as secretary to the mayor, and thus the officiant who carried out civil marriages, told me that a neighbor's wedding had been postponed until November, by which time the grapes would have been harvested, providing the household with more rubles for the wedding. Overhearing this comment, Marusha added, "and if they wait until November, the wine is good too," indicating the fact that part of the wine would be drunk at the wedding, and it would taste better after an additional period of fermentation. Indeed, the month or so following the harvest of the grapes was the wedding season in the village, partly because of the extra available funds from the grapes, partly because the bulk of the summer work had ended and more people were free, and partly because of the availability of large quantities of household wine that would be consumed at the wedding banquet by the guests. Weddings were scheduled according to this seasonal household activity.

The cash crops, onions and grapes, were of vital importance to households. Over the previous two decades, they had provided the only source of income for many families. However, planting and harvesting the crops were labor-intensive activities that relied not only on households working with the collectives/enterprises, but also on additional labor from other households. There were two sets of relationships mobilized by households in the production of the cash crops: "close" kin and kum.

It was immediate family from the household, and sometimes external to it, who provided the main labor force for cash crops. Reciprocal arrangements of labor were made only with the closest of kin. In the case of Marusha's household, help with the cash crops—the weeding of the onions in the field, or the picking of grapes at harvest time—came from a core group of seven or eight people. Apart from Kolyo, Marusha's husband, and the couple's younger son, who was part of their household, Marusha relied on her three sisters and her mother (her father was deceased), as well as the husbands of her sisters. These four households operated together: Her sisters helped her, and Marusha reciprocated when they needed her assistance for the same activities.[37] She explained: "I help them with their onions, and they help me with mine." The households often would coordinate their agricultural activities, so as to make sure that members from one household were available to help on a particular day and not clash with the activities of the other households. With such close relations, reciprocity was not always immediate or balanced. For example, in one year, one of Marusha's sisters did not work onions, but nevertheless she helped Marusha with the weeding of her onions, and then later in the year, after the harvest, with their cleaning in preparation for sale. In the wider scheme of things, Marusha would return the help in some other way or form, and "returns" could be over a very long period of time.

For those unable to reciprocate labor, or with insufficient numbers of family members, running a khoziaistvo was difficult. My host's household was such a case. Valentina had no siblings on whom she could rely for help. She also had no husband, so she could not draw on his close relatives (especially missed, given that many household tasks were seen as gender-specific and required male "physical strength"—e.g., house maintenance). Finding assistance was a constant problem. It was one reason that Valentina did not work any delianki from the agricultural organizations. She did harvest the vines at home for the first few years after her father's death, when money was needed to pay off a loan for getting the house connected to gas infrastructure,[38] but by 2014, she was contemplating no longer harvesting the household grapes, instead "giving" them to someone else (a relative, who would help her in other ways in return). She told me: "For those households which have the labor, it pays to have grapes," indicating that living alone, and with only a small network of close family on whom she could call, it made no sense to sell her grapes, because labor costs would reduce any potential profit. At the same time, as a retired government worker, she received a regular pension and was thus not as dependent on such crops for access to cash.

Nevertheless, there were other occasions when Valentina needed help. When still fit and able to work, her mother (Baba Mina) would help her own sisters, and her sisters would return the favor, when necessary, in a reciprocal labor-exchange arrangement. Once Baba Mina became too frail to engage in labor exchanges, and subsequently after her death, Valentina found herself increasingly isolated without anyone she could appeal to for help. Her relationships with aunts—both on her mother's and father's side—were not considered close, and requests for assistance were met with mixed responses. Her need for help arose on a variety of occasions, especially at times when transport was needed to collect the rent from the agricultural enterprise. Valentina could not do this herself, and was at the mercy of her aunts, some of whom were prepared to help, others who would only help for payment.[39] Speaking from personal experience, Valentina told me: You cannot depend on uncles and aunts, because "they have their own families," and therefore their own priorities and responsibilities to their own households. They were, in short, too "distant" to be relied upon for help.

First cousins provided a more fruitful avenue of assistance for households that lacked sufficient labor. As an only child, Valentina was especially close to her first cousins, with whom she had grown up. It was these cousins who could be called upon for help in much the same way as siblings.[40] First cousins were considered close family, and like siblings, they were not considered suitable marriage partners. Boryu (and his wife and family), the son of Baba Mina's sister and Valentina's first cousin, was relied on regularly for assistance. If he was too busy, she turned to his teenage boys, who were able to drive her father's motorbike and lift heavy weights, collecting sacks of grain from the agricultural enterprise. In such cases, payment was not given, but reciprocity of a form was made: The two boys were fed a good lunch for their efforts. The expectation was that labor reciprocity was required, much as in the sibling case. When you could not reciprocate, payment (usually in kind) was offered, and sometimes accepted (unlike the case with siblings). Monetary exchanges and cash were related to social distance. More distant kin (such as aunts and uncles), neighbors and other villagers could, under specific circumstances, be mobilized for help, but in such cases, they formed part of a monetary exchange system that was never practiced between closest kin.

Kum constituted a second group of people on whom the household could and did draw when seeking help with household production. Most families were in kum relationships (some couples might be godparents to more than one family), although many of these relationships today, as during the Soviet period, were not consecrated through church marriages, but operated on a more informal, secular basis between two sets of couples. The sacred associations of kum (irrespective of whether the relationship had been formalized in church or not) meant that the individuals had various symbolic importance in the reproduction of the household: at (church) weddings, at times of the birth of a child, at Easter, at name days, at funerals (they helped dig the grave and cook for the wake) and during house renovations. In short, they were associated with all ceremonial (religious) events concerning the reproduction of the household. Kum have also become important in providing labor to the household. Marusha's kum, for example, helped with the grape harvest, working alongside Marusha's sisters and their husbands.

Kum (who may or may not also be kin) were often viewed as equal in closeness to kin, and even more sacred because of their symbolic religious associations. Vito, who worked at the water irrigation station, said of his kum, who was godmother to his daughter, "A kum is the closest of all relatives." Said half-jokingly, the point was important: Kum were much like "second parents," whom "you must respect. . . . They are perhaps only second to your parents as a stately and elder couple that you respect and admire." It was for this reason that, like close kin, kum were kept out of monetary exchange circuits and never paid in cash for their services, even though it was only with their labor assistance that a household was able to reap the benefits of a cash crop. While more distant relatives might be paid for their help (if labor could not be reciprocated), the kum relationship was never—to my knowledge—reduced to the market/monetary sphere. When Valentina asked her teenaged godchild for help with the onions, and told him that she would pay him, he refused, saying, "You are my *krustnitsa*" (godmother).

In this way, he was signaling the conventional understanding that he would never dream of accepting payment. He gave his help but refused the money when it was offered. It was also why a former villager (who now lives in the district capital) did not pay his next-door neighbor to look after his chickens in the village household yard during his weeklong absences from the house. When I asked Marusha how she knew that their relationship involved no monetary transactions, she replied, "I know for a fact that he doesn't pay any rubles, because Katya [the neighbor] is kum to him . . . although he helps in other ways." Their relationship was one of reciprocal helping: He gave her some piglets to look after, and the proceeds from the animals were shared. Also, when he bought a new car, he gifted his old car to his kum. Relations with kum (as with close kin) were practiced outside the monetary sphere of exchange, even though the results of the relationship often brought or enabled cash benefits.

Much like relations between close families, relations between kum could sour. I observed a few instances where friction between families and their kum took place. One such case was in 2003 and involved our own household. Baba Mina was kum to the sovkhoz vet Kolya and his wife Galya. Valentina was godmother [*krustnitsa*] to their children, as well as being Kolya's first cousin. There was a double bond between them: kinship and kum. On one occasion, soon after arriving in Brega, I invited Valentina to come with me to Kolya and Galya's place, but Valentina refused, explaining she was "a little offended [*malko obidena*]" at Kolya. Normally, he was someone she regularly relied on: Every year, he helped her buy a piglet from the sovkhoz to raise for her household, and if it got sick, she turned to him for help. She explained that Kolya had promised on numerous occasions earlier in the year to come and castrate the piglet, but he had not come. Valentina continued: "Marusha and Kolyo [next door] got their pig at the same time; it is now 130 kilograms, while ours is barely 70 kilograms." If they are not castrated, they do not grow fat as quickly. The pig was intended for sale to cover the expenses of Valentina's daughter's studies in the district capital and could not be sold if it were only 70 kg. The issue caused trouble between Baba Mina and Valentina, as the former had become very angry with the latter for not having dealt with the pig in a timely manner. Valentina eventually found another vet willing to do the procedure. Valentina explained that the fact that Kolya had not come as he had promised cost her, a "lot of nerves and was bad for my health." It had also caused friction between Baba Mina and herself, plus they had lost money, since they were forced to buy extra winter feed for the pig, as it hadn't grown sufficiently in order to sell during the summer. Valentina emphasized that she had helped Kolya by letting him harvest the vines on their sovkhoz land. "He got a lot of money from it," yet he did not reciprocate with help when she needed him. The "obida," Valentina told me, "would pass and things will be OK," but she needed more time. For his part, Kolya explained that he had been very busy over the summer, but had tried to come a couple of times, although Valentina and Baba Mina had not been home.

In the few such cases I witnessed, breakdowns happened when help was not reciprocated, or the household's economy suffered in some way in terms of loss of income or harvest as a result of one party not fulfilling its obligations to the other household. However, in the majority of cases, the strained relations, whether family or kum, were eventually repaired.

Siblings and close family ties have always been relied upon for help in household economic activities; however, close family and kum were mobilized far more often in the contemporary period than in Soviet times. This was in response to the new burden placed on households in the provisioning of the family, and the corresponding need to increase household production. The labor had to come from somewhere. The migration of youth to cities in search of work as a result of the lack of employment possibilities in agriculture (and the war in the east of the country) had created the need to rely on people outside the household to supply labor during certain stages of the agricultural cycle. This need for labor was solved by mobilizing kin and kum from other households. The increasing popularity of kum since the 1990s could not be attributed purely to a "new interest in religion . . . now that people can engage in religion more openly," as Sasho's wife once told me. The revival of religion may have been a spiritual reawakening for some, but for many, it provided a suitable means for reaching out to other households and strengthening their labor supply.[41] Evidence for this is suggested by the fact that many of the contemporary kum arrangements remained informal and outside of institutionalized religion (having been "domesticated" during the Soviet period—see chapter 4). The traditional—if not religious—practice of kum was part of a newly developing social infrastructure in reaction to increasing labor needs of the household. It was a response to high unemployment and the corresponding new importance of household land as well as an increasing reliance on cash crops.[42]

In summary, the rising importance of household plots over the last two decades corresponds to a growing importance of, and reliance on, close kin and kum from different households. At the center of such growth and interdependence was the exchange of labor. Those households not able to reciprocate with labor—because of age or illness, having a full-time salaried position or coming from a small family—were disadvantaged, and relatively "poor" in the sense of being unable to mobilize a strong network of laborers to help work and harvest cash crops. This was the case in my household, in contrast to that of Marusha's next door. The importance of families from different households working together—whether because they were close kin or kum—was nicely described by Marusha, who told me: "Some jobs, like the onions, you can't do by yourself, and you have to do it within a fairly short period of time, so we go and help them, and they come and help us." Reference to "help," signified the nonmonetary form of labor exchange between these households.

The cash that was received from the crops that were worked with the help of family and kum allowed a household to engage in a monetary exchange circuit; however, the reciprocal labor relations that enabled the realization of the crop remained firmly outside of a cash economy or any form of commodification. In the process, the alliances between close kin and kum were reinforced through annual labor exchanges, while those kin not part of the reciprocity arrangements become more distant and peripheralized. In the latter case, such distance was evidenced in the fact that any assistance given could be monetized.

## THE CHANGING USE VALUE OF HOUSEHOLD LAND AND NEW DIVISIONS AND ALLIANCES

In considering household land as a resource, we can see the significant ways in which its use (and exchange) capacities have changed over time, that is, the way in which the resource has been revalued. Household plots were worked more after 1991 than ever before—in either pre-Soviet or Soviet times. They became central to the survival of the family and supported the cultivation of a wide range of vegetables and fruits, as well as increased animal husbandry activities. The use of the land has been extended in three senses: The land was used to grow a far greater range of crops, the area cultivated was larger and farming was more intensive. Produce from household land remained primarily of use value. In the event that households were left with a surplus, the produce could be sold, as Valentina was doing after the death of her father with the sale of the grapes grown in the household plot. However, such activities remained supplementary, as the primary objective of household land was to produce for the provisioning and survival of the household.[43] Households could engage in activities specifically focused on income generation—cash crop production—and often this was the sole means for households to earn money. Note, however, that most of this cash crop production did not take place on household plots, but relied on arrangements with the agricultural enterprises; cash crops could only be worked in cooperation with these large scale organizations. Land privatization created small-scale agricultural producers who were private landowners, but at the same time, these individual households remained very much dependent for their survival on the large agricultural enterprises, not only through the rent they received, but also for opportunities to engage in cash crop production.

Such a revaluation of land had important implications for changing relations both within and between households. The equalizing effect of Soviet salaries, that took householders away from traditional relations based on gender and age,.lk was no longer a factor after the dismantling of the agricultural collectives.[44] The lack of waged work opportunities, and consequently extended and intensified household farming activities, renewed internal distinctions within households that set gender and generation in greater relief. While my access to male activities in the household were limited (as my host household was made up of only women), it was clear from observing neighboring households that male and female tasks became more sharply delineated, as were generational differences between women (and presumably men, too).[45] A focus on the production on the staple of bread provided an insight into how internal relationships have changed within the household, with a demarcation of tasks reinforcing gender divisions and renewing hierarchies of age. Any exchange potential for households came from involvement in cash crops, but this relied on two factors: interhousehold reciprocal labor exchanges (that remained firmly outside the world of monetary exchanges) and arrangements with agricultural enterprises (also an exchange relation that took place outside the monetary domain). No longer able to rely on secure waged labor once offered by the collectives, households were more dependent than ever on cash crops, but these crops could only be worked with the help of reciprocal labor exchanges between kin and kum from other households. In this way, engagement in cash crop production—onions and vines—strengthened relations between households, creating a set of close laboring arrangements based on family members and kum. Such solidarities between close kin and a greater dependency—if not closeness—between particular households, also implied a growing social distancing with other kin/households. Kin who were not in reciprocal labor relations became more distant, as evidenced by the fact that these relationships, when mobilized, often made use of monetary payments.

In summary, the revaluation of household land and associated transformation of households into khoziaistva has resulted in new divisions and new solidarities: Internally, there has been a sharpening, if not expansion, of divisions in the family based on gender and generation; externally, household alliances have been strengthened between certain kin and kum. Such revaluations of household land—and produce from it—have resulted in changes in intra- and inter-household relations that make khoziaistva of contemporary times very different from Soviet households of the past.

CHAPTER 3

# WATER

## THE UNMAKING OF GOOD NEIGHBORLY RELATIONS

In this chapter, my focus is on water as an example of a resource that shifts value within the same category of exchange: from one form of exchange (nonmonetary) to another form of exchange (monetary). In Brega, water was a vital resource with wide-ranging importance: from its symbolic role in various ritual practices (see chapter 4), to an essential component of agricultural production, both for the large-scale agricultural enterprises as well as for individual households. My focus is on the importance of water for domestic households, a fundamental resource as recognized by Ivan, the first head of the communal company that managed the village's water supply, when he told me in 2001: "Water is a basic resource, like the air . . . and everyone needs water."

It is difficult to discuss water outside of the context of land arrangements and the organization of labor (Pradhan et al. 2000, 6; Mosse 2008, 939). It follows that land reforms have had important consequences for other resources. Over the period of a few years, as the former sovkhoz and kolkhoz wound down and extricated themselves from the provisioning of households (chapter 1), villagers were forced to grow more produce on their own household land (chapter 2). This, in turn, led to an unprecedented demand for domestic water. Thus, land reforms contributed to the revaluation of water: Water became far more important to households, and from being a resource that was exchanged for free during Soviet times, it was converted into a commodity with monetary value. With this revaluation, and in the context of unequal access, new tensions developed between neighboring households. My concern in this chapter is with the resource's revaluation and the new conflicts that this generated between neighbors.

Besides the importance of land reforms and the associated new labor arrangements, national legislation relating to water was also an important factor in the revaluation of the resource. The Water Code of Ukraine (Government of Ukraine 1995) was the main legislative act concerning water. It clearly stated that all water was the property of the Ukraine people, and that their rights over the water were exercised through Parliament.[1] However, various legislations—including decentralization laws passed in the 1990s—devolved powers to the municipalities. The devolution process extended over many years, and there were numerous amendments and even reversals of the legislation in later years, in order to make the resource more attractive to investors (OECD 2006, 8, 23).[2] Further, Ukraine's growing closeness to the EU necessitated numerous legal harmonizations in order to bring Ukraine in line with the EU requirements (Hall and Popov 2005, 6; OECD 2006, 23). The constant reforming of the system made implementing the changes difficult, complicated, and confusing for local administrators.

While water remained in public ownership, and the privatization of water in Ukraine was prohibited by law (OECD 2006, 9), decentralization created conditions for the involvement of the private sector through the management of the resource (OECD 2006, 23). The Ministry of Housing and Communal Economy was the main national body concerned with the water sector. It had departments in each oblast responsible for licensing and various other functions of the "communal" companies in the districts (OECD 2006, 23) that were charged with managing the resource. Laws limited the role of the state to supervision, regulation, and planning, while at the same time encouraged the involvement of private enterprise as a way of managing local water supplies. This opened up the possibility for the marketization of water.

The perceived rationale for water decentralization included making administration more democratic (and efficient) through reorganizing governance in order to bring decision-making powers to the local level, "closer to citizens" (Khmelko 2012, 1; Burns et al. 1994, 4), while at the same time making local inhabitants aware of the costs by giving them financial responsibility. Of course, in the case of Ukraine, as across much of the post-Soviet world, decentralization was also represented as attractive because of its ideological kickback against former socialist centralization. Further, it was a convenient cost-cutting measure for national governments: By transferring responsibility downward, national budget expenditure was reduced, while at the same time, local government was forced to seek investment from somewhere else—inevitably the private sector and/or passing costs onto users. Promotion of a market-driven commodity was part and parcel of the decentralization reforms.[3]

There were a few other general factors that bear particularly on the case discussed below and that also deserve highlighting. When the communal companies were created to manage water (and other community services) locally, the central government at the same time eliminated budget subsidies for the utilities (OECD 2006, 22). Thus, the communal companies were forced from the beginning to take responsibility for the resource without any start-up financial assistance. This forced many to introduce a metering system. The commensurability of water through a metering system that measured the resource in terms of volume used, transformed it into a potential commodity suitable for the market through a levied price per cubic meter.[4] Such a standardization took place slowly over a number of years, but was still by no means complete or universal in Brega when I last visited. Indeed, it was more than two years from when the initial idea to create a communal company was first raised at a village meeting, to the transferring of control of the water infrastructure from the former agricultural collectives to the jurisdiction of the village council, which then created a company to manage the resource.

Further, in the case of the smaller utilities, such as Brega, that is, those servicing populations of under 100,000, it was the local administration that issued licenses for companies and set tariffs. This took place in the district capitals within the oblast (OECD 2006, 23). Importantly, while disconnection of nonpaying households was not ruled out in terms of existing national legislation (Institute of Urban Economics 2004, 7), municipal councils were reticent, for political and other reasons, to implement any penalties. Indeed, local authorities banned communal companies under their jurisdiction from disconnecting nonpaying users (Institute of Urban Economics 2004,14). So, on the one hand, nationally driven decentralization policies encouraged, even necessitated, the commodification of water in order to be financially viable (given the lack of state financial support); on the other hand, fines were not imposed by local authorities for a variety of welfare and political reasons. Citizens were guaranteed the basic right to water through being shielded from disconnection. In this respect, water was unlike other utilities where penalties for nonpayment were enforced. The result was—much as Collier (2011, 26) described in the case for the Russian heating system—a "selective" intervention. In my Ukrainian case, nationally driven reforms that pushed for marketization were limited by local agendas of social protection; the national and local administrations had different priorities (with the latter trying to accommodate agendas of commercialization alongside their concerns for social welfare).

In short, state decentralization policies played an important role in the drive to transform water into a commodity with monetary exchange value. This process involved moving the control of the resource from centralized to community managed systems. It gave municipal councils responsibility for decision-making, finances and the implementation of certain functions relating to the resource. If decentralization was the vertical shifting of responsibility and control over the resource, then a horizontal movement was also implicated, as the resource was transferred from one form of public control/ownership, agricultural collective, to another, the village council. The overall effect locally was a subtle but important transformation: a decoupling of water as part of an agricultural collective system as it was passed to the authority of the council, who in turn had the legal authority to hand over management functions to private business. In this sense, the resource was owned and managed through a mixture of public and private, national and local influences.[5] In Brega, the local council "owned" water (on behalf of the nation) as a public good, but shared management responsibilities with an organization that had a commitment to commodifying the resource. The latter could only operate, however, within the social and moral limits of the community.

In the following section, I provide a general overview of the history of water in Brega in order to lay out the intimate historical connection between land and water use in pre-Soviet and Soviet times. Following the historical discussion, the rest of the chapter focuses on the way in which relations were disrupted in the process of the revaluation of water into a commodifiable resource. First, my attention is on the development of the new communal (services) company established to manage the resource in the village and some of the challenges it faced. Second, the conflicts between neighbors created by the rising demand for water are described. The penultimate section examines the solution provided by those villagers who had insufficient access to water and discusses their willingness, following encouragement from the communal company, to install meters and pay for the resource in the hope of better access and a more equitable system. Finally, I return to the issue of the revaluation of water as it moved from one form of exchange to another. The attempted creation of a market for this resource did not resolve the problems relating to access; instead, it created new divisions and antagonisms between neighbors within the community.

## THE HISTORY OF WATER IN BREGA

Many of the late evening conversations between neighbors gathered on the street during the summer months concerned assessments of their household crops: "Sonia had to buy peppers this year because she has none," Marusha, my next-door neighbor, reported to the group. Luba, who lived across the street from us added, "Tanya has lots, but they are all very small, like mine. There are lots on the bush, but they are small. . . .Whereas Luda's are a picture." "Well," responded Dasha, "naturally, she has water!" Water gained new significance after the disestablishment of the agricultural collectives and the related necessary expansion of cultivation on household land, in what was a cash poor economy with high levels of local unemployment. This in turn introduced unprecedented demands on access to water, a point emphasized by Marusha when she told me (in 2003): "Before [in Soviet times], water ran strongly and everyone had lots . . . but in more recent years, it is a problem." Villagers' memories convey an interesting picture of how water demand has changed over the decades in alignment with changing land arrangements, and with it, the emergence of water as an increasingly valued resource.

Household water needs and usage during both pre-Soviet and Soviet times were not high compared with the contemporary period. We may recall that in pre-Soviet times, householders planted very little in the household garden, as all fruit, vegetables and grapevines were grown in the blocks of land outside the village (chapter 2). Household land during this time was just an "empty space," almost "wild," according to the recollections of Baba Mina, the elderly mother of my host. Part of the reason household land was not cultivated was the lack of water; all water had to be transported by horse- or donkey-drawn carts in containers from the nearby lake. It was used primarily for human consumption and washing. Some of the luckier villagers, who lived near the creek that ran through the center of the village, might have planted tomatoes and other vegetables in their household yard, but most people were reliant on the land that lay beyond the settled boundaries of the village. In these pre-Soviet times (and the early years of the Soviet period), water was scarce, and obtaining water for household use involved considerable effort.

Tapped water became available for the first time when the communal baths were built in the years after Brega was incorporated into the Soviet Union after World War II. Water from this location was also transported home in containers by horse and cart. It was only after the households started building underground storage tanks in their own yards, from the early 1960s onward, that the sovkhoz and kolkhoz were able to deliver water to households in trucks. Nevertheless, we may recall (chapter 2) that there was no significant change to the use of household plots, nor therefore to the overall demand for domestic water during Soviet times. It is true that the householder's loss of the land outside the village—which was incorporated into the collectives—meant that villagers planted vines in their own yards as well as a small quantity of fruit and vegetables for fresh consumption during the summer months. The former were watered only by rainfall; the latter were watered by hand when necessary, using precious household water. However, the vast quantities of fruit, vegetables, and meat necessary for winter preserves—that still came from the land surrounding the village—were provided by the kolkhoz and sovkhoz. Much the same as in the pre-1941 years, in Soviet times, households did not require a lot of water; most food was produced elsewhere, cheaply available from the collectives. It was the large-scale water irrigation systems operated by the collectives (pumping high quantities of water from the lake and the underground water table) that enabled the production of crops for the provisioning of the household. Although during the Soviet period water became more readily available to households, and in larger quantities, water needs remained largely limited to domestic consumption.

In the 1970s, the village's water infrastructure system was developed further. Underground water was pumped from 90- to 180-meter depths and stored in large tanks in prime locations around the village, seven in total (five built between 1971 and 1985, while the last two were completed in 1993 and 1994). The "pumping stations" (namely, the pump and water storage tanks) were controlled by the kolkhoz and sovkhoz but have always been state owned. The water was transported to households by underground pipes installed along most of the village streets. The flow of water along the street mains could be regulated so that different streets were provided with water from the tanks on different days. However, the street pipes could also be used to carry water from another source, the lake, which provided an alternative to the underground water. There were two pumping stations at the lake, one belonged to the kolkhoz and the other to the sovkhoz, and they used the water for irrigating the fields. Occasionally, these pumps were used to supply village households with water from the lake, which was channeled through the street pipe infrastructure. It was during this same time—early to mid-1970s—that householders built new underground storage tanks located close to the street in order to make the delivery of water easier, irrespective of whether this was by pipe or transported by trucks from the collective. This was the first time households had access to substantial quantities of water. It was up to individual households to pay for and install the additional pipes that connected their own tanks with the village street mains, and most, although not all households, were connected.[6] The location of the tank was of some importance: Storage tanks were built close to the street, which made delivery easier; however, there was always a trade-off, as street proximity meant having to transport the collected water a greater distance in order to reach the house (which was located farther back from the street) or any crops in the rest of the garden that stretched out behind the house at an even greater distance from the street. (The farthest end of the yard from the access road shared a boundary with the backyard of the house in the next parallel street.)

Water was supplied to households by the agricultural collectives for free, although in later years. a small fee was charged for delivery. It was an entitlement of all collective workers as well as those in the support occupations, such as teachers and doctors. Considered together this constituted essentially the entire village. The access to water was based on an exchange: the giving of labor by employees for one of the many services provided by the collectives. Water deliveries were made by the kolkhoz or sovkhov, depending on the household's location as being either in the sovkhoz or kolkhoz end of the village. As Tanya, the schoolteacher, explained, once your name was recorded on the waiting list, "then sometime in the next couple of weeks the water would be delivered. How fast you received the delivery depended on your connections to the delivery driver and also on the other commitments of the driver, who made water deliveries in between his other agricultural duties." Since the driver was not employed full-time to deliver water, personal connections to him were useful for jumping the queue and receiving the delivery sooner rather than later.

If the delivery of water was a nonmonetary exchange between the collectives and their employees (water for labor), and connections to the driver provided another circuit of nonmonetary exchange (through an "economy of favors") that could hasten a delivery, then the sharing of water between neighbors was yet a third way in which water was exchanged. Although water was not in great demand, since the land remained largely untended, there were occasions when some households had insufficient quantities for their needs: for example, when a promised delivery was de-

**FIGURES 3.1 AND 3.2.** Baba Mina taking delivery of water. The hose from the truck is extended over the fence into the household yard where the water storage tank is located on the other side of the fence.

**FIGURE 3.3.** View of Sasho's (unregistered private farmer) household yard, with two underground water storage tanks, to the left and right of the tractor. Only the raised coverings of the storage tanks are visible.

layed, due to the fact that the deliveries were made only part-time in between the drivers' other agricultural duties, or when those on the upper side ran out of water due to the low pressure of the pipes (if water was arriving by the water main). It was possible that a household could be left without sufficient water for a temporary period. On such occasions, water was shared among households. I recorded several cases of neighboring households connecting long hoses between their yards in order to transfer water from one household storage tank to the other. The quantities shared were vast and not accounted for (in the sense that the water was not carefully measured or quantified in any way). In fact, during the Soviet years, the household where I lived had arrangements with two different neighboring households that would allow my host's home tank to be filled from those of the neighbors. Such transfers took place with the household directly across the road below us. It also took place with a neighbor whose yard was directly behind and therefore also above ours (at a higher elevation). The latter had better water access, because he lived on the parallel street above our land, which meant his house—located on the lower slope of the parallel street—had stronger water pressure. Baba Mina described in some detail how they would connect hoses between their own house and the neighbor's, allowing the latter to transfer many liters of water from his storage tank to ours. Valentina, as a council worker, did not have close connections to the delivery drivers, especially after the retirement of both her parents from the collective. The household often relied on such arrangements with neighbors when water was not delivered on time. There was no charge or "fee" given to these neighbors, it was simply part of the day-to-day general reciprocal relations practiced between the households. Clearly, when the resource was limitless and free, and household demand not high, neighbors were willing to share.

To this day, the lake and underground water provide the two main water supplies for the village. However, there was an important difference between the water from the two sources. Water from the lake[7] was good for watering household plots, and it was also pumped by the agricultural enterprises for irrigating their own crops. It was not of suitable quality for drinking. Underground water, pumped from the water table, was acceptable for human consumption, although too salty for garden use. However, and this is a complication I return to later in the chapter, there was only one set of pipes in every street; this single set of pipes had to deliver water to households from two different water sources. In addition, households generally had only one operational storage tank and could store water from only one source at any one time.

With their relatively low consumption needs primarily for domestic purposes, these technicalities were of little concern during Soviet times. However, with the collectives disestablished and the new agricultural enterprises no longer provisioning villagers, the household plots were cultivated far more intensively than ever before in the village's two-hundred-year history. This is crucial in understanding the elevated importance of water and the increasing demand for it. Households needed water in order to ensure enough for their extensive vegetable gardens and the increased amount of livestock they raised, as well as for the usual drinking and domestic needs of the family.

It is not only that land and labor shape water arrangements. Conversely, access to water determines land use and labor activities, that is, household production: what villagers plant at home as well as where they plant. For example, Tanya explained that she did not plant cabbages in her household land because this vegetable requires a lot of water, which she did not have. Baba Mina planted a small number of tomato plants and peppers at the lower end of our yard, close to the storage tank, because "they like water, and there isn't any." At least this made hand watering easier. Beyond the house, and in an increasing distance from the storage tank, lugging water by hand became too difficult. Immediately behind the house, we grew a selection of vegetables watered by a hose that was connected by an electric pump to the storage tank. The grapevines that grew beyond our house were watered only by rainfall. In short, access to water determined what was grown, how much, and where.

While water has always been a useful resource, the demand for it has increased dramatically during the past thirty years since villagers' livelihoods have depended on their household land for survival. During Soviet times, water was an exchangeable resource (nonmonetary), delivered (or piped) for free by the collectives to its employees. Through connections to the driver, individuals could move up the queue and receive a water delivery faster (another nonmonetary exchange through involvement in an "economy of favors"). Alternatively, if deliveries did not arrive on time, then water would be shared between neighbors. In each of these three ways, the circuit of exchange was of a nonmonetary form. These exchanges were part of a water arrangement that was designed to cater to the needs of households integrated within a collective system. The infrastructure not only reinforced the interdependency of households with agricultural collectives but also strengthened neighborhood relations through acts of sharing. The Soviet water infrastructure was not designed to cater to the new high water demands faced by individual households forced to cultivate the land more intensively in order to satisfy their entire annual consumption needs. Following the establishment of the agricultural enterprises and the associated new burden placed on individual households to be self-sufficient, the once adequate water infrastructure was no longer fit for purpose. Water has become a revalued resource as well as a new source of conflicts between householders in the neighborhood.

## THE MAKING OF A NEW COMMODITY

In Brega, the "social services" (including the domestic water supply) were the responsibility of the village council, rather than the agricultural collectives as in previous times. As early as 2001, the village council (henceforth "council") drew up its own plans for taking control of the water from the kolkhoz and sovkhoz. It was at the initiative of the mayor that a *komunalno khaziaistvo*[8]—"communal company," or "company"—was formed. Its name signified that in the longer term, the company would be responsible for more than just the village's water. It was anticipated that eventually the company's functions would expand and include other village services such as sanitation—including the collection of rubbish—the selling of building construction materials (e.g., sand, wood etc.), and would even be responsible for the fixing of TVs and radios. However, at least in its first two decades of operation, the company was concerned exclusively with the delivery of domestic water.

### Challenges Faced by the Communal Company

Delays—from the leader of the former sovkhoz and one of the leaders of the former kolkhoz, both of whom were reticent to lose control over the water pumps (because in the early 2000s, they still needed a regular water supply to maintain the onion crops and livestock they continued to raise)—meant that the company only existed on paper some two years after it was initially formed. However, by January 2003, at a council meeting, details were finalized as to which agricultural enterprise would give what to the communal company. The sovkhoz relinquished control over its water pumping station at the lake, the water drilling and storage tanks, a storage building, the fire engine, and a tractor for water deliveries. The four agricultural enterprises (which once constituted the kolkhoz) transferred their water pumping station at the lake, the water drilling and storage tanks, a digging machine, a tow truck, a tractor, and the communal baths. Brega's communal company became operative a few months later that same year (2003). In this way, the Soviet water infrastructure, which materially linked village houses, the school, kindergarten and the hospital with the collectives (which were the water providers), was transferred from the control of the former kolkhoz and sovkhoz to the village council.

The mayor emphasized that the company was neither a cooperative nor did it represent a means by which water was privatized, although because the company introduced charges for water and its delivery, villagers generally thought of it as a private company, even while they constantly referred to it as the "cooperative" (a term I leave unchanged in quoted passages). Operating as a public–private organization, it had a close association with the council.[9] The mayor appointed the company head (who was approved by the council), and he was assisted by an accountant and tractor driver—whose sole job was to deliver water. The company was directly answerable to the council. However, it had its own bank account and budget, and the mayor did not interfere in daily operations. All salaries were to come from the revenue from the water (one of the main bones of contention, as discussed in a following section), and the top company positions—the director and accountant—would qualify for bonuses if they performed well. Profits would be divided between the company and the council, with the company entitled to keep the first 15 percent of the overall profits in any year (assuming there were any). The remaining profit would be negotiated and possibly shared between the company and council. Water was seen as an important source of financial revenue for the council.

From its onset, the company faced a number of challenges that were rooted in the infrastructure that had been built during Soviet times and designed to accommodate a system organized along collective lines, when individual consumer demands for water were not as high.

First, there was the problem of how to deliver both drinking water and water for the gardens when there was only one set of pipes and two different water sources. This problem had not existed in Soviet times when families were not involved in any significant cultivation of their household land and thus did not require water for their gardens. Various solutions were tried, with water from the different sources being distributed through different arrangements, including pumping different types of water on different days of the week, and pumping lake water through the pipes while delivering underground drinking water by truck. Both solutions proved inadequate to the extent that some villagers

**FIGURE 3.4.** A village street in Brega, showing the sloping landscape, looking down to the lowest point and up to the other side.

**FIGURE 3.5.** Lenina Street (where Valentina, Marusha, and Luba lived). Visible is the downward slope from right to left that created such a problem in terms of water pressure.

used underground water for both drinking and for their gardening needs, even though they were aware that in the long term, this would ruin their soil, rendering it too salty to grow anything. Other villagers were drinking the lake water, which was a health risk.

A second problem related to the pipes laid under the streets. Not only were these pipes now forty to fifty years old (from the early 1970s), but they were of different thicknesses, with some pipes having a larger diameter than others. The result was an irregular flow of water. Some places did not have enough pressure, and the piped water could not reach the household storage tank or reached it only at a trickle. The problem was exacerbated by the fact that, in some places, as in Lenina Street where I lived, the pipes were installed on the lower side of the street (the village was set on two sloping hills, with a creek running through the valley in the middle). Because of the natural slope, the houses on the upper side of the street received no water, or had only very low water pressure, barely a trickle, whereas houses on the lower side of the street received much stronger flows of water.[10] The location of individual household storage tanks was also a factor: Those tanks located farther away from the street—it could be just a matter of a meter or two above street level—had greater difficulties in accessing piped water than those located closer to the street. This was especially true for houses on the upper side of the streets. Marusha's tank was barely two meters higher in her yard than ours, yet often when piped water flowed into ours, it did not reach hers.[11]

While such problems were all new in the early 2000s, over a decade later they were still largely unresolved and an ongoing source of tensions and regular flare-ups between neighbors, especially during the summer months when water was in high demand. By 2014, after years of trial and error, a roster had been agreed upon: Along our street, water flowed on Wednesdays and Saturdays, and other streets were supplied on other days of the week. The established roster did not, however, reduce friction between neighbors.

### Neighborhood Conflicts

Water preoccupied villagers' concerns every year, but the situation was particularly dire during the summer of 2003, which was, according to some, the driest they could remember in 20 years.

In the middle of the village, running north to south, is a gully. It separates the village in half (into east-west parts), with houses built on the two slopes that run down to the creek that flows along the bottom of the gully (Mavrov and Bratkov 1967, 2). In early May of 2003, Gena, who lived a few houses away from us, rushed up from the lower part of the village, to where Valentina, Marusha, and I were sitting as usual, under the shade of a tree on the street outside our home in the early evening. In an excited voice, she reported, "There's water down there [pointing to the households down by the creek]," and added somewhat unnecessarily, "and none here." From the bridge that crossed the creek, she said she saw large sprinklers in the household yards, throwing up water. They were "flooding" their plots with water. Gena continued: "Their potatoes were so high [indicating with her hand to her knees], while we have nothing. My potatoes are finished; there'll be nothing. What will I feed my children? They want to eat, too." "Exactly," responded Valentina angrily. "Over there they have water . . . they sell their cabbages and water their entire yard; we can't fill our tanks with water even when it is running [through the main pipes]."

This short exchange highlighted the two related concerns at the center of dissatisfactions. One source of tension was the differential access to what had become an important resource. Uneven access meant that some households had more than sufficient water, so much so that they could not only fulfill their own needs but also produce a surplus crop, while others struggled to produce enough to feed their own families, placing their welfare at risk. Villagers were only too aware that differences in access amounted to long-term inequalities between households with all the consequences that implied for the survival of some households.

However, it was not only that some households had water while others did not. The second and related source of tension was the fact that those who had access to water had it at the *others' expense*. It is precisely because households located at the lower parts of the village were watering their yards in abundance that there was no water left for the others at the higher ends. That is, the water consumption of one group was directly responsible for the reduced access to the resource of the other group.

On a warm night a couple of weeks after that conversation,

I heard noise from the street and went outside to see the cause of the commotion. Nine neighbors were standing in a circle in the middle of the street shouting at each other. As I approached, Marusha filled me in, explaining that Venu, the present head of the communal company, was doing the rounds on the lower side of our street, entering household yards to check if their taps had been turned off. He wanted to see if, when all the taps located on the lower side of the street were off, the houses on the upper side would receive water. As more taps on the lower side were closed, water pressure increased on the upper side of the street and started to trickle through the pipes, slowly at first, and then more strongly. At one point, Marusha's husband, Kolyo, confirmed that water was flowing strongly into their tank, and Valentina checked and reported back a similarly positive result for our household. However, one of the women from a household located the lower side of our street expressed dismay at having to turn off her tap. She asked the assembled group, "How can I turn off my tap when I get water so rarely?" Others shouted in response, "Well, we have none at all!" Marusha, who normally did not lose her temper, yelled back, "You say you have no water at all, but you don't know the meaning of this. We have NOTHING . . . you do have water, even if only from time to time, but you do have water!" The other woman responded in a more subdued tone that she gets water maybe only once or twice a week, and not enough to fill her tank. She said that her tank was empty and invited everyone to come and see. To underline her point, she repeated her invitation: "Come see my tomatoes, how wilted they are"' She deflected further attacks by throwing accusations at those not present: "If you think I have water, maybe I do occasionally, but go see Ivan, his garden is flooded. He has water all the time." The silence that greeted this comment bore witness to its truth. Valentina added that all the householders from the lower side of the street who were now with them on the street had closed their taps, "It's those not here, quietly hiding at home, that still have them open."

The above underlines the problem of different degrees of access: Some households had abundant water, others had limited access and yet others had even less—insufficient for their basic production needs. It was also evident that every household responded to their water situation in line with their own interests in terms of maximizing their water supply, and in the case of such an important issue, did so at the expense of their neighbors. It was a matter of survival.

Those households with water did not share their resource with their neighbors, a point frequently commented upon. As one woman living on the upper side of the street told me in 2003, "My neighbor has water for her tomatoes, while mine are small. Why can't I feed my children? They want to eat, too. But they [her neighbors] won't give me water, nor will those living near the kindergarten [one of the seven village pumping stations is located next to the kindergarten. Those households located close by have particularly good access and stronger water pressure]." She continued, pointing out that even when water was not in high demand, such as during the winter, her neighbors were still unwilling to share: "All I wanted was one storage tank for the whole winter, that would have been enough for me . . . for my sheep and chickens, but my neighbors wouldn't give me any." Households with water guarded their reserves and did not share under normal circumstances. In contrast to Soviet times, the sharing of water, or even simple expressions of willingness to share, was far less frequent in the contemporary period. The giving of large quantities of water through extending hoses between water tanks no longer took place. Individual households prioritized their own needs, even at the expense of good neighborly relations. When householders made it explicitly clear (in heated moments) that they cared little about their neighbors, they revealed a deeper commitment to their own households, prioritizing their own needs above anyone else.

Any offers of sharing were made only between the very closest of neighbors, although in practice these occasions were very rare. In the extremely unusual situation that water was shared, it was carefully measured out by the bucket, given in only small quantities, and only as a last resort when the need was urgent, in contrast to the large and unmeasured quantities shared during Soviet times. One day I reported to Baba Mina that Marusha next door told me that they had no water for their tomatoes. She immediately replied, "Well, we must give them some." Marusha was a distant cousin, and regular and ongoing social exchanges between the two households were a long established practice.[12] Also, we lived next door and shared a boundary. When I conveyed Baba Mina's offer, Marusha hesitated, clearly tempted, because her tomato plants desperately needed water. She accepted after reassuring us that the next day they would receive a delivery of water, making it clear this handing over of water was a one-off measure. Later that day, Baba Mina passed three buckets of water over the fence to Marusha, just enough for her to water her tomatoes and stop them from dying. If water was to be shared, it would be with these closest of neighbors: those living in proximity, with whom sometimes there may be some (distant) kinship, and with whom there was already an established relationship of reciprocity and socializing. The dynamics might not have been the same on every street, but at least on our street, sharing was less likely to take place between neighbors who were more distant, in terms of geography or social relatedness. Social relations thus defined the limits of such sharing, while geographical distance formed an outer boundary, as the transportation of water was determined by the limited capacity to carry heavy buckets of water by hand.[13]

The communal company, aware of the increasing tensions in the neighborhood, tried to address unequal access, and came up with a solution that would mean a more equitable distribution of water: the introduction of a roster system. It was first drawn up in 2003 and modified countless times thereafter. The first roster specified that water would be accessible on Monday to the upper side of the street, then the next day to the lower side (the other days it was diverted to other streets). This did not resolve the bigger problem that many households faced, that is, not receiving water at all, but at least it meant that many of the upper side would have access to some water, assuming that the lower side were diligent in turning their taps off, thus enabling a stronger water flow to reach the upper side.

While the roster seemed to offer a solution that was more equitable, the company could not enforce the system. Following complaints from the upper side of the street (first to the mayor, who referred them to the head of the company), Venu came on a number of occasions during the summer to personally check that houses on the lower side of the street had turned off their taps on the appointed day. He spent some time knocking on doors, visiting every house on the lower side of the street to ensure that their taps were turned off. I already noted one such occasion. On another, he joined the small gathering of neighbors on the street outside Marusha's place, where he reported that all the taps in the vicinity were now switched off. "Mind you," he added wryly: "I'll leave, and within an hour they'll all open their taps again." This indicated a further hurdle: While the roster system, in theory, offered a solution to unequal access, encouraging those who had little interest in honoring the roster was not easy. Marusha, at least, felt vindicated that the company head saw for himself that those on the lower end "just didn't want to close their taps." As one woman from our side of the street noted: "Those who don't want the roster system are those with water, because they don't want to share it." This was graphically articulated by a neighbor located further down the slope, closer to the creek, who made it clear in the face of neighborhood pressure that she did not care about the others: "As everyone else with water, if and when I have water, I will water. And if I had more water, I'd irrigate my whole garden; I don't pay attention to those who shout against me. I'll continue to water. Even if they threatened me with a gun, I'd still water." Social pressure from neighbors further up the hill held little sway for better located households not in the immediate vicinity.

It was precisely this disregard for, and continued flouting of, the roster that induced a number of neighbors to take the matters in their own hands. In the days following the visit from Venu, some of my neighbors from the upper side of the street agreed to walk together across to the lower side to check that their neighbors' taps were turned off in compliance with the roster (Venu could not be in attendance all the time). It was difficult to judge the effect of such neighborhood monitoring, as those on the higher, drier side continued to complain of a lack of water, even after those on the lower side assured them that their taps were off. Nevertheless, such policing methods reflected the increasing lack of trust and erosion of goodwill between neighbors. It highlighted the growing breakdown of neighborhood relations, and the lack of willingness to share, as social pressures were applied to try and curb unlimited consumption.

As the summer wore on, and water became increasingly scarce (in upper-side households), the tensions escalated, and accusations became more frequent and direct. Neighbors continued to monitor each other and accuse each other of water misuse. Drawn outside, once again, by the noise of shouting at dusk later in the summer, I found a group of ten or so women standing in the street, and three men sitting against the wall of one of the houses. When I appeared outside, Kolyo (who was a little drunk) was shouting at a woman who lived in a house further down the slope, closest to the creek. When he saw me, he explained in a loud and demonstrative voice, designed in part to shame the woman, that Nadia was watering when she should not. The confrontation had started, I learned later, because Kolyo had gone down the street to check that the houses on the lower side had shut off their taps in accordance with the agreed roster, only to find that Nadia's hose was working. He demanded to see if her tap was closed, and she refused to allow him in. Nadia claimed that the water she was using came from water already in her storage tank, not from the mains or an open tap. Others in the group suspected that she was lying and had not filled her tank with piped water the previous day, when she could have (according to the roster), because she was watering her garden all through the night, and therefore there was no time to fill the tank. She was now filling her tank using water from the mains on a day when her tap should be off. In the noisy exchange between Kolyo and Nadia, a crowd had gathered. Kolyo continued to explain his actions to the gathered audience: "I said I'd go and check her tap." Nadia intervened: "You don't have the right," and Kolyo replied, "Don't I just!" He threatened to bring a policeman, to which she retorted, "Bring two, I still won't let you in." The shouting started again until Marusha almost had to physically wrestle with her husband, telling him to go back to where the other men were sitting. Kolyo finally agreed, and things calmed down a little.

Accusations became increasingly nasty and went far beyond the issue of water access. While the water problems were seasonal, neighbors raked up years' worth of insults that created resentments that carried over into the rest of the year. One night in late autumn, Katya from the upper side of the street said somewhat provocatively to Misho, whose house was located on the lower side (directly opposite our house): "You are alright, you have water. All your life, you've had water. I've been here 27 years [as an ethnic Moldovan from a neighboring village, she had married into Brega], and for only the first five years have we had enough water, all the other years we've had nothing." Misho replied, "Is that my fault, that you don't have water? You want to come and dig up my tank and take it? Fine, do that. And I suppose it's my fault that you don't have water?" Then he added poignantly, referring to her employment in the sovkhoz as an accountant: "I may have water, but you have a lot of other things. You've stolen all your life from the sovkhoz. I see every day they are delivering something to you . . . today it was hay. . . . You stole and stole from the sovkhoz and continue to steal . . . it eventually poisoned your husband."[14] So it went on, the insults extending into unrelated accusations of stealing from the collective and the untimely death of Katya's husband, until both Valentina and Marusha intervened and told them to stop. Many weeks later, I heard this conversation repeated back between two neighbors who had not been present during the actual verbal exchange, indicating the longer-term impact to reputations resulting from such confrontations.

The new demand for, and differential access to, water led to increased tensions between neighbors, pitting the lower side of the street against the upper side, while all were against those living much further down by the creek who had unlimited access to water. It was those households without water who collectively attempted to bring about greater access via applying moral pressure on their neighbors to turn off their taps. They also became the most vocal advocates for the commodification of water—its metering and payment—as a solution, believing that payment would reduce excess usage, thus increasing their own access to the valuable resource.

## The "Solution" of Water Meters and Payments

Sitting in a circle outside Marusha's house, reflecting on the lack of water following one neighborhood showdown earlier in the evening, Gena said, "They should dig up the road and fix the problem [with the pipes]." Valentina looked at her impatiently and responded, "Just listen to yourself! How long did it take to have this [she stomped her foot on the asphalted road]? Gone are the times you say, 'Fix the problem.'" Later, after Gena had gone and most of the group had dispersed, Valentina expressed her frustration, "She [advocates] for the Soviet times." Luba, our neighbor from the lower side replied, "Well, so do I, Valentina," to which Valentina retorted, "Well, my point is that those times are gone, and now we can't expect them to 'fix the problem.' If it's important enough, we have to take the initiative."

That is exactly what some villagers were doing through their efforts to monitor their neighbors to ensure taps were turned off in accordance with the roster. In a less coordinated fashion and over a longer period of time, a second response was the growing advocacy for the installation of meters.

That villagers should pay for water was a core objective of the communal company. A village council official who helped set up the company said, "Every khoziain [owner] must have water, and the only way to ensure this is to pay for using the system." Yet, as Venu, the head of the communal company, told me in the early years, "No one wants to pay for the water, although everyone wants water." He explained on a number of occasions, both at village meetings and more informally on the street when neighbors had gathered, that the pumps in general were expensive to run, incurring high electricity costs, and were the direct responsibility of the company. He reminded people that in previous times, the collectives had paid for the running costs of water, but this was no longer the case, and the new company could not afford to have the pump running all the time as before. Despite echoing the well-worn neoliberal mantra, "There is no other alternative [to paying for water]," people in these early days remained unconvinced, and it was not an idea that was met with much local enthusiasm. The company accountant told me, when the organization was still in its first months of operation, that collecting money was an unpleasant ordeal because of the resistance and resentment aimed at her: "People aren't used to paying for water . . . and [in all fairness] they don't have the money to pay, either."

Contrary to the views of the head of the company and of the accountant, I rarely heard villagers complain about having to pay for a received water delivery. Indeed, by late summer 2003, meters were viewed—at least by those who did not have sufficient access to water—as a necessary solution. Many shared the hope that Valentina expressed: "Until they put in individual meters, there will continue to be *giurultiia* [arguments, literally translated as 'noise/commotion,' but used in this slightly different sense in Brega]. Meters will make it fair for everyone. Everyone will pay for what they use." The logic was that placing a charge on water would force those with good access to limit their usage, and this in turn would allow more water to flow freely through the pipes to other households.

However, despite the hopes of bringing about greater fairness in water access through the metering/payment scheme, the introduction of such a system only resulted in additional complications and resentments. Complaints focused on the high costs and the lack of transparency in pricing.

The first contentious aspect was the perceived charges, which were seen as too high. According to Vito, who had worked at the water station servicing the agricultural enterprises and was "in the know" when it came to water issues, those in other towns paid far less per cubic meter of water than in Brega. For example, he claimed that in Odessa and Reni, residents paid 2.5 UAH/cubic meter and 3.15 UAH/cubic meter, respectively, whereas in Brega, "We pay 5 UAH, and yet we live so close to water. How come," Vito asked rhetorically, "it is so much more expensive here? Their water comes from farther away; here, ours, is just 500 meters away (referring to the lake), so why are we paying so much?" His conclusion was, "The profit goes into the pockets of the cooperative [the company] workers." Vito went on to describe how the head and accountant say they are only getting the minimum wage, but he knows that they are getting far more (which may indeed be the case, as they are entitled to bonuses). He believed that they were able to give themselves high salaries because of the high price they charged for the water—the profit paid for their salaries. Vito was not a lone voice in this accusation. Others also expressed a belief that high prices were a way company workers were inflating their profit margins and also their salaries. Tanya's elderly mother was convinced that the high prices were evidence that "the cooperative workers are stealing from us." The present structure of the organization, which granted company leaders power to make a profit from the water and linked their salaries (and bonuses) directly to profits, was a source of both resentment and dissatisfaction. This was particularly true in the case of villagers who did not have good access to water. I once witnessed Kolyo shouting down the street after the accountant collecting the then monthly water charge: "I'm not paying your salary. You want your salary, while we have no water." Villagers believed they were being overcharged by those who controlled the resource, and this was especially riling when households could not access sufficient water.

The second concern related to differential costs. Those villagers with meters paid different prices per cubic meter; those who had not installed meters paid yet another price.

Initially, there were no water meters in the village at all. In the earliest phase of company operations in 2003, irrespective of where you lived in the village and how much water you could access or use, villagers were expected to pay a standard regular sum per month for the water. This situation did not please those who were charged but had little or no water. Several neighbors made the point: "I'm more than happy to pay if there is water, but why should I pay when there is no water?" The success of the company's operations relied ultimately on the willingness of people to pay for the service, as there was no other way to enforce the charges (see below). In addition, villagers were vocal in their complaints. Both these factors led to the system being modified in acknowledgement of access inequalities. By mid-2003, each street had one meter installed that measured the total consumption for that street. This total consumption was then divided equally between the number of houses on the street in order to set the charge for water usage for each household. However, it soon became clear that this was also unfair, given the differential access to water within each street between households. Later, prices were adjusted: The lower end of the street paid 10 UAH a month, the upper side paid 6 UAH, and water deliveries by truck were priced at 10 UAH per delivery. This also caused dissatisfaction, because it affected the upper side more negatively, as they did not receive enough water through the mains and thus needed to have additional water delivered by truck to satisfy their needs. In short, the upper side houses spent more to secure water than those households on the lower side of the street.

A decade later, when many, although by no means all, households had installed their own meters, people were charged a "standard" sum per cubic meter (but see below), irrespective of the location of the household (upper or lower street). Resentments continued, however, because the metered system assumed equality between users in terms of access to the resource, which was not the case. Installing meters did not ensure that those on the upper side of the street received (enough) piped water, even on the rostered days. If they did not receive enough, their only alternative was to pay for the delivery of additional water by truck, which was more expensive. This meant that different households paid very different amounts for water, simply based on which side of the street their house was located.

Further, the "standard" price per cubic meter also varied: Households with meters were charged different rates per cubic meter for piped water. Some, such as Vito (the water station worker mentioned above) paid 3.5 UAH/cubic meter for piped water; others, such as Marusha and our household, paid 5 UAH/cubic meter. The different tiers of payment reflected the different times that villagers had meters installed. Those who installed meters in the earlier years—soon after 2003—were charged the going rate at the time (3.5 UAH/cubic meter); customers who had meters installed some years later were charged the new rate of that time (5 UAH). Neither group has been subject to price raises since installation. In 2014, the company proposed an additional increase to bring the price per cubic meter to 8 UAH, although villagers were refusing outright to pay a higher sum.

There were others who refused to install meters. Vito claimed that a number of households on his street did not have meters and paid the general street average (or nothing at all). This was a particularly sore point for him and his wife, after it became clear a neighbor had been deliberately dishonest in concealing her water usage. This neighbor openly claimed she only had one water pump, and thus one meter. It was only when part of her garage wall collapsed, due to her having accidentally left her pump working overnight, thus flooding the garage, that the truth became obvious: She had a second pump hidden in the garage! The second pump was not connected to a meter, and she had been using as much unmetered water as she liked from this second outlet. Vito and his wife were livid when telling me this story, adding in disgust about the neighbor: "She lied, saying she doesn't have a second pump." That is why, Vito went on, they themselves do have a meter to measure their water usage, because otherwise they "would end up paying for the water used by other households in the street, many of whom don't pay any water bills at all, and don't even have meters . . . I may be naïve, but I am not that simple."

There were others who paid no water taxes as a result of their privileged positions in the community or their connections. According to Vito, and confirmed by Marusha's son, Vadika, who worked for the communal company and thus had insider information relating to the accounts, the previous mayor paid no water tax. Another villager, who frequently drove the present head of the communal company to Izmail to get parts when the machinery broke down, also paid nothing for his water. In return for these ongoing favors, he received his water free of charge. There were, according to Marusha's son, fifteen to twenty people in this category of nonpayers.[15]

For those who either did not pay or found a way to bypass the system and avoid paying full or part of the cost, there was no fine or form of punishment. The company relied on people's willingness to pay, because according to Vadika, "The cooperative has no legal authority to impose fines or force people to pay charges for the water." To emphasize his point, he continued: "At home, we could remove our meter or not allow the water tax collector to enter our property," and the company could do nothing about it because, "they have no legal rights to enter or demand payment." The company did not have the authority/ability to impose fines or force people to pay taxes for water. This became an additional source of discontent. A number of villagers expressed the view that unlike the case of electricity or phone usage, where they would be fined or cut off if they did not pay for what they used, nothing could be done with respect to water. "What sort of system is this? For every other utility there is payment and a punishment if you don't pay, except for water. It's not right," Marusha told me in 2014.

The "solution" of metering and payment created the basis for a water market in Brega. However, it was a market restricted in its operations and performance. The first restriction related to technical issues. Reliant on a Soviet infrastructure that was built to support and service a collectively organized political economy, the infrastructure was unsuited to the new conditions. The existing infrastructure was never designed to operate under the present conditions of increased water demand and usage, and was totally unsuitable for it.[16] Further, whether the company had the legal authority to punish those who did not pay their water taxes was a moot point, because the bottom line was that the Soviet-designed infrastructure made it technically impossible to cut off the water supply to an individual household. In its present state, where individual households owned and were responsible for the pipes that connected their respective underground storage tanks to the street pipes, the company could not cut off individual households from the main water supply. It was simply not doable. The company could only disconnect an entire street from the water supply, as it did on alternate days when the water was channeled to other streets. Fines were not a realistic option, since meters were not universal (as well as not politically prudent, from the local administration's perspective). Such technical (and legal) problems were one source of conflict between neighbors, especially in the summer months when water demands were at their peak.

However, access problems due to technical challenges could be largely (although not totally) overcome if households on the lower side were willing to share the water and honor the roster system. Thus, the problems were also socially generated, arising from a range of factors: a newly created demand and desperate need for the resource in order to maintain household survival; different metering and payment arrangements within the community; and reciprocal labor exchanges between households of kin and kum that created networks that did not involve neighbors, requiring them to prioritize their own needs above those of their neighbors (see chapter 2).

Water arrangements placed neighbors in a competitive relationship with each other. Some continued to use water for free and did not pay at all, while those who paid were charged at different rates. Some paid on the basis of an average user cost (measured via the common street meter), and yet others on the basis of their individually metered household volume usage. Conflicting household interests, resulting from the different access/metering/payment options, were indicators of a water infrastructure that was neither smoothly functioning nor unproblematic in its operations. Instead, the new water arrangements created new tensions and inequalities between neighbors.

Social relatedness (and degrees of closeness) constituted a form of moral pressure between neighbors, and this helped address the difficulties to some extent, but had little effect on more (socially) distant neighbors. No doubt there have always been divisions between households. (I do not make any claims that the village or neighborhood was ever a harmonious, unified community.) However, the conflicts discussed here—between neighbors as a result of unequal access to water—represented a new fragmentation that pitted neighbor against neighbor in a way that did not take place before, when water was a freely exchanged and shared resource.[17]

In attributing the blame, villagers occasionally pointed to the reforms as the source of the problem. In a moment of relative calm between neighbor flare-ups, Luda (who lived close to one of the pumping stations, on the lower side of the street where water flow was strong) defended her access to water. "Obviously," she said, "we have water all the time. If we don't, who would?" She deflected her neighbor's annoyance by pointing out that the main problem was not the neighbors who had water. She made it clear she had nothing against turning her tap off according to the roster. Rather, the problem was the reforms: "They dismantled the kolkhoz . . . and now we have such problems. We bash our heads against the wall. I'd like to bash *their* heads against the wall."[18] However, such views that attributed the contemporary problems to the reformers were few and far between. Far more common were the accusations that neighbors directed at each other, rather than at the system.

Leaving aside the question of blame, villagers nevertheless exercised considerable leverage over the communal company. Those neighbors who shared the common plight of having insufficient water access and who embraced the making of water into a commodity through its measuring and payment (in the belief it would provide a solution to the problems of unequal access and distribution) were complicit in the development of the company. Their support was evident both through the installation of household meters and their willingness to pay for the resource. Their policing of other neighbors served their own interests, but at the same time, it assisted the functioning of the company, by exerting pressure on their neighbors to respect the company's roster. In such ways, there was a limited sponsorship of the communal company.

At the same time, different access/metering/payment options provided evidence not only of a limited degree of collective village support for the organization, but from another perspective, also how ordinary villagers were able to exercise influence over the communal company's operations. The fact that different charges were levied at different times, and these tariffs were not increased or equalized for all users, suggests that local pressures were successful in dampening the company's ability to raise prices. The limiting of company operations was evident in its inability to enforce a universal or standard payment, or even to enforce the universal installation of individual meters.

There was a wide range of (inconsistent and sometimes conflicting) ways in which villagers shaped the activities of the communal company. Some activities served to support the company, some restricted and yet others undermined the company's activities. This was manifested through villagers' engagement or not in particular activities, through influencing the value/price of the good, and more indirectly, through putting pressure on neighbors to act in particular ways (such as closing their taps, etc.).

As for the company, it relied on the approval and participation of villagers in order to make a success of its business. With no legal or technical means to penalize those who did not wish to engage in the developing water market, the company head was anxious to seek solutions to the problems that addressed local concerns. For example, the roster developed by the company attempted to resolve access inequalities, but without backup from the villagers, the roster's chance of success would have been greatly reduced. Also, the pricing system had to meet with the approval of most villagers (as evidenced by the different measuring and payment levies adopted over a decade) and attain a general degree of consensus. Nevertheless, the company was in a bind: With no financial help from the government, prices needed to be high enough to maintain the infrastructure, ensure profit and discourage excess use (allowing more equal access); but at the same time, the company needed to show a degree of self-restraint so as not to attract villagers' accusations of profiteering and stealing. Villagers were aware that they could always disconnect their water meters and refuse to pay for the water, as Vadika indicated. Doing so en masse would bring the company to its knees. In the end, the company's success depended on the approval of villagers, and so far, it has been only partly successful. In other words, local relations served to define and limit the company's activities.[19]

To answer Marusha's question as to what sort of system this was: It was a system plagued with technical and social problems (the two are intricately linked), it was a system that generated neighborhood tensions and inequalities and it was an arrangement that was both shaped and limited by local relations. It was also a system that allowed villagers the freedom to engage with the developing water market as they wished: They could choose whether their household water was metered or not, whether to pay their bills or not (since there were no penalties), and there was even some flexibility in how much they paid for the same quantity of the good, even when metered! Those who wished to prove how little (not how much) water they consumed with respect to the rest of the street, which was metered as a whole, had meters installed in their respective households and participated in the commodification of water. Those with good access to water continued to resist having meters installed, as it was in their interests to be charged the standard rate based on an average street consumption (as measured by the meter that shows the water usage for the entire street). Unlimited usage, and ignoring the roster, however, meant that they had to endure the wrath from angry neighbors. It was a market that offered considerable flexibility—some would label it a "failed" or "imperfect" market—and was propped up through the participation of some and not others.[20]

It was little wonder then, that when Marusha asked the questioned that night, "What sort of system is this," her son, who worked in the company, provided her with an answer that succinctly described the situation. Vadika responded that it was a system that was both "inconsistent and unfair." I would add that it was also a system over which ordinary villagers had considerable influence. At the same time, it was also a system that has fractured relations between neighbors, creating new divisions and antagonisms between them.

## THE CHANGING EXCHANGE VALUE OF WATER AND NEW NEIGHBORHOOD CONFLICTS

Water is an interesting example of how a resource can shift from a nonmonetary to monetary form of exchange. It is also an example of how the revaluation of one resource can be impacted by another: Land privatization and the dismantling of the collective system created high rural unemployment and an associated new reliance on household production, which in turn required an unprecedented demand for domestic water. Apart from the knock-on effect of the revaluation from other resources, water was also revalued more directly as a consequence of national water reforms, decentralization policies that have kept the resource in state ownership but made possible its commodification through private management. In short, the rising importance of water as a household resource was a result of two processes: an indirect consequence of land privatization, and in a more direct way, a consequence of national decentralization policies that transferred operations/control/management of water to local administration, who in turn established a private company to manage the resource.

The Soviet (water) infrastructure was built to purpose: to service the needs of communities that were organized along collective lines. Water was provided to all citizens, who had equal rights in terms of access and received the resource for free. This was an exchange: Village households were provided with water as part of their work entitlement, a "swap" of services for labor. Water was also exchanged through another nonmonetary circuit: Its delivery by the collectives to all households was often lubricated through an economy of favors (Henig and Makovicky 2017), since connections to the kolkhoz and sovkhoz drivers were important in ensuring its timely delivery. Water was also freely shared between neighbors when household water supplies ran low and deliveries had not been received on time. Such sharing of the resources was an act that reinforced neighborly relations. All three ways in which water was exchanged were nonmonetary, operating outside of any market economy.

Water is no longer a freely accessible or exchangeable resource. It still has exchange value, but reforms have shifted water access from nonmonetary to monetary forms. With the new demand for water, and the establishment of the communal company to manage the resource (in partnership with the council), the conditions of commodification of the resource were set. In one way or another, water was metered, and most villagers paid for the service (either an average street or individual fee) despite uneven access. Water has become an unequally accessible resource that is increasingly gaining value as a commodity in a monetary exchange circuit.

To a limited degree, national reform goals have been achieved: Management and control of the resource was transferred into the hands of a local public–private company; commodification was in process as the company tried to create a profitable market from the publicly owned property; and villagers were much more aware of the costs relating to the use of this resource as help from the agricultural enterprises was withdrawn. However, from many other perspectives, the reform policies have not succeeded: The company set up to sell water operated an infrastructure (Soviet-era) that was ill-suited for the new water regime that catered to individual consumers with high water demands; the transition of water into a commodity was by no means complete; and there was no legal or technical means by which to enforce compliance from those who did not pay or did not wish to have their water metered. The company could not enforce meter installation nor enforce any punitive measures against those unwilling to pay.

Accordingly, the success of the company relied on gaining the approval of the local population, and on the active engagement of some villagers to apply moral pressure on their neighbors (which created, at the same time, conflict between them). Indeed, villagers had considerable informal influence over the company's operations, far more than they had over their land that was managed by the agricultural enterprises. The company was embedded in local webs of connectedness that placed various demands and obligations, limits and possibilities upon its functioning. In the end, the company was restrained by local spheres of moral and social influence.[21]

In the process of creating a saleable commodity, water has become the site of a new set of community tensions and was at the center of daily arguments between neighbors over access concerns, especially in the summer months. Villagers highlighted, with tinges of both irony and anger, that they had no water, despite the village's location so close to a significant body of water. As one enterprise worker pointed out at an annual village meeting: "We live near the lake [one of the largest in Ukraine], and yet at home we have no water!" Apart from access concerns, tensions also developed over the pricing of the commodity (between those who continued to get water for free and those who paid and/or were charged different rates), and the profits allegedly made by the communal company employees from the commonly owned resource. The process of commodification—through the metering of water—divided neighborhoods and neighbors, creating forms of antagonisms between households that fractured the community along new lines. The use of water did not encourage "domestic publics" (Anand 2018, 169) as much as fragment them.[22] Water, and the infrastructure through which it was distributed, might "make social connections" (Mosse 2008, 941), but it can also dismantle and divide them. The increasing importance of water as a resource, and the creation of a market for it, has not brought about the locally hoped for fairer or more equitable system, nor established a more smoothly functioning or harmoniously operating access system to what has become a vital resource. Instead, what has emerged from the growing importance of water as a commodifiable resource is increasing tensions between neighbors as they argued about, and competed over, access to the precious resource.

CHAPTER 4

# MORAL AUTHORITY

## THE PRIEST VERSUS THE REST

Unlike the previous material resources discussed so far—enterprise land, household land, and water—this is the first of two chapters that focuses on an immaterial (social) resource: moral authority. As an immaterial resource, moral authority does not have physical substance, nor can it be controlled, owned, or managed in the same way as a material resource. Nevertheless, moral authority is equally important in sustaining the community. It is "possessed" by key proponents of the moral order, a core component of the latter being the spiritual realm, which in Brega, is divided between "religion" and "tradition" (Kaneff 2018). Religion and tradition helped villagers make sense of their world at significant times in their life cycles and at key moments in the annual agricultural calendar. Religious and traditional practices were guided by those with moral authority: the priest in the case of religion, and the mayor/traditional healers (among others) in the case of traditions.

Moral authority is provided as an example of a resource that shifts within the same value category of exchange. Rather than moving from one circuit of exchange (nonmonetary) to another circuit (monetary), as was the situation for water (chapter 3), in this case, the resource is divided within the same value category. As an immaterial resource, such a division is symbolic, but can be evidenced through the separate, and occasionally competitive, circuits of exchange that were organized by the leading religious figure (the priest) on the one side, and traditionally active figures in the community (of whom the mayor was a prominent and public proponent) on the other side. The circuits of exchange involved the giving of loyalty and support by villagers to their moral leaders in return for services that provided (moral) guidance, spiritual healing, and community solidarity. Through the exchange circuits, the division of the resource was also mapped onto concrete physical spaces—the church and community buildings—as well as grounded in the figures who organized the exchanges and "possessed" the resource.

The resource's revaluation was instigated with the arrival of a priest after 1991, when the collapse of state socialism was accompanied by the new public prominence of religion. The "revival" of religion following the demise of the Soviet Union altered village life in important ways. However, speaking about the resurgence of religion masks complexities. It was, as others have noted, much more a "revival" in the sense of the need to reinsert organized religion back into public life (Halemba 2015, 178; Hann 2006, 2), rather than about a necessity to "regain" spiritual beliefs. In other words, the need was for formal religion to reclaim control over public space after decades of absence. Similarly, in Brega, the Orthodox priest was welcomed back into the village, but as described below, only in a limited way. After decades without a priest or functioning village church (the building was never dismantled, just locked up), the priest has had to work hard to reassert his authority and influence over other village elite and ordinary villagers alike.

From what I have gleaned of Soviet times, moral authority was not a contested resource (at least not in the same way as today). The three main figures with moral authority in the village at the time—the mayor and the respective heads of the sovkhoz and kolkhoz (all Party members)[1]—were secular leaders from the same ideological orientation. They also sponsored, both in formal and informal ways, the practice of traditions. Without a local priest or operational church, inhabitants were compelled to travel to the nearby district townships of Izmail, Reni or Bolgrad if they wished to seek moral guidance from an alternative source, such as formal religion.[2] The renovation of the Russian Orthodox Church (henceforth ROC)[3] and arrival of a priest in Brega after 1991 presented villagers with a second—and sometimes competing—moral leader to whom they could turn. The community has had to accommodate both moral orders—representing different persuasions—and the resource has had to be shared among practitioners of both orders (traditions and religion).

The revaluation of the resource through its sharing, which is also a division, has led to the emergence of new conflicts rooted in the nature of the exchange relationship between the villagers and the priest: contested views concerning acceptable levels of give and take between the priest and the community. Ordinary villagers deliberated as to how much control and access they were willing to give the priest in their personal lives, especially with respect to their continued practice of traditions—customs which the priest vehemently opposed. Seeking advice from traditional healers, for example, might have been dismissed as "pagan" practices by the priest, but to villagers, it was a legitimate avenue for seeking help. "Exchange" was also at the center of tensions between the priest and village leaders. The two moral orders, represented by different leading figures and the operation of distinct circuits of exchange—one run by the priest, the other by his "rival," the mayor (who upheld community traditions)—sometimes ran concurrently and in competition with each other. The leaders' rivalry for villagers' loyalty through different events, and separate exchange circuits designed to attract local interest and participation, were a way to legitimate influence and moral authority.

The following section focuses on the resource of moral authority through a discussion of the local moral order and on the split between "tradition" and "religion" as crucial in understanding the basis of moral authority in Brega. This split was at the heart of tensions between the villagers, who practiced a variety of traditions at different times of the year, and the priest (as the local leader of organized religion), who vehemently opposed many of the traditional practices. While the distinction is analytical, it is also emic, since villagers themselves insisted upon the separation between "tradition" and "religion."

Divisions created by the shifting value of moral authority, pitting the priest against the rest of the community, are the focus of the discussion in the two sections that follow. The first of these two sections looks at tensions between "ordinary" villagers and the priest. Villagers continued to carry out their traditions, despite the priest's objections that traditions often used symbols/activities that also held significance for the church, and over which the priest made exclusive claims of ownership. Another area of conflict was in terms of the priest's demands on households: Villagers felt that the priest interfered too much in family affairs, including in terms of the material demands he made on them through donations for services rendered.

It was not only ordinary villagers who came into conflict with the priest. Village leaders, the mayor in particular, also found themselves at loggerheads with the priest, and this is the subject of the second (penultimate) section. A main source of these tensions was the council's support (financial and other) for practices (often traditions) that the priest felt competed with his religious work. The discussion focuses on the events of May 22, an annually significant day for both the village council and the church. The two organizations ran different celebrations on the day, thereby competing for the loyalty and support of villagers. Villagers' participation was a way to engage in respective exchange activities offered by the council and church: They benefitted from access to specific services/assistance offered by each institution/leader, and at the same time, their support reinforced leaders' authority and influence.

At the end of this chapter, I return to the issue of moral authority and the division, which was also a sharing, of this resource. The separation of the church from the rest of the village through the operation of distinct exchange circuits by the respective moral leaders provided an "uneasy" arrangement. The priest's attempts to control village life beyond the domain of formal religion was largely unsuccessful: Villagers maintained their specific form of spirituality that combined the practice of everyday "traditions" with the carrying out of their occasional "formal religious" responsibilities.

## A NOTE ON MORAL ORDER AND THE ROLE OF RELIGION AND TRADITIONS

The reincorporation of formal religion back into public life raised moral debates and questions in former socialist states undergoing reforms (Zigon 2011, 3; Benovska-Sabkova et al. 2010; Steinberg and Wanner 2008). The collapse of the USSR was a time for the renegotiation of morality, a time when the ROC made efforts to resume its place as the "guardian of morality" (Lindquist 2000, 247; see also Zigon 2011). I follow Wanner (2007, 10) in understanding morality to be associated with a "commitment to particular practices and beliefs," that presented some resemblance of a coherent system, secular or sacred. Engagement in such activities resulted in feelings of solidarity and community membership. Every community has multiple sets of values and practices (multiple moralities) that are expressed by individuals, different groups and institutions across both secular and sacred social spaces (Wanner 2007; Zigon 2011). Struggles between competing moralities where moral relations were (re)negotiated, contested, and embodied in practice, were a feature of postsocialist society (e.g., see Rogers 2009; Zigon 2011). In the case of Brega, the social space was influenced by two main intersecting moralities, crudely drawn along formal religious and traditional lines, and encapsulated in the official figures of the priest and (often) the mayor.

Moral authority was a resource attributed to those who held office as leaders/representatives of certain organizations. However, as in the case that Halemba (2015) shows for Transcarpathian Ukraine, it was also true in the case of Bessarabia and more particularly Brega, that the ordination and charisma of office (in the Weberian sense) held by the priest was not enough to legitimize his authority. The priest needed to work hard to earn his authority,[4] which came only partly from his official position. It was also partly negotiated through his relationship with villagers. Villagers expected their priest, as a representative of the church, to be a morally exemplary figure. As one former sovkhoz worker told me, "They [priests], like the Party, should be morally exemplary . . . but they are not." The quote emphasizes both the moral accountability of the priests and the frequent disappointment expressed by villagers who felt that priests often did not measure up.

The ROC, as an upholder of the moral order, has a long history in the region that can be traced back to the original settlement in Brega. Unlike some other villages in Bessarabia settled by Bulgarians, who were accompanied by their own priest from Bulgaria (Boneva 2006, 52), in the case of Brega, the migrants adopted the ROC as part of their incorporation into the Russian empire.[5] This has had significant, long-term implications for the configuration of spiritual life in the community, which, as already indicated, was shaped by two cultural influences: a "dual" form made up of traditional practices (associated with a Bulgarian heritage) and adopted ROC loyalties (taken from Russian influence).[6] Local identity, constituted from both Bulgarian and Russian elements, is explored further in the following chapter. The important point here is that it is because the villagers' history was one of migration, and they could make no autochthonous claims to the territory in which they lived, that "traditional" practices were a core feature of their local identity (alongside history and language—see chapter 5).[7] As part of a designated Bulgarian minority in Ukraine, their identity was grounded both in their ROC affiliation and through traditions rooted in an ancestral heritage. Both religion and tradition were therefore of fundamental importance, and villagers worked with both, seeing them as parallel and compatible practices. The shared ROC-traditions are important to bear in mind as they help explain the villagers' deep commitment to both, despite the priest's opposition to traditional practices as incompatible with ROC teachings.

Thus, although the priest was welcomed back after a three-decade absence, his reincorporation into village life was not a smooth process and opened up new sites of local contestation. While the conflict between the priest and the rest of the community was carried out on a few fronts, the most important was on the basis of traditional practices.

In Brega, traditional practices were conducted in a variety of different locations in public places (e.g., the cemetery) and private spaces (home). They covered a vast range of "supernatural," or "extraordinary" activities offered by traditional healers and fortune tellers (usually elderly women in the village), as well as many practices that required no facilitator and were totally in the hands of householders. "Traditions" are what Lindquist calls "folk models of morality" (2000, 257), and what would be designated as "institutional" religion in Halemba's terms (2015). I find the distinction between "institutionalized" and "organized" religion useful in separating traditional practices from organized religion (Halemba 2015). Institutions are socially recognizable ways of acting and thinking about ritual in particular circumstances, such as during times of illness, in negotiating connections with ancestry and so on (Halemba 2015, 14). Institutional activities have no clear rules or doctrines, and no hierarchy or formal representatives of authority. Such practices are simply referred to as, "the way things are done" (Halemba 2015, 22–23) This differs from religious organizations—such as the ROC—which have designated rules and doctrines, and structure social action hierarchically through clearly defined and formalized activities. Such an analytical distinction is much in line with emic perspectives, since villagers viewed their church as quite separate—in social and physical space—from what they called their "traditions" [*traditsiia*] or "customs" [*obichai*] (to use the emic terms, as I do throughout this work). The latter were viewed as mundane and normal types of practices that were justified in terms of "what we have always done."

The priest viewed many Brega traditional practices as incompatible with formalized or organized religion (I use the terms interchangeably). From the priest's view, traditions presented a competing moral order and were a direct affront to the ROC. His views pertaining to supernatural practices are long-standing in the ROC, although they have been expressed differently at different times in history (Lindquist 2000, 272). In the context of contemporary urban Russia, Lindquist (2000, 259–60) presents a convincing case that magical/healing practices are not simply threatening to the Church because they provide a competing market and possible loss of revenue for the ROC. She also highlights deeper issues of an ideological and ontological nature, where different notions of self (and basis for agency) are expressed through the two competing forms of spirituality.[8] While this resonates with what I witnessed in Brega, my interest is on the two forms of spirituality as a source of conflict between the priest and rest of the village, and the implications this had in terms of the resource of moral authority.

Notably, often the mayor was the target of the priest's charges against the community. The mayor was not a "leader" of traditional practices (nor was the village council). Some "collective" activities had specialized facilitators, such as elderly women who were traditional healers or fortune tellers. But besides these sometimes active figures, traditional practices were often carried out by individuals at home, or in small groups that gathered at particular times of the annual calendar. Unlike ROC morality, traditional practices were a "personal morality," which were individual (Lindquist 2000, 268) and egalitarian to the extent that there were usually no higher moral figures to guide or authorize. Agency was with the practitioners. The mayor and council (as Brega natives), however, always fully supported traditional practices both in their official capacity as well as privately. They defended and upheld these practices in the name of the community in the face of criticism from the priest. The mayor and council also encouraged such activities through financial support, including paying the salary of a cultural coordinator who was responsible for organizing traditional practices among the school children as well as the community at large. It was in this sense that "traditional" practices were associated closely with the mayor and council as its sponsors.

In the rest of this chapter, I show how the revaluation of the resource, instigated by the return of a priest to the community, necessitated a renegotiation of local boundaries (secular/sacred and public/private). This was carried out largely in terms of discussions over: how much the priest gave and took from the community, and how much influence the priest had over householders lives and over the other local leaders. Moral authority as a (social) resource was attributed to, and shared between, the local leadership through the operation of distinct circuits of exchange. It was through holding separate exchange circuits that local tensions, the topic of the rest of this chapter, found some degree of resolution.

## THE PRIEST VERSUS THE VILLAGERS

Village memories are imprecise as to when the church actually stopped operating in Brega during Soviet times. An elderly pensioner said that she remembers going to church as a school pupil, but that the church in Brega was completely closed down in 1968 and reopened in 1990. However, well before 1968, services were offered in a limited way. Baba Mina (my host's mother) said that when she became engaged in 1951, there was no full-time priest, but one was shared with a neighboring village. The priest would spend one week in Brega and one week in the other village. Thus, for part of the Soviet era, the village had a priest, first full-time, then half-time, then not at all, from 1968 onward.

Before the current priest arrived in Brega in 2001, priests in the contemporary period had not lasted long. The first took up post in 1993, after the completion of the church's renovation. He was remembered fondly by Galya (a retired nurse) who said that in the three-to-four-year period that he was in Brega, he "put the church back in order after it hadn't been used for thirty-odd years." Stories attested to him being the most colorful of the priests they had been assigned. He had served in Afghanistan, and some say because of this, he "wasn't quite right in the head." Whether a result of these previous war experiences, or from other pressures, he was a drinker and behaved inappropriately when under the influence. One incident that was frequently recalled was of the priest running naked down a Brega street while intoxicated. A small circle of middle-aged and elderly women in his congregation were scandalized enough to write a letter of complaint to the regional church headquarters, who then "got rid of him." The following three priests came and went in quick succession, each lasting hardly a year. Valentina (my host and secretary to the mayor) complained especially about priest number four, the one in post in 2000 when I first arrived in Brega. She said that he was "never here." With his wife studying medicine in Odessa, he commuted backward and forward between Brega and Odessa but seemed to spend far more time in the oblast capital. What irritated Valentina the most, however, was that he required villagers to make donations—of food and money—and everyone, "was expected to give as much as they could," yet then he would, "spend his time in Odessa, taking with him everything we gave him." Priest number one, Valentina once told me, was different. "He did not take from the villagers, like the others had done." He was relatively independent and did not make such material demands on the people; to the contrary, he "did a lot for the village." This issue of exchange: How much the priest took from the village and villagers, and what he gave in return, was a major ongoing source of antagonism.

The current priest, Alexei, born in 1972 and married with two children, has been in the village over two decades. He was a

Ukrainian of mixed ethnic background—his father was from another ethnically Bulgarian village in the region, his mother from somewhere near Odessa and of Russian ethnicity. The priest did not speak the local language, Brega Bulgarian, although he said he understood some words. His native language was Russian, and this was the language he used to communicate with villagers, as well as the language of communication with his family and wife (who was from a village near Kiev and an ethnic Ukrainian). Russian was also the language used in all church services. This was significant to the extent that it designated him as an "outsider," as he communicated only in Russian, the language used in Brega at more formal/official occasions (see chapter 5).[9]

Nevertheless, villagers were pleased to hear from Alexei, priest number five, that he was planning to stay in the village, "forever, God willing." As far as I am aware, he has kept his word and is still in the post. It was a welcome sign, given the village's previous high turnover of priests during the 1990s. However, the tenure has not been without its problems. Especially in the early 2000s, after his arrival, villagers complained bitterly about Priest Alexei. "If you listen to all the priest's rules, you'd be too scared to breathe," Alyona, one of the schoolteachers, told me. While an occasional churchgoer, she was critical of the priest for being too strict and for his services that were far too long (another commonly expressed complaint). However, by far the greatest dissatisfaction that caused considerable tensions was, as Valentina once remarked, "The priest is going too far in influencing people," indicating how he was seen as intruding into parts of their lives that were not, in their view, his concern. She added that previous priests had not interfered as much as this present one.

Two aspects of the priest's meddling were seen as particularly unwelcome. The first was his opposition to the practice of traditional customs. The second was his interference in household economic activities. I deal with each of these sources of tension below.

Easter was an important time in the annual ritual calendar. In the lead-up to Easter, villagers cleaned the graves of their deceased relatives. The occasion brought back villagers who no longer lived in Brega in order to tend to their ancestor's graves. There was also a thorough cleaning of houses both inside and outside: Large open-ended waste containers were ordered so that household rub-

**FIGURE 4.1.** Luba (the kindergarten teacher who lived across the street from Valentina and Marusha) painting the street curb outside her home in preparation for Easter.

**FIGURE 4.2.** Predawn visit to the cemetery, with Marusha (left) and Valentina (kneeling) at her father's grave.

bish accumulated in the previous year could be thrown out. In addition, villagers were responsible for cleaning the street in the area immediately outside their homes—street curbs were painted, driveways swept and so on. These activities took place in the weeks leading up to Easter with the cleaning of the graves carried out in the week or so leading up to Good Friday. The preparations culminated on the night before Good Friday, when villagers went to the cemetery before the crack of dawn, while it was still dark, anytime from three in the morning onward. When one arrived at this time, he/she was met at the entrance of the cemetery by a large bonfire, while numerous smaller fires burned from individual graves. The cemetery was dotted with clusters of family members caring for the graves of their deceased. Immediate family graves were tended first: A fire was lit at the head of the grave using corn husks brought from home, fresh flowers were arranged in the vases, a cup of wine was balanced on the cross-shaped headstone, candles were lit and stuck directly into the soil of the grave and a little water was also poured directly onto the grave, "for the deceased." Intermittently, passersby were invited to ritually hand them, across the grave, the specially made little breads (*kravaicheta*) and sweets. At the same time, the giver says, "God bless X [the deceased's name]," with the receiver first crossing themselves before accepting the sweets and responding, "God bless him/her." Afterward, the graves of other more distant relatives were also visited. Villagers were quite clear as to why they were doing this: They lit fires in order to guide the souls of the deceased back home. As our next-door neighbor Marusha said, having strolled over from her own father's grave to greet us while we were at Valentina's father's grave: "Now we can wait for them to come and visit [*da doidat na gosti*]." I asked for how long they stay, and was told, "Until Spasovden" (Ascension Day, i.e., forty days after Easter).

This annual predawn visit to the cemetery and the lighting of fires was an occasion of confrontation between villagers and the priest. According to Alyona, the priest made it clear that they should not carry out this practice, and advised, "I can't stop you, but this practice is not religious." He was adamant, "This tradition is something *mestno* [local]; it is not carried out elsewhere, and it is not a religious practice."[10] He instructed her, "Go to the cemetery, but go during the day, and don't light a fire." His explanation to Alyona: "If you light a fire, and the person is in hell, then you only increase the fire of his/her hell; if the person's soul is in heaven, then you don't need to light a fire, the deceased's soul is fine in heaven."[11] Alyona surmised, "Everyone must make their own decisions as to whether they listen to the priest or not."

Many questioned the priest's advice. Valentina's view was that the priest has no business in telling people not to go to the cemetery or try to stop them from performing these practices. "The priest," she said, "is going too far in influencing people." Then she added, "The previous priests weren't like this one, they didn't interfere *in other matters*." The emphasis on "other matters" is important, because it clearly signifies Valentina's view that there were limits to the priest's jurisdiction and influence. Venu, the head of the communal (water) company, concurred and became so excited during a conversation we were having one lunchtime at the council office, in the lead-up to the fire lighting night, that he said, "Someone should stand up to the priest and tell him off . . . then he'll stop and realize he's gone too far. He can't stop me doing what I know is right and what my father and his father before him have always done." As Marusha told me on another occasion, "It's our *obichai* [custom] . . . my mother, my grandparents, all went to the cemetery and lit fires, now we are being told by the priest not to do this," then added, in justification, "but we have always done this." Luda (a regular churchgoer) was also perturbed by the priest's opposition to the practice. She spoke of the importance of recognizing their traditions, of celebrating them because, "They are old traditions, and how else can you commemorate a holiday, if not by such practices?" While I was not able to find evidence of fire lighting pre-Soviet times, people were adamant that they had always been doing this and resented the fact that the priest was trying to put a halt to it. His views created some uncertainty and anger. Alyona said that the people, "'buntuvat' [i.e., were rebelling] because the priest was telling everyone not to do this practice, a practice that they have always done." In the days leading up to the occasion, there was much discussion and deliberation between neighbors and relatives as to the best course of action. Alyona surmised, "People are in two minds; the priest has upset everyone, and they are no longer certain what to do."

Such concerns were also evident in our household, where the dilemma as to whether to listen to the priest or not was in the forefront of my hosts' minds. On the day before the proposed night excursion to the cemetery, Baba Mina told me, before Valentina returned for lunch, "As far back as I can remember, people practiced this lighting of fires *obichai* . . . even during Soviet times when the church was locked up and unused, the bell would always ring, intermittently, during the period that people went to the cemetery to light fires." She continued: "All my family, everyone would go on this occasion to the cemetery, it was unthinkable not to go." This continued throughout Soviet times. Then she added, more hesitantly, that she wasn't sure anymore. "They say that the priest says you mustn't go, so maybe we shouldn't." She concluded: "We'll see what Valentina says." When Valentina returned from her work at the village council, her response was firm: "The priest knows 'za sebe si' [for himself, in the sense that he knows what is right from his perspective], but you know for you. You've always gone, your mother before you, your grandmother. You're seventy years old, and now you are considering not going? Of course you'll go. So speaks the priest; but it's not so at all." However, later that evening, as we were packing the items to take to the cemetery, Baba Mina hesitated again: "Since we mustn't, I won't take the things for lighting a fire," at which point Valentina lost her patience with her mother, responding, "But what did I say? We will do as we've always done." Baba Mina acquiesced, but unlike Valentina, she felt less comfortable going against the priest's word. The next morning, we got up well before dawn and arrived at the cemetery in the dark (before 6 a.m.), meeting a tide of villagers already coming back from the cemetery and heading back home. Many others were still attending to the fires and graves at the cemetery. Clearly, the priest's warnings had not deterred most.

In the end, different villagers' responses varied: The majority (from what I could ascertain) paid little attention to the priest, although not without some soul-searching and discussion. Their dilemma indicated that the priest's word was not without some sway. However, ultimately in most cases, the priest's views were ignored. Villagers opted to do things the way they had always done them. Dasha—Valentina's first cousin and a former kolkhoz worker—held the view, "All I know is that going to the cemetery is a tradition, and therefore I am going." Marusha, too, who was at the cemetery well before us, noted "The priest can't stop us; we are taught to do this from ages ago." Anya, the village's cultural coordinator echoed a similar sentiment: "We've changed so many priests . . . and this one is here a year and is trying to change things that we've been doing for ages." Only the most dedicated church attendees respected the priest's wishes.[12] His small band of loyal followers (ten to twelve women) who were the most devoted churchgoers,[13] accepted his advice and did not go to the cemetery before daylight or light fires once there. Tanya, a schoolteacher and committed member of the church, was one of them. She went well after dawn, at 7:30 a.m., before continuing to school. As with others who broke with tradition, Tanya was a little defensive, and offered what would be viewed, from the perspective of others, a valid excuse or justification with which no villager could take issue: "I couldn't have gone earlier, because my mother asked me to bake bread, and I wasn't able to leave home until after this task was completed," thus hiding behind the authority of her elderly mother and a central household duty of bread baking. Another close follower of the priest had a similar excuse: that she was making the special Easter bread that morning in preparation for Easter and thus could not go to the cemetery predawn. Such reasons were a noncontentious way to sidestep the issue through providing a reason that was acceptable in nonreligious terms, while remaining true to the priest's counsel.

The priest was adamant that he was not against all Bulgarian obichai; his concern was with the symbols and practices used in traditional customs that at the same time had sacred significance for the church: red wine, the cross, fire, the lighting of candles and so on.[14] It was these specific symbols (and associated practices) that the priest was against the villagers using. It was also with respect to these symbols and objects that the priest made ownership claims as the sole property of the church. He argued for their role in "legitimate" religion, while designating any other uses of them as "not religious."[15] In trying to assert his views over local practices in this way, he was attempting to regain control/ownership over particular forms of spirituality as legitimate and under the auspices of the church, while rejecting other practices as lying outside the acceptable bounds of religion. The latter he ousted as "the devil's work." In this way, the priest was drawing a line between "proper" religion and villagers' traditional practices.

The priest also objected to the use of traditional healers and fortune tellers (or other magical practitioners). Their services, usually offered by elderly babi, were viewed by the priest as aligned with the devil, and the women practitioners were seen as, "working with the devil."[16] Much to the disapproval and concern of villagers who made use of such traditional healers, the priest refused to conduct a church service for the funeral of such elderly babi, and would not even allow the funeral procession to enter the church, although he was willing to go to their homes and say a prayer for the deceased. In his view, their activities were not in line with the teachings of the ROC. Tanya voiced the priest's view: "The priest says that we should accept the fate that God has brought us, and we shouldn't try to change our fate [by using traditional healers and fortune tellers]."

Threats of exile from the church did not stop villagers from making use of traditional healers. On one occasion, Angelica, the nineteen-year-old daughter of Vito and Olya (the former worked in the irrigation station, the latter ran a shop from home) informed the priest that her mother had visited a fortune teller. Olya frequently consulted fortune tellers when she was ill or worried about a particular issue at home, traveling to the district capital or further afield for a meeting (the city fortune tellers were more renowned than those in Brega. There was also the advantage that the priest was less likely to discover she made use of such traditional healers if she went outside the village). Olya was also a frequent, although intermittent, church attendee. She found nothing untoward with her involvement in both the church and in engaging in traditional practices. As many others in the village, she struggled to understand the priest's position. In her view, traditional healers offered an important service that was seen as quite different from, and lying outside the jurisdiction of, the church. In Olya's view, there was a place for "traditional healers" and for "religion," and the two were not incompatible.

Following Angelica's report to the priest, Olya was publicly humiliated in front of the handful of regular churchgoers who made up the congregation when the priest preached that fortune tellers "do the work of the devil," and named Olya as having recently consulted one. He had also scolded her in a private conversation following the service. The priest used his sermon as a platform to explain the church's position, and to expose and publicly admonish wrongdoing, as well as to deride traditional practices as "not religious."

Angelica's actions against her mother caused considerable friction at home, so much so that she refused to leave her room for a couple of days after a verbal confrontation with her parents. Her parents told me that they were not against their daughter going to church or being religious, but she must do this in moderation. Angelica was "going too far in her religiosity."[17] In reporting her mother to the priest, Angelica had crossed a boundary, showing her loyalty to the priest above loyalty to her parents and family. Olya angrily told her daughter that she should have left her to make her own decisions as to what she told the priest about herself. "By all means," she advised her daughter, "believe in God, but it is not necessary to tell the priest everything, confiding all family affairs to him." In this way, Olya indicated that there was a limit as to how far she was willing to allow the priest into their lives. Her continued belief in and engagement with traditional practices (of which she was all too aware the priest did not approve) should have remained—in her view—outside the priest's sphere of knowledge and influence; the priest was "overstepping" his authority and had no right to stop the practices of customs. They were considered a "family" matter and none of the priest's business. Olya said she encouraged Angelica to go to church; however, she counseled her to, "pray to an icon and achieve solace from this." There was, "no need to confess and confide everything to the priest." The basic message was that traditional practice lay outside the concern of the priest; they were purely a family matter.

Apart from the priest's disapproval of engagement in traditional practices, another focus of tension concerned economic exchanges householders had with the priest. The priest was frequently criticized in his early years in Brega for making too many material demands on households.[18] Recurrent topics between villagers concerned how much money the priest made, debates as to whether he received a sufficient salary and financial assistance from the district church as well as questions as to what was an appropriate amount of help/donations for households to give on various occasions.[19] There was a common perception that the church's and priest's economic success was at the expense of their own hard-earned security and resources. While income in Orthodox churches was never made public (Tocheva 2014, 19), and villagers were aware that priests received no salary from the state budget, they also knew that the priest's salary was dependent on a range of local sources: the "donations" he received from them for conducting religious services, blessings and the reading of prayers for the living and dead, and the food given to the church on various ritual occasions. The church—and priest—also earned money from selling candles, icons and crosses in the little booth inside the church, located near the entrance door. Such income generating activities were important for the support of the church and priest, as many villagers recognized.[20]

However, there was a limit to how much villagers were willing to give. In the summer of 2001, in the early months soon after the priest first moved to Brega, Valentina was angered when two women working on behalf of the priest walked from house to house, knocking on doors to collect money. The donations were in order to make final improvements to the priest's house: to complete the underground water storage tank, to build a fence around the house and to furnish the inside with curtains. Valentina was annoyed when she discovered that the women first spoke to her daughter, who gave them 2 UAH. Unsatisfied with the donation and hoping for more, they then spoke to Valentina's mother—who donated a further 1 UAH. Still dissatisfied with the donation, the women then asked to see Valentina. Valentina was quite direct with the women, "What more can you want? A house was built for the priest [by the agricultural collectives]; you can't and shouldn't expect more help." The women retorted that, "There is only one Priest in the village," to which Valentina quipped, "There is also only one doctor, but he doesn't expect to have a house built for him!"

Apart from criticisms that the priest had already been given sufficient support and he was going too far in the additional demands he was making of them, a related criticism was the observed zest with which the priest carried out his paid services, prioritizing profits at the expense of basic displays of respect for the villagers. For example, the priest was criticized for the manner in which he carried out blessings. Vito complained that when the priest did the village rounds, entering households who let him in to bless the house—as he did every January on Ivanovden (St. John's Day)—he walked through the houses with his muddy shoes on. Apparently, a number of people had actually complained to the priest about this, and as a result, the priest "se surdi" (was offended and upset). Vito remained unsympathetic, instead pointing out, "The priest could take off his shoes before entering the houses, but no, he's in too much of a rush to go through as many houses as possible, thus earning more donations." By not taking his shoes off, he saved time and was able to visit more houses, and in this way maximized his profits, thus giving priority to financial interests above any basic signs of courtesy to the villagers.

Olya was also critical of the priest, because he refused to give a church funeral to an elderly diado over eighty years of age, who passed away in the summer of 2003, because the gentleman did not have the 25 UAH fee to cover the costs. She went on to say that of course those who could afford it should pay, but if someone was too poor to afford the funeral expenses, then the priest should conduct the service for free. Olya concluded, for "this priest, saving the soul is less important than making money."[21] In another conversation, Valentina added her own complaint concerning the priest's inflationary prices. The year before her father died, the priest's burial services had cost 5 UAH, but the following year, at the time of her father's death, the priest had asked Valentina for 10 UAH, soon this became 20, and then in the cemetery during the funeral, she said, "He had the gall to start negotiating for 40." Religion is, they all emphasized, run like a business, and the priest's drive to maximize profits raised questions as to how genuine he was in what he preached.

Indeed, where there were signs that the profit motive appeared to trump his spiritual work, the priest's moral authority was explicitly and publicly questioned. Such questions were also raised when there were observed discrepancies between what the priest preached and what he did.[22] During an evening street conversation between neighbors, Valentina retold how the priest, having just read Mishol's (the private farmer) mother's last rites on her deathbed, walked out of the household with a live chicken under his arm, which was given to him by Mishol for services rendered. Valentina continued: "With the chicken under his arm, he told the men out in the street that they must observe Lent." She added that while it is true it was a live chicken, it is still improper to preach Lent while at the same time signaling an opposite message by withdrawing home with live meat. The sovkhoz vet summed it up in the following way: "Like the Party, priests should be morally exemplary, but they are not." Priests were always under the moral scrutiny of the people and did not always measure up to expectations. Which is why numerous villagers, especially men (e.g., Venu and Vito), told me: "I believe in God, but not so much in the priests," justifying their dismissal of the priest's authority.[23]

It was not only the relinquishing of material goods, but also the diversion of villagers' time and labor that was resented because it took resources away from the household. Vito, not a churchgoer himself, told me, "I don't mind either my wife or daughter going to church on the weekend when they have free time, but attending every day is just too much." He continued: "People need to work in order to survive. They can't spend all their time in church, because then there is no time for work." He went on to explain that he did not usually attend church services because they took too long, adding, "I have a family and children to support, and work takes up all my time." He finished: "I go to church, even if just to light a candle and then leave." His priority was clear: the maintenance of the household above any formal commitment to the church.

Villagers were well aware that increasing church attendance was in the priest's interests and part of his agenda. From their point of view, attendance was not always to their advantage; in fact, often it worked to the detriment of households, diverting time and thus labor away from home duties. I was told on various occasions by different individuals: "It doesn't worry the priest, their [referring to people who attend church] presence is good business, but it is no good for others." Church attendance was seen as a threat to the household economy. One woman at the all-night Easter church service that finished early the next morning (at approximately 6 a.m.), in the long queue at the end of the service to have her *paska* (sweet bread backed specially for Easter) blessed by the priest, complained of the length of the service. She asked her neighbor in the queue in a loud voice for all those close by to hear: "What I want to know is, who is going to milk the cow if the *khoziaika* [i.e., owner, referring to herself] is here? They need milking morning and night; it has to be done. How can this happen when I am here?" Vito, expressing concern about his daughter Angelica's loyalty to the church, told me, "It's clear that it's to his [the priest's] benefit for young people to go to church, because he lives off churchgoers; he needs more young people going to church." The more business the priest could drum up, the more young people he could encourage to go to church, the more houses he could bless, the more services that he could perform, the better for him. In short, as Vito succinctly expressed it, "He lives off his flock."

The priest also relied heavily on volunteers who helped him in his work and contributed further potential value and profits. Soon after his arrival, the priest requested the use of the land owned by the council that was located in front of the church. His idea was to cultivate the land. The relevant council worker told him rather skeptically, "You'll be the first priest to work in the garden, but go ahead." Eventually, the land was formally transferred to the church so that the priest's plans to establish a vineyard could be implemented. With the assistance of village volunteers who dug and planted the vines, the vineyard was started in the early 2000s and was well established by 2014. While he used volunteer help for the annual pruning, digging, and harvesting, all the profit from the grapes went to the church coffer, providing additional income. Such funds helped pay for his two assistants: a male helper who maintained the church property, and his wife who sold the candles at the church booth and acted as a sort of secretary/administrator to the priest.

Part of the reason Priest Alexei survived in the village, unlike his other post-Soviet predecessors, was that over the years he showed a willingness to cultivate land and thus came to rely less on villagers. Evidence of his economic success can be found in the additional land that he bought and on which he built a new house, one much larger than the original house he was given to live in. The new residence was conveniently located across the street from the first house (which was itself next door to the church). The priest worked the household land with the assistance of his brother-in-law and family, who moved to the village and acted as church assistants while living in the smaller house. With their help, the priest set up his own *khoziaistvo*, grew food and became self-sufficient. He became a *khoziain* as well as a priest. This was partly why, over the years, the tensions between the priest and ordinary villagers gradually declined. While he worked the land with a lot of assistance, including with help from village volunteers, it was the one way in which he earned limited respect and a nod of acceptance from even his most avid critics. He became, at least in this one way, one of them. At the same time, and much to the villagers' approval, this made him less dependent, and less of a drain on other village households and their resources.

As of the early 2020s, the priest had served in Brega for over 20 years. During this time, the relationship between him and the villagers was negotiated, and the worst of the friction resolved. When they needed him, villagers paid the priest for his services—for funerals, christenings, and the like—and the more dedicated helped him with the maintenance of the vineyard and in other tasks requiring volunteers. Those who wished made donations at specific times of the religious calendar. He maintained his position and established authority in the village in part at least as a result of the early years of negotiation with the people and his realization that he needed to create his own garden and not rely entirely on donations from villagers. In other words, priest number five achieved with some effort what priest number one was praised for. People spoke most fondly of the latter because "he had done a lot of things [for the village] and he wasn't always dependent on the village; he looked after himself." However, while the more recent priest's material conditions flourished and he no longer "lives off his flock" to the same extent as in the early years, the number of dedicated followers did not increase. It remained constant, consisting of a handful of elderly women.

At the same time, I never heard anyone in the village say they wanted the priest to leave. Organized religion had an accepted role in the community. Attendance on the two biggest days of the Orthodox calendar—Easter and Christmas—were respectable; in fact, the church was usually full to capacity. There clearly was a place for the priest in the village. Nevertheless, his influence and authority were more limited than he would have liked. Villagers restricted the extent of the priest's "interference," with respect to traditional practices and household (economic) activities. Traditional practices continued to be relevant in a way that formal religion did not. In 2014, I spent an afternoon with Valentina's daughter and unwell six-year-old granddaughter, seeking help from a village fortune teller and then a traditional healer (in the morning, we had taken her to the doctor). The younger generations continued to show a preference for, and to seek out, traditional practitioners during times of illness. They turned to the church for major life cycle occasions—christenings, marriage, and death; traditions had an everyday relevance for more run-of-the-mill events such as everyday illnesses. Thus, interactions between the priest and villagers were well defined: Exchanges took place within the domain of "formal religion," and there was a limit to how often villagers engaged with the priest and the extent of the exchanges. The priest's influence did not extend into the domain of traditional practices (and he kept his distance from such activities) nor were his activities allowed to drain the economic resources of the household. Such an arrangement suited both parties for different reasons. The division was clear: Villagers had their responsibilities; the priest had his. As Marusha expressed it: "Let him carry on with the regular church services, but without us," which at the same time as acknowledging the need for a church, made clear that its functioning had a limited role in their lives. It was the priest's responsibility to conduct church services, and they were happy to let him get on with this, as long as his influence over them was contained.

## THE PRIEST VERSUS THE MAYOR

May 22 was a significant day in the village calendar and celebrated by two events that took place concurrently. The first, *Den' Sela*, "Day of the Village," was a festival organized by the council with the support of other leading figures from the agricultural enterprises and village businesses.[24] This event coincided with a church holiday that commemorated St. Nikolai, the patron saint of the village church after which it was named. The priest held special rituals annually on this day to bless the church and honor St. Nikolai.[25] Both celebrations were new to the extent that neither were celebrated during Soviet times and were only performed from the mid-1990s onward. In the early years, May 22 was at the heart of community divisions between the priest and the village council.

Tense relations had been mounting between Priest Alexei and other village leaders in the days leading up to May 22, 2003. Many of the customs practiced by the villagers around this time of year relating to the anticipated harvests and need for rain were dismissed by the priest as "pagan" and "the devil's work." He spoke out against such practices in his sermons and often had sharp words with the mayor and the agricultural enterprise heads for sponsoring and participating in such activities. One such case that arose in the week before May 22, and to which the priest was vehemently opposed, was the tradition of *paparuda*, a custom that included homemade crosses being carried from household to household on May 15 by groups of usually elderly women who would chant a prayer. The custom was believed to bring rain and good harvests (see Kaneff 2018). In this practice, which Luda described as a "stara Bulgarska traditsiia" (an old Bulgarian tradition), participants who carried the cross and sang for each household they visited were given money (attached to the cross) and various foodstuffs, including red wine, feta cheese, and flour. They also visited the village council and the agricultural enterprise headquarters and were equally warmly welcomed and rewarded. The priest opposed the ritual because of what he argued was the sacrilegious use of the cross, which he said should not be thrown away into the lake at the end of the day (as was the custom). He was also opposed to the ritual on the grounds that it offered an alternate way of "praying for rain," which from the priest's perspective, competed with his own efforts to offer prayers for rain. If people wanted rain, he argued, instead of supporting the traditional custom, they should come to the church and pray.

The priest used every opportunity to speak against people's involvement in paparuda: In church services, he preached against the practice; he berated Anya, the village's cultural coordinator (a position paid for by the council) whom he met on the street one day, for organizing a group of girls from the school to partake in the custom; and he also admonished village leaders when they convened to finalize organizational matters relating to the May 22 celebration.[26] At the meeting, he accused the mayor and heads of the enterprises of sponsoring paparuda, which he termed "pagan devilry" [*iaeicheskaia besovskaia*]. He went on to say that if they wanted rain, instead of sponsoring paparuda, they should help him in his own efforts to pray for rain, by carrying the church cross to the end of the village and to the fields. The priest was also critical of the mayor for permitting a visiting circus (which had set up camp in the week leading up to May 22 and gave daily matinee and evening performances) to give a final performance on the evening of May 21, as it clashed with his own evening service on the night before the big events of the following day. Thus, in the lead-up to May 22, the priest and other village officials were already at loggerheads, and relations were strained.

As plans for May 22 were finalized, it became obvious that activities would run concurrently, and villagers would have to choose to go to one event or the other, but it would be difficult go to both. The church's celebration of Saint Nikolai was to begin with a special three-hour church service, from 8 a.m. to 11 a.m., and was to be conducted by one of the three priests invited to attend the day, the head priest for the district. The latter was to be assisted by Brega's priest, as well as another two priests visiting from neighboring villages to honor the occasion. Unlike everyday services, a choir would be present to sing. The service would culminate with the circumnavigation of the church by the congregation, with the

**FIGURE 4.3.** The church service on St. Nikolai Day.

**FIGURE 4.4.** The kurban following the three-hour service, attended by villagers and guests who accompanied the visiting priests. The priests ate separately at Priest Alexei's house.

priests in front carrying church banners and the cross, in a conclusion to the blessing of the church. Afterward, the visiting priests would retire to Priest Alexei's home for a meal, or *kurban*,[27] while churchgoers would feast outside, in the church grounds, where tables had been laid out for the occasion. The kurban was open to all villagers, as well as to the entourage who had accompanied the other priests to Brega for the event. Roast lamb constituted the main food on the menu, as it was the traditional food for this day. The lambs were donated by two village men as a thanksgiving for having recovered from serious illness during the previous year. The individuals also provided bread and other essentials, while the priest's followers (those who attended church on a regular/weekly basis) contributed various additional dishes.

The village council's activities for their Den′ Sela were of quite a different nature. The events took place in the school quadrangle (the assembly area outside the main entrance) and were planned to begin with a concert midmorning, at the same time as the church service was in progress. Most of the concert performers were children from the school, singing contemporary songs and reciting poetry. It drew a crowd of supportive and proud parents and grandparents. There was also a performance by the village folklore group, as well as a dance performance by a guest artist (a young girl) from Izmail. Ice cream featured highly on this day, and the two-hour concert was followed by a competition held to see which of three young contestants could name the most ice cream flavors, with the winner receiving an ice cream! The music part of the event concluded with a karaoke competition between six schoolchildren. The applause from the audience determined the winner, but there were prizes for all six participants. A lunch was planned to follow the concert, to be held in the school canteen, and to which all those who had helped with the organization and sponsored the event were invited: the mayor and village council workers, the heads of all the agricultural enterprises and communal (water) company, the private farmers, and the local business proprietors—shop owners, the owner of the mill, among others. Following the banquet, later in the afternoon, a football match was scheduled in the village stadium, as well as a raffle. It was this latter activity that captivated the interest of most villagers and was the most anticipated and well attended of all the events. With 700 tickets and 700 prizes, everyone who bought a ticket was guaranteed to win. Valentina made a point of telling me that while the tickets sold for 3 UAH (thus bringing in 2,100 UAH to the village council in funds), the value of the goods had been calculated at 2,800. Her point was that the council was not making an overall profit; the real benefit was in favor of those who entered the raffle. The most coveted prize, drawn last, was a calf donated by the former sovkhoz. The sovkhoz also donated five piglets, and another ten were donated by the other agricultural enterprises and two of the private farmers. Other donations given as prizes included: 300 kilograms of sugar (100 kg from each of the former kolkhoz enterprises), 60 liters of sunflower oil (20 liters from each of the enterprises) and 60 geese, ducks, and goslings donated by private farmers. One of the private shepherds donated two lambs, the other a bucketful of feta cheese in brine (from sheep's milk), while the privatized cultural house—now a disco and bar—and the village shops donated various items: groceries (including packets of rice, pasta, tea, washing powder, toothpaste etc.), toys, clothes and so on. Angelovski, a successful local businessman, who owned three village shops and the petrol station, was one of the biggest donors on the day. The delay in drawing the prizes, pushed back to allow first the concert and then karaoke to finish after a late start, did not deter the large number of villagers, many of whom milled around for hours waiting for the drawing to begin. Most of the prizes were collected from the council the following day, although smaller prizes, such as the gosling that I won and named "Nikolai," were collected outside the school on the evening of the raffle.

The Den' Sela program, finalized only the day before the event, did not go according to plan because of a two-hour delay in the start of the concert. According to Valentina, the holdup was due to Anya losing her temper with the council workers for not having organized the prizes for the karaoke participants in advance. After a shouting match, Anya stormed out of the building, leaving the council organizers in the lurch, before cooling off and returning a couple of hours later to conduct the concert.[28] The delay had a knock-on effect of pushing back all events, including the lunch, which was deferred to the evening. This was probably fortuitous, as the school kitchen was being used by the church for its lunch

**FIGURE 4.5.** The school folklore group performing at Den' Sela, organized by the village council.

**FIGURE 4.6.** The raffle draw concluded the Den' Sela program and proved to be very popular.

**FIGURE 4.7.** At the end of the day, the organizers and those who donated or contributed to the event were treated to a feast.

preparations. Having to share the space, under the circumstances, would have been less than ideal.

Even with last-minute hiccups to the program, attendance at Den′ Sela far exceeded the number at the church event. Perhaps more would have gone to both events if it were possible. However, those who were waiting for the concert to begin were unable to attend the church's kurban, had they wanted to, which ran at the same time. Even though the council's banquet was postponed until the evening, the visiting priests and their entourages were unable to attend (even if they had been invited) because their prearranged transport to take them home departed in the early afternoon. Thus, there was little mixing of the audience between both events.

During the actual day, and in the days that followed, there was much bickering between the two camps: the priest and his followers, and the mayor and the council workers.[29] Comparisons with the way in which the day was celebrated in the previous year served to underscore to all present the current escalation of tensions. The 2002 celebrations had also run events concurrently—the church service took place at the same time as the council's entertainment program. However, unlike 2003, everyone came together in the one feast held for the whole village at lunchtime. The joint feast, attended by the clergy (and their visitors) and other villagers alike, was held at the school, with food provided by the agricultural enterprises. The holding of two—rather than one—feasts in 2003 was thus a particular point of contestation. Tanya complained that this year's event was "badly organized," and elaborated: "You can't expect the church congregation and visitors from other villagers to wait until the evening [for the start of the banquet]." In her opinion, it would have been much better to bring together everyone at a lunch for the whole village, as had been the case the previous year, rather than exclude the priest and churchgoers. She believed that the banquet should have been for the entire village—those participating in the church event and citizens at the council's event. Tanya blamed the mayor and agricultural heads for the delay to the proceedings,[30] and consequent rescheduling of the feast to the evening, and for therefore having deliberately separated the "church from the rest of the village through holding two separate feasts." However, the council workers, and the librarian in particular, were adamant that the priest himself had wanted the separation, and the holding of two feasts was not the doing of the mayor or council (something Tanya refuted). They told me that on the actual day the priest had confronted the mayor, informing him that Den′ Sela should be moved to another day so as "not to interfere or distract from St. Nikolai Day." The priest's request was given consideration by the mayor that night at the evening banquet, which was not attended by the church followers or priests. The mayor raised the issue with those sitting near him, in order to gauge opinions. Those present were so intoxicated by that time that there was little interest in the discussion, and no opinions were offered.

The blame both groups accorded each other, with the priest's followers claiming it was all the mayor and council's fault, and the council workers claiming that the priest himself wanted a separate event, reinforced and strengthened the split between the church and the village council. Deteriorating relations were evidenced in the formalized monetary exchange transaction that took place when the council charged the church 25 UAH to make use of the school kitchen facilities in preparation for their kurban. This was an additional source of anger among church followers. Olya, a shop owner who had made a donation to the raffle, refused to join the evening banquet as a sign of protest. She said she was "surdita" (upset/offended) with the mayor and council for not helping the church with the kurban and for charging a fee for the use of the school kitchen. She told me that this was not "proper. . . . They should have been given use of the kitchen premises for free." The charging of a monetary payment for the church's access to the public facility, which was available without cost to other local organizations, was a clear sign of the church's differential treatment and its separation from the rest of the village.

The division in the community was evidenced not only in the holding of two feasts as well as in the charging of the church a fee for the use of the kitchen. It was also evidenced through the two separate events that were in essence large exchange circuits: the church event, where followers donated food and partook in the service in exchange for a spiritual blessing and the ongoing spiritual protection of the church, and Den′ Sela, where villagers participated in a range of cultural and entertainment activities in return for various material rewards and public recognition (this exchange was also a form of redistribution of goods/livestock donated by local agricultural producers and businesses). It was via villagers' participation (or nonparticipation) in respective events and exchanges that the moral authority of the leaders was ultimately legitimated (or dismissed), and loyalty to a particular organization expressed.[31] In effect, because it was difficult to attend both, a competition between the two leaders and institutions ensued, both vying with one another for village interest and participation. This served to set the boundaries of moral authority in terms of social space: The priest was restricted to the domain of formal religion and the church, the mayor to everyday community activities/traditions and the council.

Moral authority was restricted in another sense: It was important for the exchange activities to be seen as "equal," or more precisely, reciprocal. Within the very different exchanges that took place on the day, which provided distinct circuits involving food/gifts, skills/spirituality, one party should not be seen to profit from the exchange at the expense of the other. Moral authority, as a resource, should not be part of a profit-making (monetary) exchange circuit. To do so incited accusations of corruption, or comments about inappropriate behavior, and as such, threatened the leaders with a potential loss of influence. If a moral leader engaged in exchanges that were seen to be driven by personal gain, then his or her authority was questioned. This was why it was important for the council to be seen not to be making a profit from the raffle, and why Valentina made a point of informing me that the value of the prizes exceeded the total money collected through the tickets. Similarly, when households engaged in exchanges with the priest, such as providing payment for services, these must always be perceived as "donations," thus rendering them both voluntary and also "fair," and not profit-making endeavors (Tocheva 2014, 18). Conversely, if the priest was seen to charge too much or to place his "business interests" above the spiritual well-being of the people, then villagers criticized the priest's practices as being economically motivated, out of line with religious teachings, and thus of questionable morality.[32] If an unequal exchange was deemed to have occurred (such as when the priest went through houses with muddy boots to save time, and in so doing maximize his profits), then his behavior was questioned, and moral authority was eroded. Thus, alongside the limitations to moral authority as a shared resource (restricting the influence of the priest and mayor to separate social spaces), exchanges that reinforced influence took place through transactions that were perceived as reciprocal (and balanced) and nonmonetary in form. This kept the leaders mindful: They knew that an unequal exchange would lead to criticisms, possibly even a withdrawal of participation, and this would ultimately restrict or put their authority at risk.

No one could deny the council or other village organizations' support for their priest. After all, it was in the early 1990s, before decollectivization had been fully implemented, that the kolkhoz and sovkhoz built the house for the priest, with the village council contributing some of the building materials. The priest paid no rent for the property, which was transferred to church ownership. Further, it was the mayor who was the driving force behind the renovation of the church, and in the early years at least, the council paid the salaries of the priest's two assistants. The village council also granted the priest land for cultivation. Undoubtedly, there was a place for the priest in the village, and he was welcomed and given all necessary support to fulfill his duties by the council.

Nevertheless, the priest's authority was confined to the sacred business of the church (the realm of formal religion) and held at an arm's length from the rest of the village and its institutions. The delineation of authority that accompanied such a division was stated explicitly by Valentina, who once remarked, in defense of the mayor and agricultural leaders against criticisms from the priest at the time of the paparuda confrontations, "Praying [for rain] is the priest's work." She went on to explain that it was not the "job" of other officials in the village to pray for rain. "They have far too much else on their plates with the running of agriculture and the village and shouldn't have to worry about the priest's work, too." She ended by saying, "It is not their job [to pray], it is the priest's," but then after a moment added, "although the other leaders would be willing to help if asked [by the priest]." Valentina was speaking specifically with respect to the praying for rain during paparuda, but the more general point holds: It was the priest's role to carry out regular church services and prayers. Those villagers who wished could support the priest in his prayers by attending his services on a regular basis and were free to do so. However, for the vast majority, everyday events that required spiritual/healing practices were carried out at home or through consulting traditional practitioners: the inviting of elderly women involved in the custom of paparuda into their homes to pray for rain in the late spring, consulting a fortune teller for advice at times of uncertainty and so on. For villagers and the village council, traditional and religious practices were seen as separate yet complementary activities. Traditions were not believed to compete with or be seen as a threat to formal religion (contrary to the view held by the priest). The priest had his responsibilities and duties, and the villagers had theirs.

On May 22, 2003, the separation of formal religion from everyday practices came to a head, and this arrangement has not changed significantly since then, at least not in the two following decades. The separate circuits of exchange and engagements between the priest/church and mayor/council continued, reflecting the separate spaces of moral order in the community. Paparuda, the traditional prayers for rain, still took place, despite the priest's ongoing although much subdued campaign against this practice.

Similarly, in the contemporary Den′ Sela celebrations, no role was given to the church. The event remained focused on cultural entertainments—a concert, folklore dancing performances, games for the children—and continued to be financially sponsored by the agricultural enterprises and local entrepreneurs. Unlike other locations in the region,[33] the church and council events in Brega remained separate, with no shared activities including the holding of two feasts. The priest as a figure of moral authority was welcome, but only within designated domains of village life. The church remained separate from the rest of the community.

## THE DIVISION OF THE MORAL AUTHORITY RESOURCE AND NEW COMMUNITY TENSIONS WITH THE PRIEST

As a resource, moral authority has been revalued, divided up between religious and traditional practitioners who guided Brega's spiritual world (and the local moral order). The sharing of the resource involved a difficult and confrontational negotiation process between the returning priest trying to carve out his niche in the Brega spiritual world and the rest of the community.[34] From the priest's perspective, villagers' traditional practices were a threat to the ROC and in competition with his own services. From the villagers' perspective, the priest and formal religion was one important dimension of their spiritual world, and he was welcome as long as his practices ran alongside (and not in opposition to) traditional customs. The negotiated solution was the division of the resource of moral authority.

It was through the operation of separate exchange circuits that practitioners (and perceived representatives, such as the mayor) of tradition and religion were able to stake out the limits of their authority. At the same time, villagers' involvement in church/council exchanges was a way to display support for the authority of respective leaders: Their engagement in respective circuits of exchange were a means for leaders' influence to be legitimated or conversely dismissed (through nonparticipation).

Therefore, exchange was central in the division (revaluation) of the resource and also central in the negotiation of relations between the priest and the community. First, there was the question of what the priest gave to, and how much he took from, the village and its people. Villagers were concerned that the priest made too many material (financial) demands on them and was also a drain on household resources in terms of labor and time. Aware that the priest's livelihood depended on their donations and various forms of help, they were mindful as to how much they gave, and also critical of those occasions when they observed his zest for profit making. Similarly, at the community level, the council kept its relationship with the church formal and required that the church pay for any communal services it used, in order to ensure that exchanges did not deplete public resources.

Second, and of considerable importance, exchange was also at the center of the tensions over villagers' engagement in traditional practices. The priest's attempts to carve out his authority in the village took place largely in terms of his crusade against villagers' traditional practices, trying to convince them to not participate in such activities. Through his sponsorship of some practices as "true religion," and the rejection of others as the "devil's work," the priest attempted to reassert his control over the wider spiritual domain of village life, delineating the boundary between "sacred" and "secular" through an attempted monopoly on what constituted "sacred." His opposition to traditions put him in conflict with ordinary villagers and leaders alike. Most villagers carried on despite the priest's objections, although with much preliminary questioning and deliberation. What the priest failed to understand was the fundamental role of traditions in grounding local identity: Traditional practices as "what we have always done" provided villagers with a direct link to their Bulgarian ancestral roots and gave them a sense of continuity over time (unlike the ROC and Brega priests, whose presence had not been a constant in the village's contemporary history).[35]

A separation of the priest and church from everyday (traditional) practices was, in the end, the only way to go forward. The view of the villagers—leaders and ordinary citizens alike—was that the priest's involvement in such practices was "interference" and unwelcome. For very different reasons, the priest did not wish to be involved in traditional practices, seeing them as incompatible with ROC teachings. This set the limit to the exchanges that villagers were willing to have with the priest (and indeed vice versa). The solution to the dilemma was one of restricted acceptance, in which the priest's authority was curtailed and did not extend into influence over traditional practices. Such a separation between the priest and the community was symbolic but also could be mapped out in physical space through the institutions of the council and the church, as well as through the distinct exchange circuits operated by figures with moral authority. It provided the particular Bregan configuration of public/private and secular/sacred social spaces.

On occasions, such as May 22, engaging in both council (traditional) and church (religious) events was not possible, but in many other instances, the possibility was present. Villagers turned to the priest at certain times in the annual calendar—Easter and Christmas—and at crucial moments in their life cycles (especially christenings and death). When villagers wished to engage with the priest in a circuit of exchange—donations for services rendered—it was up to them to request/invite him to their homes or to attend his services in the church. To this extent, there was, and continued to be, a role for the hierarchical and prescriptive practices provided by the priest and the ROC. Like traditions, the ROC was also grounded in Brega's past, part of the migration package that was adopted by the first settlers, who were given sanctuary from the Ottomans on newly won Russian territory. Alongside this association with the ROC, villagers also maintained their practice of traditions. Traditions reaffirmed a moral community based on equality between villagers, commonly owned and controlled practices in which every individual household could engage, and which were under the "protection" of the council/mayor.[36] Traditions also created a solidarity that grounded the villagers to their distant ancestral past and their Bulgarian origins. Customs that connected villagers to their Bulgarian heritage operated alongside the formalized religion of the ROC. Moral authority remained a shared resource: The negotiated settlement was for traditions and organized religion to operate in parallel (though sometimes in competition), as distinctive and constitutive parts of the Brega spiritual world and local identity.

CHAPTER 5

# IDENTITY

## BREGANS AND OUTSIDERS

In the previous chapters, the focus has been on how resources are revalued *within* use or exchange categories. In this final ethnographic chapter, the attention is on identity as an example of a resource that jumps categories: from having use value to also acquiring exchange value. As a social resource, identity provides villagers with a sense of belonging that is grounded in particular language and history characteristics (as well as in traditional practices, see chapter 4). A Bregan identity oriented and distinguished the rural inhabitants with respect to other villages in the region, as well as nationally and beyond. It gained heightened importance and was revalued following the collapse of the Soviet Union, when seismic shifts in "belonging" were instigated as Bregans transitioned from Soviet citizens to citizens of the newly independent Ukrainian state. As a consequence, new exchange possibilities, and associated potential alliances, were created both regionally and transnationally via migration, marriage, educational and employment opportunities. At the same time, a Bregan identity had only limited national exchange value (and in this sense, the designated minority status was a source of exclusion). Thus, the chapter highlights how at least in some contexts the resource has jumped value categorization from having only use value during Soviet times to the new (potential) exchange value following Ukrainian independence. It also presents an example of how a resource can be simultaneously attributed different values in different contexts, creating alliances/solidarities in some contexts (regionally and transnationally), and acting as a source of exclusion in other contexts (nationally).

When I first arrived in Brega in 2000, I asked Valentina, my host and secretary to the mayor, about the ethnic makeup of the village. She told me that the village was predominantly Bulgarian, although there are a few minorities—Gagauz,[1] Russian, Ukrainian, and Moldovan[2]—but she added, "They are small in number."[3] At my expression of amazement that after 200 years the village was still overwhelmingly Bulgarian, she explained that when outsiders moved to the village, "they must learn our language [that is, (Bregan) Bulgarian]." This arrangement applied not only to language but also to the village's customs and practices. By the same token, Valentina continued, "If we go to their village, we learn to speak their language. That is fair." Thus, when Bregans moved to another village, they adopted the native language and customs of the new village, be this Moldovan, Gagauz, Russian or Ukrainian. With a few exceptions (discussed below), most newcomers complied with this general regional rule and learned the Bulgarian language; any Bregans who moved to another village learned the ways and language of their new home. The practice of adopting the local language and customs maintained the apparent integrity of the monoethnic makeup of the village, despite intermarriage being common. In my host family, for example, Valentina's daughter (the offspring of an ethnic Bulgarian mother and Gagauz father), who was still at school when I first arrived in Brega, graduated as a qualified accountant, and married an ethnic Russian Ukrainian. She and her husband lived 70 km north of Brega in a village that was dominated by two ethnicities: Russian and Ukrainian. Whenever the young family—with a five-year-old daughter (in 2014)—visited Valentina, she only spoke Russian to her granddaughter, never Bulgarian. The granddaughter was being raised, as regional tradition demanded, to speak the language(s) of her community: She was raised as a Russian Ukrainian speaker and was not versed in any of the languages of her family from outside the community in which she lived.

The arrangement indicates the significance of language—and by association a particular history in which language practice is grounded—as crucial in understanding local identity and in the conversion of "outsiders" to "insiders."[4] It is this arrangement of adopting local language and customs that has ensured, according to Bregan natives, not only the survival of the Bulgarian village, but also provided a principle for the peaceful coexistence of the multiethnic, multilingual region for over two centuries.

Villagers claimed that they gave little thought to their Bulgarian heritage during Soviet times, as it was secondary to their Soviet citizenship. In practice, both aspects of their identity were in play: As bilingual speakers (Bulgarian and Russian), the Bulgarian language and many of the traditional customs were practiced in the village in nonofficial contexts and also often carried out with the support of local state bodies (e.g., the village council). Ancestral connections to Bulgaria were formally recognized in their Soviet passports, where their ethnicity was recorded as "Bulgarian." Various studies have shown how the USSR's policy with respect to minority languages was often inconsistent and fluctuated over time, connected as it was to the country's nationalities policies (e.g., Van Meurs 1994, 124–25). Yet at least in Brega—and much of southern Bessarabia—incorporation into the USSR after World War II did not require drastic realignments. Since its initial settlement in the early 1800s, southern Bessarabia was a province in the Russian Empire, and Russian, if not a lingua franca, was part of the region's language portfolio (through necessary engagement with administrators and the Russian Orthodox Church [ ROC]) well before entry into the Soviet Union. Thus, local identity required little renegotiation in the transition period between pre-Soviet and Soviet times: The blend of local Bulgarian and wider Russian influences was a point of historical continuity.[5] I do not wish to imply that the juggling of Bulgarian and Russian cultural influences was always tension-free during pre-Soviet and Soviet times. Others have shown how complicated and ambiguous the dual identities between a Soviet identity and national/ethnic identity could be (e.g., Bassin and Kelly 2012). However, in the case of Brega—and probably other villages in the region—the dual identity based on particular language and history selections were compatible with USSR ideology. Villages had always juggled a belonging based on two cultural influences—Bulgarian and Russian—and this in essence continued, although the latter transmuted into a more encompassing "Soviet" identity.[6]

The construction of a unifying "Ukrainian" identity, in the process of building an independent nation-state after 1991, was a complicated and ongoing concern for successive national governments given the considerable linguistic, historical, ethnic, cultural, religious and geopolitical diversity between the regions that made up the country.[7] Ukraine, as it has been pointed out numerous times, is divided by language, geopolitics and history (Marples 2007; Schlegel 2019) and locality is crucial in questions relating to history and identity (Richardson 2008, 21). The "borderlands" conceptualization, so frequently applied to the case of Ukraine,[8] provides a suitable metaphor for the acknowledged diverse history and geopolitical alliances of different parts of Ukraine. The situation was no less complicated in the region of this study. The makeup of the three administrative districts that I consider "the region," or "southern Bessarabia," was multiethnic (and ethnic groups coexisted together in the townships), although rural settlements were predominantly (self-designated) monoethnic—most often Bulgarian, Moldovan or Gagauz.[9] Notably, Ukrainians and Russians—the two largest ethnic groups in Ukraine when considered as a whole—were in the minority in the rural areas of the region. The nationally designated "minorities" were a majority in rural southern Bessarabia.

The obvious difficulties experienced in unifying the nation through any commonly sought criteria of belonging go beyond the considerable geopolitical, linguistic, and historical diversity in the country. Economic hardships following the collapse of the Soviet Union compounded the problem. As is the case with many other areas in former East Europe, this region of Ukraine was an economic loser following the collapse of state socialism (Kaneff 2021). Economic marginalization was partly a result of Kiev policies that largely ignored the region in terms of investment or development in the decades since the country's independence in 1991. It is only in more recent years, with the rising strategic importance of the ports on the Danube and Black Sea following the loss of Crimea, that some investment—from the EU—has found its way to district townships, if not the villages. Alongside lack of investment, the economic hardships of the local population were compounded by neoliberal reforms that were enforced through conditional loans from the World Bank, IMF, and EU, which demanded the privatization of the land (and other resources). As discussed in chapter 1, privatization of land and the associated dismantling of the Soviet agricultural collectives resulted in the unemployment of 90 percent of the working village population. An entire generation have not had salaried employment since they lost their jobs in the collectives, while many of the younger generation were forced to migrate in search of work. At the same time, a range of vital services provided during Soviet times were gradually shut down, including the village hospital (which once had a staff of 17 medical workers and 25 beds). Given the real decline in services and facilities, coupled with majority unemployment, it was unsurprising that villagers associated the previous thirty years of an independent Ukraine with economic hardship. Local disenfranchisement was exacerbated by the ongoing and escalating war in the east of the country, which heightened already evident divisions.

All the above factors—language diversity, geopolitical and history differences, decades of economic struggle and pressures of war—are an important backdrop to understanding identity issues from the perspective of those living in the region, in appreciating the disillusionment of citizens in "marginalized" regions, such as in southern Bessarabia (Kaneff 2021).

Further, while Ukraine was constitutionally committed to a policy of multiculturalism and the protection of minority rights, this commitment was countered in practice by nationalist concerns that sought to unify all Ukrainian citizens under the same umbrella of selected criteria. These two contradictory processes at the national level were manifested through state support for the prominence of the Ukrainian language (and associated culture and history), and the principle of equal rights for members of all ethnic groups (e.g., Kulyk 2006). In July 2019, the law "On Supporting the Functioning of the Ukrainian Language as the State Language" came into force (Verkhovna Rada of Ukraine 2019).[10] It enshrined the Ukrainian language as the only state language in the country, as the dominant language in all media, state bodies and educational institutions.[11] This law was only one of numerous political attempts to find a suitable pathway between having one state language while paying homage to the needs of the country's "minorities," which, since ethnicity and language did not always align, meant that the vast number of Russian speakers included ethnic Ukrainians, ethnic Russians, Bulgarians, and others as well. History—as a politicized selection and contested set of events espoused in national debates and state institutions—was a second important criteria used in the construction of a national identity. Particular (regional) events in the past were given national prominence through the media, the agendas of different political parties and educational institutions. Much like language, history has also proven to be a contentious field for the negotiation of a national sense of belonging over the past three decades. The point is that considerable diversity in terms of language and history was sidelined, if not ignored, in the drive to create a national unity through the support for only one language and only one history.

The multiethnic arrangements in Bessarabia make it difficult to generalize, even at a regional level of analysis, but with no autochthonous links to the land to ground the inhabitants to territory on the basis of ethnicity, language and history played a particularly crucial role in the construction and maintenance of identity (alongside traditional customs, which are given less attention here but were covered in the previous chapter).[12] Irrespective of their ethnic background, Bessarabian inhabitants shared a common history of resettlement and migration (Kaneff and Heinz 2006). At the same time, and unlike other regions in Ukraine, the historical enemy were the Ottomans, and the protector and provider of sanctuary, the Russians. The challenge in contemporary times for Bregans (as for other Bessarabians) was to accommodate the legal requirement for the insertion of another language (Ukrainian), and to accept a very different set of historical events as the main points of reference, when neither the language nor the newly designated national history had any local precedent or relevance.

Since 1991, villagers have had to reassess and negotiate anew their belonging as part of a newly designated "Bulgarian minority" in an independent Ukrainian state. The changes were commented upon by villagers. Valentina told me that she had never felt "Bulgarian" before (i.e., in Soviet times), whereas now (in 2003) she felt "more Bulgarian" because of the government's efforts to promote the issue of minorities. While hopes were high in the early days of national independence that villagers' particular dual cultural heritage would be respected, they have increasingly found themselves at a disadvantage. This served to marginalize many Ukrainian citizens living in southern Bessarabia, because their own cultural and linguistic characteristics were part of a geopolitical history that was quite distinct from the one privileged by Kiev (and in national debates) in the project of building a unified nation. Thus, in the course of exploring the way in which the resource of identity had shifted from use value to also include exchange value, the chapter also throws light on some of the challenges faced by a minority population in contemporary Ukraine.

The chapter's discussion is divided into two sections, reflecting the two main sources of identity: history and language. The following section is concerned with the first of the two main sources for local identity—history—and highlights how the particularities of Bregan history had little resonance with a history put forward nationally. A Brega history—that gave positive value to Russia, that did not experience the 1930s' famine or have any direct involvement in World War II—had little in common and simply did not fit into the dominant Ukrainian narrative given national prominence as historically relevant. Bregans felt excluded and marginalized, aware that their own history had little national currency or recognition. Marginalization did not, however, result in open tensions. Instead it was voiced locally as resentments, as villagers struggled to find a pathway for social mobility when coming from a position of historical (and linguistic) disadvantage. The second section of the chapter focuses on another source of local identity—language. It highlights how, with the rearranging of borders and nation-states, villagers, as Bulgarian-Russian speakers with added Moldovan and Gagauz skill sets, had a potentially rich range of new ways in which to engage regionally and transnationally. It is in these two domains (regional and transnational) that local identity gained new impetus, with considerable nonmonetary and monetary exchange value. In regional and transnational contexts—if not nationally—villagers found alternative means for acceptance; new alliances were made possible through their particular language/history grounded identity that allowed them to engage in various exchange opportunities.

At the end of the chapter, I return to discuss the findings in terms of use and exchange value. The local Bregan identity based on two sources—history and language—was revalued with the creation of an independent Ukraine: It was a local resource that had use value but little exchange potential nationally; however, it had acquired exchange value both regionally (through marriage and trading) and transnationally (through migration, education, and cultural engagements). A focus on identity highlights how with a shift in circumstances—the rise of a new independent nation state and the creation of a new "minority" group—the resource with use value could also acquire exchange value, thus jumping categories. It also provides an example of how the same resource could be simultaneously useful and exchangeable in certain spheres of social life—regionally and transnationally—while less valuable in others (nationally). The resource created alliances in some contexts and was a basis for marginality in other contexts. [13]

## LOCAL IDENTITY AND NATIONAL EXCLUSION

In 2001, a cultural center was opened in the district capital. Its design reflected the ethnic makeup of the district, with rooms in the new complex allocated in proportion to the sizes of the different ethnic groups in the district. Funds for the cultural center building were available from the government, but these were insufficient, and the head of the center spent some of her own personal savings carrying out the renovations. Most of the items displayed—from embroidered clothes to ceramic pots, religious icons to woven kilims—were donated from inhabitants in the township as well as from the surrounding villages (including Brega). Some donations came from abroad: The books and most of the informational materials on Bulgaria came from donations from the Republic of Bulgaria. Apart from its role in exhibiting and educating visitors about the district's ethnic populations, the center also served as a meeting place for local inhabitants, with one room of the building designated for seminars, lectures, and language classes. There was also a small library that contained books and other educational materials.

The efforts of the district capital provided some of the much-needed impetus for the establishment of a far more modest center, a “museum” in Brega, which was opened in the same year as the district center. Officials from the district capital had first pick of the objects collected in Brega; what did not go to the district cultural center ended up in the Brega museum.[14] There were no government funds at the village administrative level for this project. In Brega, financial support for the museum came from the agricultural enterprises, and from the village’s most successful businessman, who voluntarily made a contribution once he had seen their initial efforts.

It was the mayor who had put forward the idea to create a village museum in 1991, and he asked Valentina (secretary to the mayor, and trained as a librarian by profession) to collect information and items for exhibit, a task she carried out over a period of the following decade. Apart from numerous trips to the district capital to search for information, she also knocked on doors and asked countless villagers for donations, anything that would be appropriate for the museum: old plows or agricultural equipment, traditional embroidered clothes, photos, old furniture, kitchen utensils and so on. The received items were stored in the basement of the kindergarten building, before one of the younger and more motivated schoolteachers in the village, Alyona (who taught Bulgarian and Ukraine language), with the assistance of two pupils, established the museum in the school in an empty room allocated for this purpose.

I was first invited to see the display while it was still in preparation. As I wandered around the room, it seemed to me that the collected objects were arranged in a way that had no overarching narrative. Indeed, Valentina and I were invited in part because Alyona was struggling with how to display the items and wanted our advice. In the large, rectangular room, one wall displayed an odd selection of clothing: everything from traditional embroidered dresses to a soldier’s uniform from the contemporary period. The second wall conveyed a brief history of the village in poster form; it also displayed framed embroidered items and old pottery and other bits and pieces found during archeological digs in the village. At the very end of this wall was a poster depicting the four Russian parachutists who were killed after accidently landing in the village during World War II when the territory was behind enemy lines (occupied by Romania at the time). The poster described the parachutists' fate and included a photograph of the monument erected next to the village municipal council building in commemoration of the tragedy. The third wall contained several larger domestic household objects: an old dresser and mirror decorated with more embroidered cloth, a 1920s gramophone player, large ceramic pots once used for pickling food and a religious icon in the corner. The last wall contained very little: a glass case with a few World War II passports and some embroidery remnants. The floor was strewn with a variety of ancient objects—old irons, cauldrons once used to carry water, a large plow, pitchforks used for moving hay, a spinning wheel, and many photographs. The latter, as well as other documents, had been collected by Valentina during a number of trips to the district capital archives.

Alyona was stuck as to what she could display on the fourth wall. As I struggled to make sense of the way in which the items had been organized and the message it conveyed, I questioned whether there was any chronological order to the display. Valentina immediately latched onto my question, which she interpreted somewhat differently, and said, "Yes, Deema is correct, you need to display these items in chronological order." We decided that the first wall would present all the archeological items from the earliest period, as well as the material documenting the early settlement. The progression of history would continue along the second and third walls until the last wall, which would represent the contemporary period. I had not intended to influence the proceedings in such a direct way, but now, fired up by the idea, we left Alyona with a much clearer idea as to how a narrative could be realized through the objects. The large items would remain in the middle, around which people could walk. Alyona noted the lack of objects for the contemporary wall and in response I offered to take photos of the village that could be displayed on this fourth wall. The women liked this idea, and when I asked them what I should photograph, they both agreed on one particular location from which one could gain an excellent panorama of the whole village—of the church, the school, and the lake (see fig. I.4, Introduction). It was this view that they wished me to photograph. Valentina also suggested that I could photograph modern agricultural machinery

**FIGURE 5.1.** Alyona in the early stages of setting up the museum.

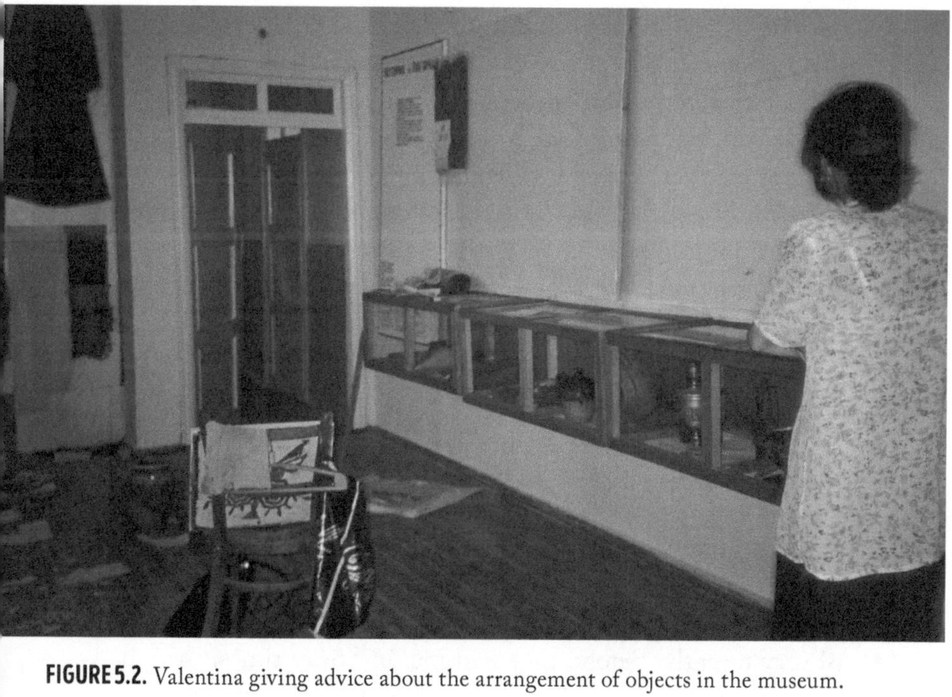

**FIGURE 5.2.** Valentina giving advice about the arrangement of objects in the museum.

**FIGURE 5.3.** Some of the objects collected for the museum.

used by the "cooperatives," which would poignantly contrast with the photos and old agricultural implements already collected for the display. The linear process of time and evidence of progress became the central scaffolding for the display.

The creation of a village museum demanded reflections on the village's past heritage in a way quite different from previous times. The rise of regional/local cultural museums and centers (and the introduction of teaching Bulgarian at school) was part of a new government initiative that required citizens to reflect on their newly designated "minority" status. Until this time, villagers, by their own admission, had not thought much about their "Bulgarianness." Indeed, when I asked the all-female staff of administrators at the village council soon after I first arrived in Brega whether they felt like Bulgarians, Russians, or Ukrainians, one of the women, accompanied by nods of support from her fellow workers, said "We don't feel like anything." They explained that they spoke Bulgarian and carried out Bulgarian customs because, "That's the way it has always been," but they had not really reflected on it until very recently. Before, they told me, in Soviet times, there had been no funding for Bulgarian books and for the language to be

**FIGURES 5.4 AND 5.5.** Getting some order into the exhibition.

taught at the school (they themselves had never learned Bulgarian grammar or the language in any formal capacity). They were, first and foremost, Soviet citizens, and never thought much about being Bulgarian. They emphasized that the Bulgarian language was "not discouraged, it's just that it was not given particular attention during Soviet times."

It was this particular "attention" to their ethnic background that was now underway in the early years after Ukrainian independence. The exercise of constructing a museum represented, in part, a move away from being Soviet citizens with an officially acknowledged Bulgarian ethnicity that was recorded in every passport but required little reflection or articulation (although it was constantly being practiced through language and daily activities), to being Ukrainian citizens with minority status (Bulgarians being the fifth largest minority in the country). The creation of the museum demanded local reflection on the past and on Brega's position in the new Ukrainian state. (A similar process of reflection took place with respect to their traditional customs, when the priest, in admonishing villagers for the practice of some of their village traditions, motivated villagers to think about, and defend, their taken-for-granted, everyday customs [see chapter 4]). Such new demands for reflection were a challenge, at least for Alyona and Valentina, who led the construction of a new historical narrative for the village. It necessitated a coherent story that would align the local past with the broader national narrative.

The village mayor, who was not burdened with the intricate details of creating the narrative, was quite clear as to the purpose of the museum. He identified the objective (in 2001): "Let the people know when they come to this region that here we have our own language, our own culture." In other words, he was concerned to inform outsiders about Brega's unique linguistic and cultural characteristics. As for the villagers themselves, the mayor said, "it is important that our children know what is behind us. We must let our children know about our history." The educational purposes of the museum were also emphasized by Valentina in a comment she made to Sonia, who donated an old loom to the museum. When Sonia apologized for its sorry state (the wood was rotting in a few places), Valentina responded, "It's fine. The museum is there for our children, to teach them how it was before, in our grandparents' time." Thus, the museum's aim was to provide an insight into the village's past: to inform outsiders as to what it was that was specific and special about their community, and to educate/inform the younger village generation as to their heritage.

It is in considering the particular historical circumstances that led the Bulgarian migrants to settle in this land that we can understand how it is that Bregans had their "own language" and their "own culture." Described below are some of the most important historical moments in the village's past that have provided the basis of Bregan belonging and identity. The information presented is not intended to be a thorough history of the village or region; it remains, as are all histories, inevitably a selection. However, I present this information as a means to highlight some of the most important features of the history, many of which were explicitly referenced in the museum display, and in two locally authored histories (written in Soviet times), as well as in conversations I had with villagers over the years. In providing this history, the point is to highlight the significant ways in which Brega history differed from the national "Ukrainian" state-sponsored history that has been under construction since 1991.

Although under Ottoman rule since the sixteenth century, historical sources present the area as sparsely occupied until the late 1700s.[15] It was the Russian struggle against Ottoman domination that served as the core reference point around which local history was oriented. Various campaigns by the Russian Army (often working in alliance with the Habsburg Empire) in the eighteenth century were unsuccessful, and it was only in the early 1800s that the Russians finally gained dominance, and the Ottomans were forced to the negotiation table. The Bucharest Peace Treaty was signed in 1812, formally transferring the territory to Russia, thereby ending three centuries under Ottoman control (Van Meurs 1994, 43–46; Schlegel 2016, 19). By this date, and from the end of the 1700s onward, the region that was the most southerly area of what was known as Bessarabia (see fig. I.2, Introduction) was settled by refugees seeking a new life outside of Ottoman rule.[16] As Bulgarian (and Gagauz) migrants moved into the area, escaping persecution and reprisals from the Ottomans who still controlled territories further south, including Bulgaria, the Russian Empire was consolidating this region as a new frontier of its territory (Brandes 2011, 272). Brega was established in 1812, with settlers welcomed, given sanctuary and granted land by Russian officials working on behalf of the Russian tsar, eager to have the area developed as a new outpost of the Russian Empire (Mavrov and Bratkov 2006 [1967]). Archival materials following settlement, primarily letters now located in the museum, contain some of the earliest documents relating to this period. One letter is from a Russian administrator asking the Russian authorities on behalf of the Bulgarians to grant them permission to remain; other letters are from the Bulgarians themselves requesting permission to settle and be accepted into the Russian Empire. One letter (no date) was from a Russian general written in the name of the Russian Tsar Alexander I, who reigned from 1801 to 1825. It said, "Those migrating . . . in order to escape the Turks are being granted land and are also free from all other obligations [e.g., from serving in the army]. The land is granted for an initial period of three years, but this period could be extended for longer and the Bulgarians need not pay taxes on the land. The people can choose the land they want to live on. . . . [It] is being given to them in order that they can establish their new lives. . . . These privileges are granted in the name of the Russian Tsar" (DK translation). While freedom from Ottoman rule remained the main attraction for settlers, the granting of land, exemption from taxes and military service, as well as the conveying of autonomous status to Bessarabia provided additional benefits for Bulgarians and other migrants to the region (Van Meurs 1994, 47; Schlegel 2016, 19). The capital of the province was Chisinau, heralding an ongoing strong influence of Moldovans in the region, despite the influx of Russian officials and administrators into the regional capital.

It is worth highlighting that the village's foundation was a result of its inhabitants sharing a common enemy with Russia: the Ottomans. Bulgaria proper did not achieve independence from the Ottomans until 1878, some seventy or so years after the initial exodus of Bulgarians to Bessarabia. Bessarabia itself became an important base for the continuing revolutionary movement fighting for Bulgarian independence. Local history notes the presence of the exiled Bulgarian revolutionary hero and poet Hristo Botev, who was based in Bessarabia in the 1860s and early 1870s. He worked as a teacher but also collaborated with Russian revolutionaries (Mavrov and Bratkov 2006 [1967], 9). Bulgarians from Bessarabia were actively involved in providing assistance to their ancestral homeland in a number of ways: sending financial and other resources, as well as providing infrastructural support to the Russian Army. Bessarabian Bulgarians thus played an important strategic role on the side of Russia against the Ottomans for decades after their initial settlement in the territory. The final stand and successful war against the Turks in Bulgaria signified Bulgarian independence after 500 years of Ottoman domination. It also had implications for the southern parts of Bessarabia, which having been transferred to Romania under the Paris Treaty of 1856, were returned to Russia in the San Stefano Peace Treaty that marked, finally, the end of the Russo-Turkish War (1877–1878) and helped liberate the Balkans. A letter dated April 6, 1881, stated that 333 rubles had been collected to mark the momentous occasion: The funds were set aside as a contribution toward the building of a national monument at Shipka Peak in the Balkan Mountains in Bulgaria, close to where several key battles in the Russo-Turkish War took place, to commemorate the country's independence. The monument, which remains a popular tourist pilgrimage site in contemporary times, was funded from donations from people all over Bulgaria, but also included financial contributions from the Bulgarian diaspora in Bessarabia—documents reveal that Brega was one of the villages to have contributed.[17]

In 1845, the village population was 1,093 and there were 148 houses. Records show that for the earliest years of settlement at least, Russian Empire administrators were not present on site in any permanent capacity. The recording of vital statistics—births, deaths, and marriages—was performed by the ROC, which acted in lieu of a full-time state administrator (Schlegel 2019, 55). Unlike some other Bulgarian settlements where it appears that the migrants were accompanied by their own Bulgarian priests (see Boneva 2006, 52), in Brega, the ROC with a Russian priest was established from the first settlement. The village church was completed in 1814. Villagers accepted the ROC into their lives as part of the matter of course, a way to solidify their place in their newly adopted home under the protection of the Russian Empire. Membership of the ROC meant that they were christened with Russian names (often the closest to the Bulgarian equivalent), and these

Russian names were used in all subsequent official documentation, while the Bulgarian names were used in everyday life. This dual naming system provided the beginnings of the development of a bilingual arrangement, one that has gradually melded Russian language (and associated cultural practices) with Bulgarian traditions and language. In contemporary times, the two influences operated together to create a distinct local Bregan identity.

The first half of the twentieth century was a tumultuous time that included two world wars, which in the case of southern Bessarabia also meant that the region shifted between Romanian and Russian control. It was not until the area became part of the Soviet Union in 1944 that relative stability returned to the territory. The early Soviet years were remembered as particularly hard due to a drought in 1946 and a lack of suitable agricultural equipment—attributed by a local history to having been taken by the retreating Romanian Army (Mavrov and Bratkov 2006 [1967], 14). However, Bulgarians, perhaps more than the other ethnicities in the region, found acceptance and success as new Soviet citizens. This was partly because of the rehabilitated position of the Republic of Bulgaria following the Bulgarian Communist Party's victory and the subsequent establishment of Bulgaria into one of the USSR's closest allies. This had knock-on positive implications for Bulgarians in the USSR. The other reason was, as Bregans themselves told me, they were more successful than their Moldovan and Gagauz counterparts in their linguistic integration, speaking Russian well (and without an accent, unlike the others) because of the relative closeness of the Bulgarian and Russian languages. The Russian language was already familiar to them, although most had had little opportunity to receive any formal education in pre-Soviet times.[18]

From its initial settlement some 200 years ago, the region, and more specifically Brega, has come under the influence of different powers, first as part of the Russian Empire, then after World War II, as part of the Soviet Union, and now as part of an independent Ukraine (1991). During most of the two-century period, Romanian/Moldovan influence was also present to various degrees alongside the ongoing Russian ones. Population upheavals were common with every change in external governance. In the two brief periods that Romania gained formal control of Bessarabia

(1856–1878 and 1918–1944), there were large emigrations of Slavs, giving Moldovans greater numerical dominance, while the Slavs' subsequent return after the territory reverted back to Russia again reversed the ethnic balance (Van Meurs 1994, 117, 119). The end of the second period of Romanian control (1918–1944) was particularly unsettling: Taken by the USSR briefly in the early part of World War II (one year), it was lost again to Romania for another three years (1941 to 1944) before the final victory of the Soviet Union against the Germans transferred the territory to the Soviet Union, where it remained until the breakup of the USSR.[19] At this time, in 1991, the southern part of Bessarabia, which included Brega, was incorporated into the newly independent Ukraine.[20] Apart from obvious political and economic reforms, Ukrainian influence was primarily felt in the need to adapt to new linguistic requirements, since by law all government documentation was only available in Ukrainian, a language that until 1991 was never used in the village or region (although taught in class at school during Soviet times, alongside German and Russian).

The above regional history, by necessity a mere skeleton, suggests significant divergences from the grand national "Ukrainian" narrative under construction since independence (see Wanner 1998). While acknowledging the complexity of any attempt to construct a national history in a country where regional and even district variation is considerable, contemporary accounts have identified "defining moments," or reference points from the first half of the twentieth century as crucial in any presentation of a "Ukrainian" history (Marples 2007, xi). Inevitably, accounts have engaged with two events that are given privileged attention: the famine of 1932–1933, and the years prior to and following World War II, especially with respect to the activities of organizations that claimed to have fought for an independent Ukraine, the Organization of Ukrainian Nationalists (OUN) and the Ukrainian Insurgent Army (UPA) (e.g., Marples 2007; Wanner 1998).[21] The highly politicized and contested nature of debates concerning these events (and related details), debates that often coalesce around the west Ukrainian "nationalist" position versus the east Ukraine view of history (seen as closely aligned to pro-Soviet views), are not my concern here.[22] Rather, I wish to highlight that a national preoccupation with these particular events over and above others loses sight of the fact that in some regions of the country, these privileged occurrences had little significance at all. This was the case for southern Bessarabia, and more specifically Brega, where local history did not align with the designated nationally significant events.

First, it meant that in the case of Brega, which was not part of the USSR at the time, there were no narratives of victimization and suffering with respect to the 1930s famine. Debates that dominated the first decades of independent Ukraine surrounding the causes of the famine and how many died (and whether or not it was a genocide)[23] had little relevance in southern Bessarabia. Whether the famine was due to (resistance to) Soviet collectivization policies,[24] or unfavorable environmental and climatic conditions, was also a moot point, as southern Bessarabia was under Romanian rule at the time. Thus, the famine, as a reference point for the construction of, and debates surrounding "national" narratives since 1991, was irrelevant for this area that was not incorporated into the Soviet Union until almost two decades after the famine.

Second, the national concerns relating to World War II in terms of the heavy loss of life, as well as the intricacies of the OUN and UPA activities both during and after the war, again, had little resonance for Bregans. The organizations, irrespective of their activities—whether in alliance with or against the Germans and Soviet Army—held minimal significance for a population that was excluded altogether from active fighting in the war. Bregan fortunes took a number of turns during the war, and villagers found themselves in a very difficult situation, with opposing forces moving through their space at different times: the Romanians supporting the German side, and the Soviets on the side of the Allied Powers. Bregans were trusted by neither side: The fact that the Bulgarian village had been under Russian rule for so long made the villagers untrustworthy in the eyes of the Romanians, and according to Brega history, the men were rounded up and sent to work in mines and agriculture in Romania during the war (Mavrov and Bratkov 2006 [1967], 13). The Bregans were also not trusted by the Soviet Army, which claimed, then lost, and then reclaimed the area. As ethnic Bulgarians (recall that Bulgaria, like Romania, was also on Germany's side during the war), the village men were not accepted into the Soviet Army, and no one from the village fought on the Front.[25] A significant event in Brega's own World War II history indicates the difficulty of their position: Four Russian parachutists who accidently landed in the village when the territory was behind enemy lines (occupied by Romania) were killed. Although local history remained silent as to who actually killed the soldiers, villagers or occupying Romanians, the war memorial erected in the village during Soviet times that was the site for annual May 9 commemorations paid homage to the soldiers. The ongoing significance of the occurrence for the community, as the single event of disloyalty to Russia/USSR, was evident in the fact that the museum allocated a special place for the recounting of the tragedy. After the war, with the territory's incorporation into the USSR, village men were once again sent to work, this time to the "Labor Front" in 1945, in parts of the Soviet Union as far away as Chelyabinsk (Southern Urals, now in present-day Russia) to work in the coal mines and other industries. The men's labor, it was explained to me by a villager, was in demand following heavy losses of Russian/Soviet lives during the war and the deficit of men.

Thus, while the war experience differed for every village in the district according to different perceived ethnic, historical, and cultural alliances, the Bulgarian population, including Bregans, was viewed with suspicion and as untrustworthy by both sides. As such, the men did not participate directly in fighting in the war on any side. It explains why Tanya, the schoolteacher, once told me, "People here aren't as emotionally committed to the war, unlike in other places."

The exclusion of the village from fighting in the war meant that Brega could not easily join in any national collective history of suffering framed around participation in the Front. Instead, local history recounted the community's exclusion from fighting as a consequence of war alliances that were not of local making. The May 9 celebrations that were celebrated across the Soviet Union to mark the end of World War II and continued to be celebrated in Ukraine (until very recently), were relatively low-key in Brega, since, as Valentina explained, "Bulgarian men in the village were never directly involved in the Front." The handful of men in the village who were honored as active fighters in village commemorations were "not from our village," they were ethnic Russians who had moved to the village after the war (usually through marriage).[26] The annual war commemorations in Brega were largely formularistic and relatively subdued. Informal memories of the war gravitated around elderly villagers' recollections concerning various demands—for food, clothing, or other assistance—made by the armies as they marched through the territory. While such memories of all three forces—German, Soviet and Romanian—diverged as to which army treated them better or worse, the unifying narrative of all was one of exclusion from participation in the fighting. Bregans were neither trusted nor aligned with either side.

The position of Bregans in terms of both nationally designated historical events discussed above—the famine and World War II—diverged significantly from the "national" rendition. Bregans—and I would venture southern Bessarabians more generally, especially Gagauz and Bulgarian communities whose history was one of being given sanctuary by the Russians—held a diametrically opposite view from the negative value attributed to Russia/USSR in other parts of Ukraine. Russians were not seen as colonizers or foreign oppressors, and there was no strong anti-Russian/Soviet sentiment. Independence from Russia was an alien viewpoint to the migrant non-autochthonous population, which remained grateful for the offered sanctuary, protection, and a permanent home in the new lands of the empire. Russia was also honored for liberating, some decades later, the Bulgarian "motherland" from Ottoman rule. In this sense, Bregans found themselves, along with other southern and eastern parts of the country (although for very different reasons), at odds with what were attributed as west Ukrainian understandings of the past.[27]

Such a divergence from the dominant national version of the past was rarely a topic of conversation in Brega until the more tense days of 2014, when the war in the east and the loss of Crimea ("annexation" was not the way it was locally understood) was prominent in villagers' minds. In one animated conversation on the street one early evening, a villager said, "I don't understand why they [west Ukrainians] are so against Russia. Russia freed them from the fascists; they should be grateful."[28] This conversation developed out of a longer discussion during which the gathered neighbors expressed their concern at the country's shift toward the EU and "the West," and further away from a Russian orbit. Inevitably, Kiev's anti-Russian stance was seen as evidence of the country's shift to "the West" and the EU.[29] There was a general consensus that "Ukraine has always been anti-Russian, and Europe backs them up," and people pointed to the hegemonic role west Ukrainian versions of history have played post-1991 in both Ukraine itself and abroad. The refusal to give the Russian language equal prominence, something that directly and negatively impacted Bregans, was seen as one root cause of the conflict in eastern Ukraine. "What would it have hurt," one neighbor asked, to nods of agreement from the others present, "to accept Russian as another official language?" Returning to the topic of the general reorientation away from Russia, yet another woman added with more than just a touch of sarcasm, "Now we are entering the EU; we'll blossom." Meaning the exact opposite: Prices were expected to rise and living standards to fall.[30] Zina, a village native working in administration in the district capital and one of the leading figures involved in the agricultural reforms in Brega, told me after visiting Bulgaria in 2014: "After joining the EU, they [Bulgaria] are still poor. The EU brought them nothing; they are the rubbish of the EU." The fact that in Bulgaria, "Things aren't any better, they are as poor as us" (to quote another villager who had been to Bulgaria twice in the past decade), provided further justification for questioning the closer political and economic alignment being cultivated by the Ukraine government to "the West."

A designated Ukrainian history based on negative appraisals of Russia/USSR—a position that dominated formal or mainstream media, political and educational institutions—had few supporters in Brega. The core events given central national attention, the 1930s famine and World War II conflicts, lay outside of local experiences. Even if there were opportunities, perhaps regionally and in less formal (private) spaces, for multiple voices and perspectives to be expressed (as seems to be the case in Odessa, Richardson 2008), these debates still relied on some form of assumed engagement or position taken with respect to nationally designated "significant" past events. Those whose experiences lay well outside these privileged national events were excluded from this dialogue. Minority status had become, for Bregans, not an opportunity to have their "own culture" and "own language" acknowledged, but instead a form of silencing and marginalization from the nation building project, which was constructed on the basis of a very different collective memory and history from that known or experienced locally.

The village museum was only open for a brief two-year period. Since then, it has remained locked, gathering dust, a relic that testified to a brief time in the very early years after independence when villagers tried to find a way to represent themselves to outsiders and to fit themselves into a broader national narrative. The lack of state sponsorship contributed to its closure. Alyona, the custodian, was not paid any salary, and as she told me, "You can't work these days for a *spasibo* [Russian for "thank you"]. So, I've resigned. Either they have to pay me for my efforts, or I can't take it on." Soon after this conversation, in 2003, she migrated to Odessa with her husband and found work as a shop assistant. The museum has not been open since.

Much like the example of the museum, Bregans found few means to fit themselves into a wider national history. The newfound interest in their Bulgarian minority status lost much of its earlier (pre-2000) impetus. State rhetoric claiming support for minority groups was not matched by financial or other forms of support. At the same time, the government's preoccupation with tensions and conflicts in other regions in the country where Russian dominated (in terms of language and historical alliances) made any Bregan efforts at identity expression difficult, given their own pro-Russian historical solidarities. Despite national laws that guaranteed the freedom of minorities, there has been a lack of state support for local identity. The fate of the museum was one example. The folklore group was another example: Sponsorship was entirely from village sources, from the agricultural enterprises (rather than from the government). Any public support for a local history or for expressions of their particular heritage and identity came from within the community and remained restricted to it.

The past, as one of the sources of attempted unified identity, provided few opportunities for Brega incorporation into the national project, and few points of commonality existed on which a local-national conversation could take place. The Ottomans represented an important collective regional historical "enemy" against whom local identity was constructed, while the Russians an equally important positive "savior" to whom villagers remained eternally grateful. A Brega history had no value in the national Ukrainian arena, and little chance to be incorporated into the new history of the nation-state. To recall the words of the mayor, who after informing me of the purposes of the museum added, "In the last years, history has changed by 180 degrees—it was one, now it is another." At the time he said this to me, in 2001, I assumed he was referring to the villagers' history. Now, I understand he was referring to the construction of a new national history that was revised so dramatically that it was "turned around" by 180 degrees (in line with many other rewriting and revaluations of national history throughout eastern Europe—see Kaneff 1998; Verdery 1999; Marples 2007). A teacher who taught history at the village school said something similar: "Before, we used to learn about Russian heroes, now the history has changed, and we learn about Ukrainian heroes." Villagers found it difficult to connect to the new national history. When the mayor went on to say, "The children must know how to live with their neighbors, they mustn't argue with their neighbors, but must live as friends," I was under the definite impression he was referring to the extra efforts and sensitivities necessary to survive in a situation where local history aligned poorly with that advocated beyond the region, nationally. Ukrainian independence, constructed on the basis of a particular set of past events more closely aligned to other regions of the country, served to emphasize to Bregans their own peripherality and exclusion. Their history was marginal, even oppositional to the extent that it was based on experiences and values that contrasted sharply with those sponsored in Kiev, and that dominated the nationalistic agenda of the media, formal educational and political institutions in the country. The villagers' history held little national currency and provided no exchange potential. The safest response, especially under the given circumstances, was silence.

## LOCAL IDENTITY AND REGIONAL/TRANSNATIONAL EXCHANGES

Local identity was a complicated mix of several cultural influences that provided villagers with few discernible national assets but did have exchange value in other contexts. In this section, I first describe the multifaceted identity before turning to discuss the exchange potential of local identity both regionally and transnationally.

It was many months into my stay in Brega that I first realized that almost everyone in the village had two first names: a legal name that appeared on all official paperwork, and an everyday Bulgarian (undocumented) name, by which they were known in the village.[31] The former was used in all official correspondence—passports, land titles, marriage, birth, and death certificates and so on. However, this name was never used in everyday village life, which was why it took me months to realize that such a situation existed. My host's mother was addressed as "Mina," and out of respect, most called her "Baba Mina." Having lived with Baba Mina for many months, I never knew her by any other name, as our relationship was not one that was played out in any official bureaucratic spaces. My next-door neighbor was called "Marusha," the only name by which I knew her. In both cases, the names "Mina" and "Marusha" were used in everyday situations, and these were (and are) Bulgarian, not Russian names.[32] Both women were recorded in their passports with the same Russian name: Maria. When I eventually learned of the dual naming arrangements and asked about it, Baba Mina told me she and Marusha "are both officially written as 'Maria' in our passports, but we are not called that by other villagers." This situation was relatively standard in the village, although there were some exceptions, such as individuals who were given names that overlapped and were the same in both Bulgarian and Russian, thus requiring no second name. For example, Valentina, often shortened to Valya, was a common name in the village that was used both in formal documentation and in the community, irrespective of context. However, in cases where Russian and Bulgarian names did not coincide, villagers had two first names. This practice had its roots from the earliest time of settlement when villagers were christened with ROC names that were used in all documentation and bureaucratic interactions and constituted their official persona, while retaining their own Bulgarian names for everyday use.

Such a dual naming system provides a first indication of the complicated relationship between the two cultures that was at the core of Bregan identity: Russian was the language in which one engaged with the "outside" world, while Bulgarian was reserved for those considered "insiders." Another example serves to underline the nuances of this insider/outsider delineation. One morning, I answered the phone, and the person at the other end greeted me and said, "It's Lena here." I looked quizzically at Valentina, who was also in the room, because I did not know a "Lena." It was only after I had spoken to her for a short while that I recognized the voice as belonging to Alyona, the schoolteacher I had met recently and was getting to know through her efforts to establish the village museum. Afterward, Valentina explained to me that she was (to make matters more confusing) "Elena" in her passport, and "Lena" was the abbreviated version of "Elena," while her Bulgarian name, by which I knew her, was Alyona. I cannot recall the original circumstances when I first began to address her as Alyona, but I probably used the name I had heard others use, including Valentina, with whom I lived. We had gone together to the museum to help Alyona, and it is during that first meeting that—imitating Valentina—I started addressing her as Alyona. Lena's use of her formal, passport name, but with an added touch of casualness, through the abbreviation, denoted the type of relationship she felt she had with me at the time that I answered the telephone: not quite that of strangers, but also not close enough to warrant the use of her Bulgarian name. It defined our relationship as less formal than one between strangers, yet not so close as to make use of the Bulgarian "Alyona." It was only when we got to know each other better, over the following months, that she herself made it clear I should call her "Alyona."

The formal/informal delineation in naming practices that determined how people addressed each other in different contexts based on their degree of social closeness was largely unreflected upon, although at times it was a deliberately employed strategy (as detailed below). In all cases, language choice established and confirmed social distance between people. As the schoolteacher, Tanya, who I had engaged to give me Russian lessons, told me: "You only speak Bulgarian with 'blizki,'" those to whom you are close. This essentially included the entire village, although the situation was far more nuanced than this—as I discovered through my growing friendship with Alyona/Lena/Elena. Generally, Bulgarian was used in everyday situations (when no outsiders were present) within the village: at home, the school, the shops, the council, the kindergarten, the streets and so on. However, even within these spaces and contexts, the two languages were used strategically and carried different connotations. For example, Tanya explained that there was a huge difference in which language a teacher chose to use when scolding a misbehaving pupil at school. "If you do it in Bulgarian, then the telling off in the more familiar language of blizki is a way to scold in a more good-natured and friendly way. If you scold the misbehaving pupil in Russian, then this constitutes a more formal or severe reprimand, and thus should be taken more seriously." The same principle held in other everyday situations in the village: Good-natured, friendly exchanges between village and local officials took place in Bulgarian, but if Russian was used (usually in some official site, such as at the village council building or school), then it added a degree of authority, reserve, and formality to the interaction.

Russian created, in Tanya's words, a "distance based on formality." It was the language one used with those perceived to be socially more distant (including strangers). It was spoken: at official functions, where one was more likely to encounter other ethnic groups or strangers; at meetings that included officials from the district (e.g., the annual council meeting); in the bus that operated between the villages and district capital (although fellow travelers from the same village spoke their native language to each other); and at formal public events, such as school functions when parents and guests from outside might be present. In summary, reverting to Russian usually took place in official sites, at times that necessitated a degree of formality and on occasions where a common interethnic language was required.

Using Russian was often also an indicator of status and thus used on occasions when an additional degree of legitimacy was desired. For example, during heated exchanges between villagers arguing over land or taxes, villagers frequently lapsed into Russian, which gave an extra degree of authority to their arguments. Another example was when my elderly next-door neighbor Diado Shiro agreed to meet and tell me the history of the village (a more structured and formally organized meeting than our usual casual banters on the street). In this instance, he spoke more Russian than on other occasions. The use of Russian gave an additional degree of legitimacy to his retold history. The higher status of Russian language also made it the language of preference for a few individuals in the village who spoke primarily in Russian, with occasional additions of Bulgarian words. This was true in the case of the head of the sovkhoz. I noted that he spoke predominantly in Russian at village council meetings (sometimes mixed with some Bulgarian words and phrases), unlike the other village officials who relied far more on Bulgarian. When I asked about this afterward, I was assured that it was not an issue of him wishing to be above the others, but simply because he had a Russian wife, spoke Russian at home and had forgotten much of his Bulgarian, despite living full-time in the village. I suspected that both factors were significant: He was married to a Russian, and thus household arrangements played a part. At the same time, his position as head of the sovkhoz, the government's model agricultural collective organization seen as a showpiece to locals and foreigners alike, provided little incentive to relearn Bulgarian, as speaking Russian reinforced his position of authority. Further, marriages between Brega Bulgarians and Russians/Ukrainians were less likely to result in the latter learning fluent Bulgarian than marriages with Gagauz or Moldovan speakers. This suggests an ongoing hierarchy of languages, with Russian and Ukrainian (especially post-1991), having primacy.[33] Despite some individuals' greater reliance on Russian due to the circles in which they moved, most spoke Bulgarian to each other, with different degrees of "purity." Even the head of the sovkhoz made an effort to include some Bulgarian words when responding to queries from other officials at meetings. It was a gesture that brought him closer to other officials, who also, in an attempt to accommodate him, moved between Bulgarian and Russian. Bridges were always extended between linguistic chasms without hesitation. Notably, the priest was the only person in the village who operated exclusively in Russian, both in the church during services and when interacting with villagers in their own homes to perform a rite. He said he could understand some Bulgarian, but I never heard him utter a word. I believe this was to some extent a deliberate strategy: Through his exclusive use of Russian, the priest established his authority and distance both spiritually and socially from the rest of the village.

Russian was also an indicator of a higher level of education. Those with tertiary educations were far more likely to speak a version of Bulgarian that incorporated more Russian words, as opposed to those less well educated. For example, my neighbor from across the street, Luba, a kindergarten teacher, used more Russian words in her everyday Bulgarian speech than Marusha, my less educated neighbor, who had worked as an unskilled (field) laborer in the kolkhoz. However, because Bulgarian was the language of social closeness, even university educated figures in the village made efforts to speak Bulgarian on everyday occasions. Tanya explained how at home, before she started school, she spoke Bulgarian. Then, when she was a pupil at school, almost everything was in Russian, and for her at least, by the time she went to university in Kishinev (as it was still known in Brega) and then fulfilled her assigned post-training teaching (she was absent from the village for a total of six years—three years of university, and then three years of state service teaching in Kishinev), she had "forgotten" her Bulgarian. To indicate how dominant the Russian language had become for her in the course of attaining a tertiary education, she said that when speaking Bulgarian on her return to Brega, she had to first translate her thoughts from Russian, because Bulgarian had become so unfamiliar to her. Unlike the head of the sovkhoz married to a Russian, once she was back in the village, she set aside time to relearn Bulgarian, although she acknowledged that often she slipped in a Russian word when she could not think of the Bulgarian one, or did not know it. She, like other tertiary educated villagers, felt more "limited" in Bulgarian, and better able to express herself in Russian. However, for the vast majority in the village who did not complete tertiary education, Brega Bulgarian, with far less reliance on Russian words, remained the language of everyday communication.

The language arrangement described above was unique to Brega. It was clear from what I saw, and from what Bregans and villagers from other communities told me, that every village in the region had its own particularities, borrowing from Russian and the local ethnic language in a way that was presented as specific to their own community.[34] Such a uniqueness was evident in the distinct way language and kinship terminology were blended, and also extended to various customs and practices.[35]

The choice of language, the particular context, and dialect (see below) highlighted the sometimes strategic and always situational nature of language use. This in turn gave identity, rooted in language, a multidimensionality: operating at a range of local, national, and transnational levels (see also Dickinson 2010).

In Brega, there were three important ways in which language served as an identity marker and presented opportunities for exchange. First, it distinguished Brega, as a Bulgarian village, from other villages with a different ethnic background in the same administrative district and the region more generally. That is, it distinguished Brega from the Moldovan and Gagauz villages in the region, as well as the less commonly found Russian and Ukrainian ethnic villages. Every interaction between inhabitants from different villages was an occasion to reinforce the uniqueness of each community. At a marriage that I attended in 2003, between a Bulgarian woman from Brega and a Moldovan man from a nearby village, guests from both villages were very aware of the mixed practices and customs that constituted the two-day wedding. What was notable was that everyone present knew exactly which customs were Bulgarian and which were Moldovan (and the wedding borrowed customs and music from both). Guests accepted each other's practices and showed a willingness to accommodate them. Frequently, the different customs were identified and commented on—these were the "Bulgarian" parts, and these were the "Moldovan" ones. After the registry ceremony and the laying of flowers at the war monument, for example, there was a short *khoro* (dance) to music provided by a band of musicians. My Brega friend, with whom I attended, commented on the difference in the way the Moldovans and Bulgarians shouted—that shrill call to prompt and urge on the dancers: "We Bulgarians," she said, "shout differently."' Russian, as the lingua franca, mediated all exchanges between the two parties. Any lapses were brief and corrected: Earlier in the day, at the bride's house, the bride's sister fell momentarily into Bulgarian before being gently reminded by the groom to, "Speak in Russian." After their marriage, I was told, the couple would speak Russian at home, but eventually the bride would learn (at least some) Moldovan. Their future children would speak Moldovan and Russian.

Second, language was also the source of identification between villages within the region that were of the same ethnicity. I was frequently informed of a selection of words used differently in other Bulgarian villages in the region from the way they were used in Brega. For example, the verb "gulcha" in Brega was used to mean "to speak/to tell"' According to villagers in Brega, neighboring Bulgarian villages, did not use gulcha in this way. This difference, regularly brought to my attention by them, helped distinguish their community vis-à-vis other nearby Bulgarian villages. Customs were used in a similar way: to highlight uniqueness between Bulgarian villages in the region. Driving through a village near Bolgrad that I did not know well, my Brega friends pointed out to me the flowers painted on the gates of the houses, which apparently indicated how many girls there were in the household. If the flower was white, the daughter was still young, and if red, then the daughter was of marriageable age. This practice, they told me, was specific to that Bulgarian village and not practiced in Brega. The preference to use a dark green color in the Bolgrad District for painting house exteriors, while in the Reni District blue was preferred, was another example of common practices that distinguished villages of the same ethnicity. Such everyday markers served to underline, in ordinary, everyday ways, practices that set apart one Bulgarian village from every other in the region.

Third, at the transnational level, language also helped distinguish Brega, and Bessarabian Bulgarians more generally, from Bulgarians in the Republic of Bulgaria. Most villagers picked up quite soon that my Bulgarian was a shade different from their own. I was frequently informed that their Bulgarian was "more pure" than the language spoken in Bulgaria. My neighbors, for example, reasoned that their language was better "preserved" than modern Bulgarian, because it reflected an older spoken version of the language. "Our Bulgarian" they told me, "is preserved from 200 years ago." Valentina even told me that one French researcher (she had no reference I could follow up) confirmed that their language and customs, "are pure and reflect an antiquity." When I queried in what sense was it more preserved and pure, as to my ear it contained Russian words, while other words were clearly a mixture (Bulgaria roots with a Russian declension), I was told that the Bulgarian spoken by them was, "less influenced by Turkish." The explanation was that they had been under Ottoman rule less time than Bulgaria proper, and as a consequence, their language was more "pure and authentic." Purity in language was directly connected to the lesser number of years spent under Ottoman domination. While they readily acknowledged that their language incorporated some Russian, this was dismissed as a recent addition, "and actually, the pure Bulgarian remains." Further, "we have preserved the language in a way that the Bulgarians have not, despite our Russian additions." The verb "gulcha" was again a frequently cited example. In present-day Bulgaria, the verb means "to tell off/to scold," but in the sense used in Brega, the original meaning remains, "to speak/to tell" (According to Valentina, modern Bulgarian uses a borrowed Russian word for "to tell" [*govoria*]). The etymological accuracy of this view is less important than the fact that villagers used such narratives of difference to distinguish themselves from Bulgarians in the Republic of Bulgaria. I even heard one villager—admittedly rather drunk at the Den′ Sela banquet—claim that in Bulgaria they speak a "dirty, unclean form of Bulgarian, while here [in Bessarabia] we speak pure Bulgarian." The core of the village's identity harkened back to a perceived "purity" that was ultimately defined in terms of the lesser number of years they were under Ottoman domination than Bulgarians from the Republic. Struggles against the Ottomans remained key to understanding local identity among Bulgarians in this region.

Such "purity" theories were reinforced at times when Bessarabian Bulgarians came into contact with Bulgarians from the Republic of Bulgaria. On one occasion in 2001, when the mayor was expecting guests from Bulgaria to inspect the new cultural center in the district capital with an additional stopover in Brega, the mayor instructed the village council workers to organize the singing group because "we sing songs that the Bulgarians have forgotten." Later, he added, "In Brega, we have traditions that Bulgarians have forgotten, but which are still maintained here." Those who traveled to Bulgaria found further confirmation of the purity of their own language. Mitko (the first private farmer in Brega), married to a woman from the Republic of Bulgaria, noted that when he had been in Bulgaria in the mid-1980s, one Bulgarian said to him, "You are more Bulgarian than my father-in-law in Sofia!"

Claims to being "Bulgarian" and "more Bulgarian than the Bulgarians [in the Republic of Bulgaria]" were founded on a self-definition of "Bulgarianness" constructed on the basis of the community's shared linguistic and traditional practices that displayed greater distance from Ottoman influences. It was an indication of the strength and importance of language and traditions which outweighed any biological features in the definition of identity and determined who was accepted into the community as "Bulgarian" and who was seen as an "outsider." One villager, herself born in Chelyabinsk, Russia, where her Bulgarian father was sent to work after the war, told me she was married to a Ukrainian, but then she added, "He moved here with his family at the age of six and speaks very good Bulgarian." She claimed it was on this basis that he was accepted into the community.[36] Since identity was grounded in the practice of language and customs, then anyone, in principle, prepared to adopt the language/customs could become a Bregan Bulgarian. Indeed, it was because of this arrangement that Brega has remained predominantly "Bulgarian," as confirmed by the statistical data that recorded the village's ethnicity as 90 percent Bulgarian. Indications of the ethnic mix of the village, based on the origins of some of the village surnames that were rooted in Polish, Russian and Romanian (as in the case of my landlady and next-door neighbor Marusha), as well as some very standard Bulgarian surnames (such as Popov and Mitev; I was told that the former could also be a Russian name), did not present a problem for villagers. After my elderly neighbor finished listing the diverse ethnic background of Bregans, as evidenced by the different surnames, he concluded by saying, "We are all Bulgarian now." The practice of the Bulgarian language (and customs) formed the basis of an "insider" identity and acceptance as a Bregan.

The language arrangements described above made the situation in this part of Ukraine significantly different from other regions where Russian and Ukrainian dominated (e.g., Wanner 2014; Bilaniuk 2005).[37] It also made the situation different from the multilingual and multiethnic context of Transcarpathian Ukraine (Dickinson 2010). The interethnic language in southern Bessarabia, where there was no precedent of Ukrainian language, and where national "minorities" constituted the rural majority, was Russian. Russian was spoken in combination with at least one other ethnic language: Bulgarian, Moldovan, or Gagauz. Ukrainian was never spoken, although it was taught in language classes at school. It also had an increasing presence in villagers' lives in a written form, through government legislation. During the period of my fieldwork, the local use of Ukrainian was restricted entirely to the domain of bureaucratic paperwork; it was by law the written language for documents in the formal public domain.

Such a language portfolio (Russian and at least one ethnic language) reinforced the lack of exchange possibilities nationally. Irrespective of how much schooling in Ukrainian villagers had had, everyone expressed an inadequate knowledge of the language for the regular official purposes for which the language was increasingly required and demanded.

Villagers were all too aware of the importance of language and surprisingly malleable in their efforts to embrace their new circumstances when dealing with government bureaucracy exclusively in the Ukrainian language. Nevertheless, on numerous occasions I witnessed the inconveniences faced by villagers in having to negotiate the new legislated linguistic challenges. Aside from the difficulties of navigating through legal documents available only in Ukrainian, the villagers' official names were also changed to Ukrainian ones in their (internal) passports in the early 2000s requiring them to sign documents in an unfamiliar script. This was seen as an inconvenience, rather than an assault on their basic human rights.[38] They frequently commented on how they had to "practice" their signatures, as it was easy to make a mistake.[39] For example, I was at the village council when a young couple—the woman was heavily pregnant—came in, so as to complete the necessary registration forms in order to get married. As the man was filling out the application form, it was clear he did not know how to write in Ukrainian: On two occasions, I saw him look across from his passport to another piece of paper and then back to the form, in order to copy out his name and other information correctly from the passport, taking care to not make a mistake. Sometimes, as in this case, villagers were completing legal documents, often not fully aware of the details of the document they were signing. For local administrators, it was a nightmare, as mistakes made in translations from Russian to Ukrainian created ongoing and long-term problems, especially, one official informed me, when most people (including local officials themselves) did not know Ukrainian very well. Luba, my middle-aged neighbor, told me that she only did one year of Ukrainian at school, and she found it hard to even sign her name in Ukrainian. She said when she goes to the unemployment office (as a kindergarten teacher, she was occasionally unemployed due to lack of heating or other resources that forced the kindergarten to close for temporary periods), she had to "fill out the form a few times because I automatically sign my name in Russian and not Ukrainian . . . or I forget one letter, or mess it up in some way." Valentina had completed three years of Ukrainian language at school, as well as some additional training after she took on the official position of secretary to the mayor, and she confessed, "I still can't read it properly," although her comprehension was good. In short, villagers faced new barriers when exercising their rights as Ukrainian citizens and state employees.

Bregans met such external bureaucratic challenges with passive resignation. Some—especially teachers and officials—took courses or tried to improve their language skills, with the knowledge that those who did not were disadvantaged in public life and could lose their jobs. They made every effort to learn the Ukrainian language to a suitable standard. State sector employment depended on having good Ukrainian-language skills, and more often than not, also on having a tertiary education. Attaining a university education posed new challenges for young Bregans, insofar as since 1993, entrance examinations were conducted in the Ukrainian language (Wanner 1998, 84). Not having had the advantage of it being part of their historical heritage, villagers struggled to attain the necessary minimum Ukrainian-language requirements. Obstacles also existed at school, as in the decades after 1991, Ukrainian-language teachers were scarce and unavailable in rural areas. Those who were available were usually not native speakers. The deficit of Ukrainian teachers in the rural region compounded the problem of lack of access to Ukrainian-language training and had long-term implications for the younger generation, who were at a clear disadvantage in negotiating or engaging in present-day Ukraine, where tertiary education and state jobs (among numerous other occupations) required good Ukrainian-language skills.

Villagers tried to adapt to contemporary language demands. The legislated need for Ukrainian added a further language to an already multilayered identity: Russian remained the lingua franca, Ukrainian became the written language of officialdom, and Brega Bulgarian remained the everyday language among "insiders."

Adopting new languages to their repertoire was the way rural inhabitants survived two centuries of external governance: Russian, Romanian, Soviet, and most recently Ukrainian. Yet, survival did not imply thriving. As in the case of a national history, in the case of a state language also, villagers were often excluded or hindered due to not having "the correct" skill set. This did not result in open tensions, but it was a source of local resentment and frustration; villagers were all too aware that it was restricting their (and their children's) opportunities, excluding them from access to a range of institutions that were crucial for social mobility and a better future.

The variety of language skills possessed in Brega did, however, provide exchange opportunities for villagers, locally and transnationally if not nationally. Indeed, it was the same set of language skills that were denied national worth that conversely presented exchange opportunities in other contexts.

The languages at the disposal of Bregans are best captured by my next-door neighbor, Marusha, who had only the most basic of educational qualifications, yet she had a wealth of language "capital." Marusha was born in 1949 in Reni, which was where her parents met and married. Her mother was Gagauz and her father Bulgarian. At this time, and into the 1950s, Moldovan was still the main language in the town. Her family spoke Moldovan at home. They moved to Brega after her grandfather died and left his son (Marusha's father) the house. It was only after they had moved, when Marusha was still a child, that they switched to speaking Bulgarian at home. As an adult, Marusha spoke perfect Bregan Bulgarian, was fluent in Russian and Moldovan, and also understood Gagauz (which she learned from her mother). Her surname was Moldovan, her first name, officially "Maria," was Russian, and in everyday life, she was known by her Bulgarian name, "Marusha." Marusha, had no doubts as to her ethnicity: She was Bulgarian, and this ethnicity was recorded in all her relevant official Soviet paperwork. Her range of language skills beyond Bulgarian—Russian, Moldovan, and some Gagauz—did not detract or deny her Bulgarianness. She was, in the end, Bulgarian (out of all the range of ethnic identities at her disposal), because "at home," in her household and in her community, her everyday language was Bulgarian, the language her family adopted when they moved to the village. She was also Bulgarian because of the traditional practices she engaged in and the history she shared with co-villagers: an eternal gratitude to Russia for refuge from Ottoman domination two centuries ago. Associated with this gratitude were cultural, religious, and linguistic commonalities with Russia.

Marusha's situation was not unusual to the extent that many, if not most, villagers had a bank of language skills. Bregans' language abilities associated with their ancestral ties to Bulgaria, as well as long-term Russian and Romanian influences,[40] provided an important asset in their identity that offered multiple avenues for different types of exchanges in contemporary times.

Before turning to some of the contemporary exchange opportunities provided by local identity, it is first necessary to briefly discuss the established and multiple connections and networks that were developed during Soviet times and continued being important after 1991. These networks were lubricated by language skills, and included work, educational, military and travel based ties, each of which are dealt with in turn.

First, work produced one important source for long term connections even in the case of a rural community such as Brega. Village networks spanned from the German Democratic Republic and Czechoslovakia (where agricultural collective heads and specialists were sent for long periods of work experience) to Kazakhstan (where some village families worked in the 1970s), and from Leningrad and Moscow (where many villagers were sent on work placement [*komandirovka*]) to Estonia (where Baba Mina's husband visited while fulfilling his job as a lorry driver for the sovkhoz, delivering agricultural produce).

Work connections often arose from participating in educational or other training programs. Bregans were educated in various parts of the Soviet Union: Most commonly, villagers went to towns in the region, but some were trained in Moscow, Odessa, Leningrad, and Kishinev. This, in turn, led to long-term associations with these places: For example, both of Tanya's sisters went to the university in Kishinev, and following their marriages to Moldovan Bulgarians, have remained in Moldova. They lived in a town that had a significant ethnic Bulgarian population, including some other Brega natives. Anya, the village's cultural coordinator, was an ethnic Russian originally from the Caucasus. She moved to Russia, completing her five-year degree in Leningrad, and was then sent on work placement to Odessa, where she met Georgi and ended up moving, after her marriage, to Georgi's native Brega. Petur, the former head of the kolkhoz and leader of one of the agricultural enterprises, received his tertiary education in Odessa (as did the other enterprise leaders). His brother attended a university in Moscow, married, and remained there. After years of study for a degree (in, for example, medicine or teaching), graduates were sent for three years to work in another part of the vast USSR once their course was completed. Tanya told me, "You had to go wherever they sent you," which she explained was often to faraway places that needed teachers or doctors. You were well looked after during these work placements, provided with accommodation and other facilities. It was only after this service was over that it was possible to return to your home region.[41] Following graduation, the Brega doctor (retired in 2000 and never replaced) had been assigned to work in Siberia. There he had met his future wife, also a doctor, and they returned to Brega after their first child was born. Villagers educated in the port towns of Izmail or Reni often found employment aboard ships, as in the case of a neighbor's son who graduated as a doctor and was rarely home, spending long periods at sea working as a ships' doctor. As Tanya, who was also very well-traveled said, education, training and work sent villagers to "all ends of the Soviet world."

Military service was also a reason for high mobility among the youth and sometimes led to marriages and further webs of connections between Brega and locations in the former USSR, and even beyond. In at least one case, the brother of the former sovkhoz veterinary surgeon, while stationed in Moldova as a young soldier in the 1970s, met and married a woman who was born in Moldova but of German ancestry. Her ancestry qualified her to migrate, and in the early 1990s, the couple moved to Germany with their two young sons. The latter are now grown and also married to women who are Russian speakers of German ancestry living in Germany. The family made annual trips to Brega to visit relatives.

Travel for pleasure or personal reasons also created opportunities for networks. Some villagers told me about their package holidays to various parts of the USSR (mentioning how cheap it was to fly to Moscow from Odessa). Travel for the purposes of visiting kin stationed in different parts of the Soviet Union (for work) was another common reason for travel. Marusha told me on a number of occasions about her trip to Kazakhstan in the mid-1980s, where her sister and family were based for over a decade (a dozen families from Brega went in the middle to late 1970s, drawn by the attractive salaries, but most returned following the collapse of the USSR).[42] The trip to reach Kazakhstan took two days: a train to Odessa, then a flight to Moscow where they had an overnight stay. They were met and entertained by a fellow villager living in Moscow. He had moved permanently in 1947 and still returned to Brega every summer as a pensioner in the 1980s. He showed them the sites of Moscow and took them shopping. It was on this shopping trip, Marusha said, she saw an escalator in a department store for the first time (at the time there were no escalators in Odessa). Where else, she laughed, would she see such strange wonders, such as "electric stairs?" From Moscow, she took another flight to Almaty. Her children had also traveled; their earliest trip was a school excursion to Leningrad. They joked that the elder brother went to Leningrad, while the younger one, two years later, went to St. Petersburg! Marusha's now adult children bemoan that their own children do not have such travel opportunities.

Villagers' extensive networks established through work, education, military service, and travel during the Soviet period, and facilitated by their language skills, have become, since Ukrainian independence, an asset presenting a wide range of possible monetary and nonmonetary exchange opportunities. My focus below is on two: trading and cultural/educational activities.

First, trading and barter were made possible through established kinship/friendship/marriage connections. The lack of an established market for produce (after the Soviet market was dismantled, with no other alternative distribution/exchange infrastructure in place) meant that for the handful of private farmers, and all households reliant on cash crops, connections based on kinship, marriage or friendship were of vital importance in finding a market for their produce. Much like the household alliances that were strengthened between close kin for the purposes of producing cash crops (described in chapter 2), regional alliances between kin and friends gained new momentum and importance in enabling trading opportunities, both locally and transnationally, as Bessarabian connections extended into Moldova. In the 1990s, before the nearby border with Moldova was fully stabilized, villagers turned to their broader Bessarabian connections to find a market for the household cash crop of onions. Small traders from Moldova would come with their cars and buy up the stock. The buyers were often either relatives living in Moldova or friends of relatives. This was possible in the early years, because as Marusha said, "There was free traffic flowing and no border controls." Such trading links were curtailed after the borders between Ukraine and Moldova were more fully operationalized. Nevertheless, trading did continue, at least in an informal sense. The brother of Vito (the latter worked for the water irrigation station) dealt in importing cars from Germany and selling them in Ukraine. He boasted that he had been to Germany at least fifty times, but the arrangement was hindered by international borders and was eventually reorganized in a more localized way: Vito's brother crossed the neighboring border to Moldova and brought the cars back from there; his contact in Moldova, who had EU citizenship (and could thus pass through the other states freely) did the other leg of the trip, from Germany to Moldova.

Villagers also used their kinship connections to establish links with other parts of Ukraine in order to organize trading or bartering. However, they were limited by lack of government investment in infrastructure: The poor road conditions served to largely isolate the region and reduce the number of such economic activities with other parts of the country. With the continued lack of any external market for local produce during the early 2000s, and new borders restricting access to Moldova, trading between villages in the district became the most viable option. I regularly witnessed cars from neighboring villages driving through the village either wanting to buy particular items (sheep skins, scrap metal) or sell certain items. Those from neighboring townships would buy grapes produced in household plots in order to make their own wine.

Second, Brega's historical ancestral-based transnational connections continued with the Republic of Bulgaria. The frequency of contacts increased over the years. These were primarily cultural and educational, providing contemporary opportunities for monetary and nonmonetary exchanges. Some of the cultural exchanges, broadly defined, had practical benefits for the local population. For example, in 2002, at a time when the region was starved of government funding, the Bulgarian Association in Odessa arranged for a cardiologist from Sofia to come to the region and give free consultations in a number of local Bulgarian towns and villages. The doctor spent two days in Brega treating villagers with heart conditions, referring them for further treatment in Odessa or Sofia when necessary. More traditional cultural exchanges included literature and traditional/artistic performances. One village, in the District of Bolgrad, boasted the best Bulgarian library in the region; it was established in 1990 and, by the time I first visited in 2000, it held 40,000 books—most of which were Bulgarian, but there were also some Russian and Ukrainian materials. In Brega, I found copies of *Rodno Slovo*, a Bulgarian newspaper for "Soviet Bulgarians." Most copies dated back to 1990, although the earliest was from 1988. The village folklore group began expanding its repertoire to include Bulgarian songs;[43] some additional Bulgarian traditional customs, such as those practiced at Christmas, were revived. While most of the adult population had no formal education in the Bulgarian language, the village library contained books in Bulgarian, most of which were attained through private means from individual donors in Bulgaria and the region (rather than through Ukraine government sponsorship, financial or any other).[44]

Such cultural exchanges served no direct commodity or monetary purpose but helped reinforce identity and renew long dormant historical associations and solidarities. Bulgarians from the Republic of Bulgaria also traveled to the region for various cultural engagements, including organized school trips by children who performed folklore songs in Brega and other Bulgarian Bessarabian villages. Marusha told me about her impressions from one such visit in 1997: The teenage Bulgarians, "drank coffee and smoked—even the girls!" This observation was more than just a faintly disapproving commentary on teenage behavior. The drinking of tea or coffee was a further marker of evidence of Bessarabians' "purity"—drinking tea was associated with Russia and drinking coffee with Turkey. One of the village council administrators once told me, "In Bulgaria, they prefer to drink coffee, but here we like to drink tea. This is one difference between us." The way in which alcohol was drunk provided an additional distinguishing feature that was commented on and separated Bregans from Bulgarians from the Republic. Luda observed: "Bulgarians don't drink like us. They just take sips, put their glasses down, then sip again. When Bulgarians see us drink, they explain it by saying, 'They are Russians!'" Such practices served as additional reinforcement of locals' identity by highlighting significant differences with their counterparts in Bulgaria.

Other cultural exchanges led to monetary forms of exchange, such as the selling of cultural objects. In the early 2000s, individuals from the Republic of Bulgaria made frequent trips, buying up local embroidery, kilims, and other such craft items that they told Bregans would be displayed in museums in Bulgaria as "traditional" exhibits of craftwork. Marusha described one occasion when two Bulgarian women who had arrived by car drove from house to house buying lace curtains and embroidered items. They had told her the objects were destined for museums, although Valentina (quite correctly, in my opinion) expressed her doubts as to the final destination of such items. She added, "My heart aches when I hear such things, and I wouldn't ever sell anything, all that work that Mama put in these things." Marusha, forever pragmatic, and without the luxury of a regular government salary, just shrugged her shoulders and said, "The babi won't ever use these things; they might as well sell them."

Bulgaria remained a popular tourist destination for Bessarabian holiday makers; Bregans continued to go on package tours to Bulgaria, as they had during Soviet times, engaging in economic exchanges. A form of tourism—educational tourism—was intensified and extended after 1991 as Bregans sought to educate their children in Bulgarian universities. The daughter of the priest's "secretary" completed her five-year degree at the University of Plovdiv in 1998 in Bulgarian philology (but on her return, was unable to get a job teaching Bulgarian, and had to retrain to teach the Ukrainian language). In Bulgaria, she met and married another (Bulgarian) Ukrainian studying in Plovdiv, who was from Crimea (his mother was Bulgarian, his father Russian). Thus, educational exchanges led to other exchanges, such as when Brega students married ethnic Bulgarians (from Ukraine or Bulgarians from the Republic). Some of them remained in Bulgaria, creating further opportunities for long-term transnational exchanges with Brega. In 2014, a former mayor of the village came to see me while I was in the village; to ask for advice and the addresses of any contacts I could give him in Bulgaria for his grandson, who was planning to study information technology at the university in the city of Veliko Turnovo in Bulgaria. The requested contacts were just a precaution, he explained, in case the boy got in trouble and needed help. While studying in Bulgaria was already taking place in the 1990s (as an attractive option, where Ukrainian language was an entry requirement that excluded village youth from domestic universities), it seemed to me that this was happening with far more frequency in 2014, especially among young men not wanting to be called up to join the Ukrainian Army in order to fight in the war in the east of the country. The war provided an additional and more recent impetus for migration. With the expansion of the conflict, there has been a large exodus of men from the district to Bulgaria for educational reasons, preferring this to accepting "invitations" from the Ukraine government to fight in the war, which for them was a war of "brother against brother," and in which they did not wish to participate.[45] Families with migrant sons told me that the young men planned to return when the war was over (which seems, with the passing of each year, less likely).

While educational migration was one reason for exchanges between Bregans and Bulgarians, labor migration was another important factor. A small number of villagers applied for Bulgarian passports—easy to do, given they could prove their ethnicity, which was recorded in their Soviet passports.[46] These passports were sought, I was told, in order to have access to the EU labor market. There was no point in going to Bulgaria, because things there "are not much better" (for the same reason ethnic Moldovans did not go to Romania). As with educational migration, language skills and historical connections played a fundamental role in determining migration patterns, which were heavily skewed toward migrating to places where language posed no barriers. Internal migration was directed toward Russian-speaking cities, overwhelmingly to Odessa in Ukraine, where villagers could find work in semiskilled jobs such as in public transport or as shop assistants. However, much of the migration was to Russia itself. Tanya told me (2014), and this was backed up by my own observations, that youth went to either Odessa or Moscow. When I asked, "Why not Kiev?" She answered after a moment's thought: "Odessa is close, and somehow we are more oriented to Moscow." By "close," Tanya explicitly had in mind geographical distance, but closeness was also grounded in shared history, cultural and linguistic factors that made Odessa or Moscow the preferred locations. She added that people gravitated to Moscow in Soviet times because it was the "capital," and the attraction of Moscow continued after 1991. Network migration drew villagers to where they already had long established connections (and the language skills), and it seemed to me that almost every second family in the village had a family member in either Moscow or St. Petersburg, or somewhere else in the former USSR, primarily Russia. Apart from the war, which was one of the drivers of migration, migrations also took place for economic reasons: The young men were attracted by the higher salaries in Russia, and they usually found work in the construction or transport industry. Luba's son, for example, worked for a construction firm outside Moscow. He originally left to avoid being called up to the war, but he was also happy with the good money he could make in Russia.[47] Connections established during the USSR played a role in this. The owner of the firm, originally from Brega, went to Russia during Soviet times, and eventually established a construction company outside of Moscow. Luba told me that the boss paid well, and he preferred workers from Brega because he trusted them. There were three to four other men from Brega also working for him. The boss periodically returned to Brega and on these occasions brought presents for the village—on one occasion a television, and on another bicycles—which in both cases were gifted to the kindergarten. Thus, the exchanges were not only limited to labor-for-income arrangements, but such migrations also resulted in benefits for the wider community.

Villagers' multilingual skills, and the connections made over the period of many decades to various locations in the former Soviet Union provided an opportunity and foundation for a range of present-day local and transnational exchanges. In other words, identity, based on language skills, was a local and transnational resource. The Bulgarian–Russian nexus, with additional Moldovan and Gagauz skill sets, was useful in enabling exchanges within the region and beyond it, to Bulgaria and Russia. Often exchanges were of a nonmonetary kind: marriages between villagers from neighboring communities or further afield, or cultural and educational exchanges that took place between the region and Bulgaria. However, such nonmonetary exchanges frequently also presented potential monetary exchange options: marriages, especially between family members between different villages in the region or across the border in Moldova, presented trading opportunities that were fundamental to the economic welfare of households within and between villages. The sale of cultural objects to visiting Bulgarians provided an example of how identity attained monetary exchange value. Trading conducted across borders, and migration opportunities to Russia for employment, were also examples of the monetary exchange value of the identity resource. In all cases, such exchanges reinforced identity while at the same time created new (or strengthened established) alliances and solidarities, both within the region and transnationally.

## THE REVALUATION OF THE IDENTITY RESOURCE AND TRANSFORMED RELATIONS WITH OUTSIDERS

Identity is an example of how a resource that has use value under certain conditions—such as the establishment of a new nation-state following the collapse of the USSR—can also attain exchange value and jump categories from use to exchange. Such a jump was evident in the case of the resource both regionally and transnationally, where Bregan identity has undergone a shift that has given it new exchange possibilities, which in turn strengthened and created opportunities for (new) alliances through a range of activities, including marriage, educational attainment, economic practices, and migration. The jump from use to exchange did not take place in the national arena, where local identity presented few exchange opportunities. The case is thus also an example of how a social resource can have different values at the same time in different contexts: exchange value regionally and transnationally, yet no such value nationally. In the latter case, the lack of exchange opportunities has led to locally expressed dissatisfactions and experiences of exclusion. The resource's revaluation therefore creates new solidarities in some contexts and new marginalization (and tensions) in other contexts.

In considering the Brega identity as a resource, it is important to not lose sight of the wider context within which nation-building in Ukraine took place. Threats to sovereignty through the loss of Crimea, and an ongoing war in the east of the country meant that Kiev has been preoccupied and made few gestures of support to its designated minorities. However, this has not served the minorities well, nor the country more generally. It may be that the Ukrainian constitution endorses a multiethnic state, and that minority cultures and languages are protected by law, yet a privileging of a "majority" ethnicity (through attributing dominance to particular language and history elements) can exclude or estrange the others (Schlegel 2017, 204). The political, historical, and linguistic regional differences across the country make the construction of any identity aiming at national unity a challenge. Attempts to find a unifying national narrative on the basis of a shared history (Wanner 1998, 75), while understandable in the quest for state building, seem futile and ultimately provide evidence for the need to consider the history of different parts of the country separately (e.g., Magocsi 1996; Golczewski 2011). Since state building takes place through a unity that relies on arrangements that are monolinguistic, and a privileging of particular events in the past (1930s famine, participation in World War II), then engagement in these "validates belonging in a shared Ukrainian state" (Dickinson 2010, 74), while those unable to participate in this state building project on such a basis are excluded. Crimea and eastern Ukraine are examples of areas where issues of identity have caused severe tensions, arguably contributing to war, but there are also other regions that have struggled to find commonality with the espoused national "Ukrainian" narrative.[48] Southern Bessarabia is one such region.

Bregan identity was both complicated and multifarious. It was an identity founded in Bulgarian ancestry, blended with elements from their Russian host who offered them a permanent homeland some two centuries ago. Yet the villagers distinguished themselves from both to a certain degree through linguistic arguments of "purity" and social distance (respectively). It was an identity partly overlapping with other ethnic groups in the region, that is, other Bessarabians, with whom they shared a migratory past, a similar Christian (usually ROC) religion and a similar pro-Russian orientation alongside a view of Ottomans as their historical enemy. Yet Bregans also distinguished themselves from other Bessarabians on the basis of the particularities of their Bulgarian language and traditional customs. It was an identity that has been shaped by various external ruling powers that have controlled the region at various times in the past two centuries: Russian, Romanian, Soviet, and now Ukrainian. Given such a wealth of diversity, engagement in the contemporary Ukrainian national project that gave prominence to one language and a history with selectively rooted reference points proved to be a challenge for Bregans, who like others in Bessarabia, struggled to find a way to represent themselves, their history, their language, and traditions in a way that was compatible with nation-state demands.

While I have never heard anyone in Brega, or for that matter in the region, express a wish to be anything but a citizen of Ukraine, Bregan resentments have been increasing over the years as enforcing and privileging the Ukrainian language alongside particular historical events (or debates about this history) has exacerbated the gap between national and local positions. Bregans were hesitant to speak out, worried that any expressions of their "Bulgarianness" or pro-Russian orientation could be misconstrued as a threat to the state. Nevertheless, the national historical orientation that represented a "180 degree turnaround" (to use the mayor's words) from Soviet times devalued what in Bregan terms was held positively and core to their own identity. Their (transnational) historical and linguistic advantages became a (national) liability. In a formal sense, Bregans were given national acknowledgement as part of a recognized "minority." In this restricted capacity, local identity had a use: It allowed, at least on paper, for the Ukraine government to fulfill its legal responsibilities as an aspiring democracy by acknowledging its minority groups and paying lip service to the guarantee of their rights. However, this did not translate on the ground to any real benefits or advantages. In the early years of Ukraine independence, there seemed to be some encouragement for Bregans to develop their "minority" status through public portrayals of their heritage and identity, such as through the cultural center in the district capital (for which limited government funding was provided) and the establishment of a museum in the village (for which there was no state support). Villagers seemed relatively satisfied with arrangements. In more recent years, however, dissatisfactions were expressed far more often, and tensions grew (at least as witnessed in 2014), as villagers felt increasingly under pressure to be "Ukrainians" in the narrow sense espoused nationally. With the escalation of the war, there was growing local uncertainty and disquiet. From the village perspective, their identity—rooted in a special blend of Bulgarian and Russian—was being threatened by a nationalism that made few concessions to, or acknowledgement of, alternate visions, and was monopolized by influences from western Ukraine (Galicia in particular), backed by foreign interests from the West (EU, NATO, and USA). In this configuration, a Bregan identity held no national currency: It had no exchange value that brought advantage or social mobility opportunities, be these educational, financial, or symbolic. The new marginality Bregans experienced, grounded in linguistic and historical exclusions, took place through a lack of access to tertiary level education, and this had longer-term social mobility implications. Bregans also faced ongoing and daily difficulties in accessing institutions and government resources that should have been, in theory, basic entitlements to all citizens. In short, minority status, as experienced, was a label of marginalization and exclusion, rather than a means to gain acceptance through an appreciation of diversity or the attainment of any material or other advantages. One villager expressed the perceived exclusion from a longer-term perspective: "Under the Russians, we could be Bulgarians in Russia; during Soviet times we were Bulgarians in the USSR; but now in Ukraine, we have to be Ukrainians." Variations of this statement were expressed frequently in 2014. Another villager told me, "Today we are not allowed to be Bulgarians; we have to be Ukrainians." Bregans experienced life in their country as both excluding, and in some respects, oppressive.

However, southern Bessarabians have a long history of engagement in various local and transnational cultural and economic exchanges (Schlegel 2017, 206) determined by the particular historical period and external powers in place. As I have shown in the case of Brega, identity attained newly acquired exchange value in particular social spaces: within the region and also transnationally. Their anti-Ottoman and pro-Russian history (and their linguistic assets) were valuable in giving villagers a shared sense of belonging with others in the region as "Bessarabians," and this provided a range of alliance and exchange possibilities. It was also an identity that provided a basis for transnational exchanges with Russia, Bulgaria, and other countries to which the local people were connected through history and ancestry. The resulting solidarities were numerous and varied. The establishment of a district cultural center and the village's own museum, the expanding activities of the folklore group, the continuation of everyday traditional practices and customs, the wealth of available languages, the library with its supply of Bulgarian literature, the archival and newspaper/journal collections, and the cultural and educational engagements with the ancestral homeland—all activities funded by local and/or transnational sponsors—were means of reinforcing the local identity and community, as well as solidifying exchange opportunities. As Schlegel (2017) shows for the region more generally, ethnic minority associations—and I would add, the range of activities and actors noted directly above that were not always formalized through an organization—played an important role in transforming local identity into a resource with considerable regional and transnational exchange value. Establishing their particular "place" in the region as (Bulgarian) Bessarabians and transnationally with respect to the Republic of Bulgaria created exchange possibilities that were carried out through marriage, kinship ties, and trading at the regional level, while migration served transnationally to provide educational, cultural and employment opportunities. These alliances (based on the multilayered identity of the villagers), some established many decades ago and some newly operationalized, gave Bregans particular opportunities within the district, within the region, in relation to the Republic of Bulgaria and in terms of their (historical) association with Russia. Such assets have proven vital in the previous three decades of economic hardship and political marginalization in Ukraine, strengthening (and creating new) solidarities regionally and transnationally.

This is not the first time in their history that Bregans have found themselves in a difficult position with respect to the ruling powers that have controlled Bessarabia. Their response, as in previous times in the past (especially during World War II), was to tread carefully, and despite their own particular alliances and values, avoid taking sides (at least this was the case up until about a decade ago with respect to the war that had erupted in the east of the country). As they have done for the past two centuries, Bregans continued to comply and acquiesce with the directives imposed from the outside. At the same time, they upheld their "own culture" and their "own language," making good use of their identity, regionally and transnationally, if not nationally.

CONCLUSION

# A MODEL FOR ANALYZING SOCIAL CHANGE

It is difficult to overestimate the effects of the dismantling of state socialism across eastern Europe and the former Soviet Union, a process that initiated socioeconomic turmoil across the continent: Institutions that had been established some fifty to seventy years earlier were broken up, property ownership transferred, resources reallocated, histories rewritten, the political sphere remodeled, ideologies turned around 180 degrees, and economies transformed. The impact of such changes, which are arguably still felt today, reverberated globally in the creation of a new world order, but the direct impact was most severe on people in the former socialist states. The tragic wars that followed in the wake of the breakup of state socialism across Eurasia—in the former Yugoslavia, parts of the Caucasus, and more recently in Ukraine—are the extreme and most brutal end of the range of conflicts that are a consequence of the attempt at total political-economic transformation. In a less dramatic but equally devastating way, ordinary citizens have endured their everyday social, and often physical, landscapes being pulled apart and subject to reorganization, with individual lives shattered and relationship renegotiated as well as communities transfigured and often fragmented.

Given such upheaval, it is unsurprising that social change has been an important backdrop, if not central concern, for anthropologists working in the region. Focus has been on explaining and understanding the changes: how the reforms were received and implemented locally, how they have impacted communities and determined social relations—often in devastating ways—and how they have led to unintended consequences and local forms of resistance. With the hindsight of over three decades since the onset of the reforms, I have suggested that a focus on resources through an exploration of their valuation and revaluation provides a useful lens through which to explore processes of social change. For it is partly through the mobilization and revaluation of resources that the reforms designed to dismantle former socialist structures and build market-oriented economies have taken place. While the value of resources is always under negotiation, this is particularly true in periods of extreme turmoil, such as those experienced in the former Eastern Europe since 1989–1991. The subsequent decades have been a period of massive resource valuation/revaluation.[1]

My thesis rests on an expansive conceptualization of resources, one that considers social alongside natural resources, because it provides the necessary broad platform from which to explore the changes, one that goes well beyond the narrower area constituted simply by "natural" resources. The concern has been to explore the significance of the valuation/revaluation of resources through a focus on their use and exchange capacities. Such an analytical framework provides a way for examining the changing status of resources, as they move within and between systems of use and circuits of exchange. Resource revaluation, in turn, disrupts social relationships. A study of the shift in resource valuation, therefore, offers a means of investigating the impact of political-economic reforms during periods of intense social change, and provides a way of talking about the resulting conflicts, tensions, divisions, and also new alliances.

## THE (RE/UN)MAKING OF RESOURCES

A focus on resources and their valuation/revaluation through use and exchange provides one possible way to reconsider and give suitable analytical precision to processes of social change, enabling cross-cultural comparison, and yet remaining true to ethnographic detail and context. These features are not well accommodated by the concepts we have been using to date, such as "postsocialism" and "privatization" (see Introduction).

In this section, I wish to highlight three discernible pathways/processes in the revaluation of resources. These are derived from the previous ethnographic chapters relating to my Ukraine case, but I believe they have broader relevancy, applicable to other post-socialist contexts and beyond.

## Systems of Use

First, the revaluation of resources may take place within what I call, "systems of use." Former collective land serves as an example of how resources have shifted from one form of use to another (see chapter 1). In Soviet times, kolkhoz and sovkhoz land was controlled and worked collectively. Clearly, it had huge significance as a resource—the community's livelihood depended on it, as it still does. While this land had exchange importance at the organizational level,[2] my focus was on the impact of the revaluation of the collective land for Brega households. During Soviet times, the use value of the land was expressed through a variety of entitlements and rights: Households gained, apart from employment for family members, or rather through employment, guaranteed access to a huge variety of subsidized foods, as well as access to a range of services, health care, education, and so on. These entitlements and rights were nontransferable and non-tradable. In the broadest sense, they were primarily a means of provisioning the household and its members. However, workers were also paid a salary for their labor (on top of the entitlements), and this gave them access to the Soviet market. The land therefore had use value as well as presenting opportunities to engage in the market. The agricultural enterprises that replaced the Soviet collectives after 1991 no longer provided any of the previous entitlements (there were no more food subsidies or various services delivered), nor did villagers receive a monetary income from their land. The enterprises gave relatively little support to the community, although they paid householders, now private landowners, "rent" for the land worked. Importantly, rent was nonmonetary, in the form of tons of grain with which householders fed animals for household consumption, and from which they made bread, also for their own personal consumption.[3] Thus, much as in previous Soviet times, the use value of the land was defined in terms of household reproduction. Rent was paid to landowners through the direct transference of produce to households that enabled their survival and provisioning—although the extent of the benefits was vastly reduced, since the enterprises did not provide households with fruit, vegetables or animals produce, nor did they supply the range of services they once did. From the perspective of ordinary householders, the land was now outside any exchange circuit: They received no monetary benefits from the land as they once had via salaries (and a legal land market was nonexistent for the first three decades after independence). In short, the use value of the land was transformed and reduced. Such an arrangement provided one source of new tensions in the community, between "ordinary" villagers and a new agricultural elite: the majority who owned the land and yet were excluded from receiving a monetary income from it, and a minority who worked the land and profited from it. This division was further exacerbated by the lack of determination owners had over their land, while lessees had exclusive control over the resource.

Similarly, household plots, discussed in chapter 2, provide another example of how resources have shifted from one form of use to another. In this case, the plots had an expanded usefulness corresponding to the decline of former collective land. In Soviet times, plots were used primarily for the raising of a low number of small-scale livestock for household consumption, the tending of some rows of grapes for wine, and producing a small quantity of vegetables sufficient for fresh consumption over the summer months. The vast quantities of vegetables/fruit/meat needed for the long nongrowing season were provided by the collectives. With the disestablishment of the collectives, plots vastly expanded their use value, as villagers (most of whom lost their employment under the new enterprise arrangements) no longer received produce from the enterprise's harvests, and were thus forced into working their household land in order to produce the necessary foodstuffs for their annual consumption. The use of the land was extended in three senses: The land was used to grow a far greater range of crops, the area cultivated was increased and farming became more intensive. The result of this revaluation of the household land and its expanded use was a transformation in household/family relations. It created an increasing importance of, and reliance on, kin, whose additional labor contributions were crucial for the survival of the household and its members. Internally—within households—there was a discernible reinforcement, if not expansion, of family divisions based on generation and gender. Externally, relations between households of kin and kum (godparents) were strengthened through the need for additional labor in order to engage in cash crop production (the only source of income for many). New household solidarities resulted in reinforcing certain kin as "close;" whereas relations between those households who did not exchange labor were weakened, and the kin perceived as more "distant."

In both above cases, the resource maintained its use value, although the form of use had shifted: The use value of enterprise land remained vital for household provisioning, yet reduced in the sense of the range of types of produce and support it provided for households; in the case of household plots, the use increased in intensity and the size of area cultivated, as well as in terms of the variety of what was grown.

## Circuits of Exchange

Second, a revaluation takes place when resources move within the same value category of exchange, that is, from one exchange circuit to another. Water provides an example of this (chapter 3). As the water supply did not reach all individual households, families had water storage tanks in their homes' yards. During Soviet times, water was delivered to households, whose use for this resource was minimal and largely for domestic purposes, that is, washing and drinking. The water was managed by the kolkhoz and sovkhoz, and since the vast majority of villagers belonged to one or the other, this free resource was effectively an entitlement to all, exchanged on the basis of their labor as collective employees. When deliveries from the collectives ran behind schedule (as they sometimes did), then connections to the delivery driver were called on in order to fast-track an individual through the official queue to hasten delivery. In this way, access to water was part of another circuit of exchange that operated in part at least through an economy of favors. The sharing of water between neighbors served as an additional means by which the resource was obtained at times when household supplies ran low and family members did not have the necessary strong connections to the driver to ensure a timely delivery. Such sharing represented a third nonmonetary circuit of exchange in which the resource was embedded during Soviet times. With the disestablishment of the sovkhoz and kolkhoz, subsidized foods and other services previously provided by the collectives were gradually phased out, while at the same time, the majority of villagers found themselves unemployed. This resulted in a dramatically increased demand for water, as villagers were forced into more intensive farming of their own household land in order to produce foodstuffs for their survival. As water passed from the jurisdiction of the former collectives to the village council, which was expected to commodify the resource (and thereby gain an income), the resource shifted in value. Under the new conditions, the resource moved away from being a nonmonetary exchange resource and became a commodity in a monetary circuit. The attempt to commodify the once-free resource, the inability of the Soviet water infrastructure to sufficiently meet the new increased water demands, the push for the installation of water meters, unequal access to the resource, and a differing water price regime resulted in new tensions between neighbors all vying for the precious resource.

Chapter 4, on moral authority, provided another example of a resource's revaluation through participation in different circuits of exchange. In this case we did not witness the replacement of one exchange form by another (as in chapter 3), but the division of the social resource, creating a second exchange circuit that ran alongside the first. This happened with the arrival of the priest, a second supplier of moral authority in the community; the first were the various practitioners of tradition (with the mayor as community leader frequently the leading sponsor). The priest's attempts to carve out his influence took place largely in terms of his crusade against Bregan traditional practices. This placed him at odds with the community because of the integral importance of traditional customs in everyday village life and local identity. Religious or traditional circuits of exchange organized by those with moral authority became the focus of tensions and competition as leaders vied for public authority and influence. The exchange circuits relied on villagers' attendance and participation in the religious/traditional events, in exchange for (moral) guidance, spiritual healing and community solidarity. These circuits operated in parallel, and sometimes in competition with each other. While villagers engaged in both traditional and religious circuits of exchange (most divided their involvement between the two as necessary), the priest's authority was limited to the "formal religious" domain, and any attempted "interference" in everyday traditional practices was not welcomed. In other words, the resource of moral authority was shared between the priest and traditional practitioners, but it was not an "equal" division, in the sense that the priest was limited in terms of the access he had over villagers' everyday lives. Tensions between the priest and community were negotiated and ultimately resolved through the division of the resource. While this was a symbolic division of the immaterial resource, it was evidenced in the operation of separate nonmonetary exchange circuits and mapped out through the constructed separation between the community/council and church (i.e., secular/sacred space and traditional practices/formal religion, respectively).

Water and moral authority provide examples of how resources can be revalued through mobility within the same value category of exchange. In the case of water, during Soviet times, the resource was exchanged through three distinct nonmonetary exchange circuits. After the water was transferred to the control of the village council following reforms, the resource entered a monetary based circuit of exchange. In the case of moral authority, the return of religion and the priest to Brega (from the previous Soviet situation, when there was no religious presence in the village) introduced a degree of competition for influence between the local leaders of the spiritual world, that is, tradition and religion. Those with moral authority offered services/rewards that were part of two distinct nonmonetary forms of exchange, operating in parallel. The process of revaluation resulted in the sharing of the resource, although this division granted the priest only limited access.

## Jumping Valuation Categories

A third form of revaluation is one that jumps valuation categories, such as a movement from use to the attainment of exchange value.

The social resource of "identity," discussed in chapter 5, provided evidence of such a shift in value. The movement from use to monetary exchange is commonly associated with entry into a capitalist economy and related processes, such as privatization. However, in the case of identity, the formation of a new, independent Ukraine was also a factor in the revaluation of the resource. During Soviet times, the Bregans were denoted in their passports as ethnic Bulgarians. This had some use, in the sense that it oriented their citizenship via their ethnicity while at the same time giving them overarching rights and belonging in the USSR as Soviet citizens. Their ethnic designation was still useful in post-1991 times, in a different way, as a designated minority in the newly independent Ukrainian state. However, exchange benefits were limited nationally because of the selective linguistic and historical portfolio touted as fundamental to a "Ukrainian" identity. It provided few opportunities for Bregans whose identity was based on a different linguistic skill set and historical alliances. At the same time, identity based on connections with their ancestral homeland and historically close alliance to Russia gained new exchange potential, both regionally and transnationally. In part, as a response to economic hardship and marginalization, Bregans pursued, even extended, their exchanges regionally—such as through marriage, kinship and other forms of relatedness that opened up opportunities for trading and barter. Transnational activities were strengthened (or newly established) through their historical associations with Russia and the Republic of Bulgaria. For example, Bulgarians from the Republic of Bulgaria bought local handicrafts from (ethnic Bulgarian) Ukrainian villagers. These handicrafts were held in high esteem in Bulgaria, because the skills needed to produce such items were no longer practiced, and at the same time were highly valued signifiers of Bulgarian heritage. Such a material exchange between Bulgarians and the Bulgarian diaspora in Ukraine was only one of a range of new exchange activities. Other exchanges were based on marriage, education, and employment. A Bregan identity provided many opportunities, both regionally (within Bessarabia) through different forms of relatedness (marriage, etc.), and also transnationally, through various cultural and economic exchange activities.

The example of the resource jumping categories was evident

as identity became more than just useful, but also presented, post-1991, (monetary and nonmonetary) exchange possibilities, at least in particular contexts, regional and transnational.

It was through the revaluation of resources between and within systems of use, and circuits of exchange, that new resources were made, others remade, and still others unmade. In every case, the new valuations/revaluations were articulated through, and shaped by, the previous uses and forms of exchange of the resources. Importantly, such processes were neither smooth nor clean. As others have observed, and I believe my own empirical material shows, the reforms that drove such revaluations were tentative, often divergent in their effects and limited in their deployment (Collier 2011). Recall the example of water (chapter 3): The resource was an emerging commodity in a market, yet different pricing arrangements, different degrees of support for meter installation, unwillingness to penalize those who did not pay their water bills, and so on ensured that the market was by no means wholeheartedly embraced or engaged with by everyone in the community.

Apart from the above three main pathways by which resources can be revalued, we can also draw from the ethnographic chapters some further insights into the conceptual nature of resources (see also Introduction). One insight concerns how the shifts arise, the circumstances under which resources are made, or their value is enhanced. Two possibilities come to mind. First, mobilization can be achieved directly through legalized reform. An example was the legal dismantling of the agricultural collectives and privatization of the land. This was a direct way to initiate a revaluation of land. Second, the mobilization of resources can have the knock-on effect of creating new resources, through the creation of new needs and wants. For example, following the dismantling of the agricultural collectives, additional importance was given to two other resources, household land (chapter 2) and water (chapter 3). A new demand for these resources—a direct consequence of the collapse of the Soviet agricultural collectives that ended the provision of subsidized food and resulted in the loss of paid employment, forcing individuals to be more reliant on their own household land—has turned water, as well as household plots, into a far more important and needed resource than in Soviet or pre-Soviet times. In summary, as well as the direct revaluation of resources instigated through the passing of new laws and implementation of related policies (e.g., land privatization, water decentralization, changes in borders and citizenship status, etc.), resources can also be changed more indirectly by the creation of new wants and needs, or by changing existing ones, which transforms the value of resources to satisfy these new or altered situations. This also highlights the interdependency or interconnectedness of resources: When one resource changes value, others are impacted in a knock-on effect.

A second insight concerns how resources can operate at various levels simultaneously. The same resource can have use and/or exchange value in multiple operations at the same time. For example, identity (chapter 5) was useful and exchangeable in certain spheres of social life (regionally and transnationally), while at the same time less valuable without exchange value in other domains (nationally). A second example: Water (chapter 3) was exchanged in a couple of different circuits that operated concurrently in Soviet times when water deliveries were running late—in an economy of favors between the water delivery driver of the collective and individual householders, and in sharing practices between neighbors. A third example was when the same resource had use value for some and exchange value for others from the same community. This was the case of former collective land, which after privatization had use value exclusively for the ordinary villagers, while at the same time also had monetary exchange value for the small number of villagers still working or leasing the land and profiting from it through harvest sales (chapter 1). These examples highlight how the operationalization of resources in practice could reinforce (or create) different interest groups and sets of relationships that served to include/exclude, and this in turn was a source of solidarities/tensions. The three examples show respectively that the same resource could: be attributed different value for those in different spaces, within and outside the village; be exchanged in different circuits within the same space, reflecting different relationships between workers from the same collective; and finally, have distinct (use and exchange) values for different interest groups within the same organization (the agricultural enterprise), depending on whether the villagers had a salaried position or were simply landowners entitled to rent. In each of these three cases, different sets of inclusions/exclusions were evident, and generated different solidarities/tensions.

A third insight concerns the division of resources. It is not only material resources with physical substance that can be subdivided. Nonmaterial resources can also be split up—as evidenced in the case of the social resource of moral authority (chapter 4). The division of the immaterial resource was manifested symbolically: for example, through the separation of public space into "secular" and "sacred" zones, or ideologically through a division of practices into "traditional" and "formal religious." Such symbolic divisions were evidenced through the operation of distinct exchange circuits taking place in physical spaces and grounded in the figures who "possessed" the resource through their leading positions of influence. The more general point is that while many material resources can be sectioned off into tangible units (e.g., land can be subdivided, water can be shared out through distribution mechanisms), immaterial resources can also be divided, their separation carried out symbolically or ideologically. Such a division may have spatial or temporal implications, and as in the case of material resources, can also be a source of tensions or solidarities.

A focus on resources and how they are revalued gives ethnographic substance to (rather than replacing) other analytical approaches that are used to understand social change. The macro perspectives of others (such as Harvey 2005) are vital in highlighting general trends that have led to significant concentrations of wealth at the top end of the elite classes, alongside rising inequalities and poverty, both globally and regionally. Such processes have been directly correlated with the implementation of neoliberal policies/reforms over the previous decades (Petras and Veltmeyer 2011, 19–30). However, conceptualizing social change in terms of resource revaluation (shifts in use and exchange value) provides us with an insight into the intricacies of the transformations that followed the dismantling of state socialism, when the more typical description of these processes, within the framework of "postsocialism" and "privatization," appear inadequate or insufficient. A focus on resource revaluation can help us fill in the gaps, to develop a more nuanced and grounded understanding of the nature and basis of these inequalities and concentrations of wealth. In short, it can provide an appreciation of the complexities and shed light on how such processes actually happened. In my Ukrainian case, for example, reforms attempted to thrust more and more resources into circuits of monetary exchange. This is not a novel finding; we do not need to apply a theory to recognize that the reforms were designed to create a market economy through the creation of private property, as this was the explicit and well-articulated strategy of political leaders, global financial institutions and their economists, among others. However, it is a finding grounded in detailed ethnography, and through such empirical data, we can see the intricacies and complications of such processes. The findings show that while reforms may be passed in law and even implemented, on the ground, the changes may not be evident or at least not in the anticipated way (a common finding of anthropologists who have detailed knowledge of workings at the grassroots level). Further, my approach reveals that the mobilization of resources changes relationships between people: Relationships are disrupted and transformed. As a result, new conflicts/tensions emerged between, for example, ordinary members and new elite working in the agricultural enterprises, or neighbors competing for water, and so on. Although in an overwhelming number of examples, the disruptions to relationships were manifested as conflicts and tensions, a disruption could also result in new alliances or solidarities. Examples of the latter case were the new strengthened relationships between certain kin working household land together, developing exchanges with new moral leaders, or even establishing connections transnationally on the basis of an identity that brought material and other rewards. Thus, while the tensions may be a source of new inequalities and exclusions, there are also other possible outcomes. Social change can also result in new alliances and solidarities that operate alongside new divisions.

In summary, the valuation/revaluation of resources alters relationships between people and triggers social change. The approach I propose unmasks the intricacies (the new tensions/alliances) of this process on the ground, while at a broader level, it reminds us that inequalities are not the only possible outcome. A focus on social change allows us to see inequalities as one vital development, but there are others. Social change is complex, and the very important inequalities identified by macro perspectives provide only part of the complicated story.

Despite the important comparative possibilities offered by macro contributions, Ganti (2014, 100) is correct to underline problems of "scale, comparison, representation and relevance" that such "broad, encompassing analytical frameworks" such as "neoliberalism" or "postsocialism" often present. What is masked are the very strengths offered by an anthropological inductive approach that is grounded in important ethnographic details and meanings. In this respect, my approach to resources can provide some benefits: Resources are contextualized through an examination of their *particular* use and exchange values in time and space, thus giving greater nuance and complexity to the findings provided by other approaches. It also has the potential advantage that a vast range of ethnographic sites and topics can be considered within the same framework, allowing us to draw connections and make analytical comparisons cross-culturally. The approach I propose is both more nuanced and context-specific, and also broader and more encompassing than existing perspectives. "Use" and "exchange" have long been a part of the tool kit of economic anthropologists across a wide range of ethnographic sites worldwide. A focus on social change through a resources framework thus draws on already established (although perhaps not always analytically precise) concepts. In addition, the approach has interdisciplinary application, it is a useful way to enter into conversations about resources and social change across disciplinary boundaries.

It is tempting (although perhaps a little imprudent without additional empirical data from other locations) to take the argument a step further and speculate about the connection between resource revaluation and different types of political economies. Others have already highlighted the important association between resources and different forms of capitalist expansion. Franquesa writes that resources, "are intimately connected to changing regimes of accumulation," and also with the reordering of global hierarchies (Franquesa 2019, 82; see also Zimmerman 1933). There is clearly a connection that requires further reflection.

Resources, I have argued, are central to understanding any organization or reorganization of society. Further, what constitutes a resource and the value it is given—through the way it is used or exchanged—varies in different social milieus. The mobilization of resources takes place in all societies all the time, but the impact is more intense during times of extra pressure coming from a drive to "reform." Twice in the last century, eastern Europe has undergone such a dramatic process: the foundation of state socialism following the Russian revolution (and after World War II in the case of other East European locations) and then following the collapse of state socialism in 1989–1991, when there was a reversal of many of the previous reforms. On these occasions, we can presume that the restructuring of political economies and social life was much more radical, and the impact on people's lives far more dramatic than at other times, such as the reforms that were a constant feature of state socialism (Dale and Fabry 2018, 236; see also Swain 1992) as governments fine-tuned policies to meet an economic and political agenda.

This makes a lot of common sense, but it raises other questions. For example: Were the "postsocialist" reforms applied in eastern Europe since 1989–1991 different from the "neoliberal" reforms that were implemented in various locations across western Europe from the late 1970s onward? That is, were the reforms and resource revaluations in essence the same, with the main difference the specific context to which they were applied (with the former East European reforms introduced into a setting that had a very different starting arrangement, because public ownership/control of resources was far more widespread)? Also, can we characterize different political economies on the basis of predominant pathways of resource valuations (identified in the previous section)?

Without further comparative study, it is difficult to answer any of the above, although based on my own ethnography, I can offer some tentative insights. If socialism can be characterized as placing many basic resources outside of a monetary exchange circuit (keeping firmly within use value or nonmonetary forms of exchange, as was the case for land and water in the Ukraine case discussed here), and gave prominence to exchanges anchored in personal relationships that gave a non-anonymous dimension to the exchanges, then can we characterize capitalism as pushing exchanges into anonymous forms that rely more often on market (monetary) exchanges? The history of Western colonialism suggests that this may be the case. Previous ethnographies from various parts of the world present substantial evidence of this amongst communities coming into first contact with capitalism and being incorporated into a world economy (e.g., Bohannan 1955; Taussig 2001). In all instances, local (nonmonetary) exchange circuits were disrupted, and resources became increasingly incorporated into monetary exchanges. Similar processes can be witnessed in my case from Ukraine, where the reforms of recent decades appear to be pushing more resources into a particular direction toward a specific type of exchange, that is, monetary circuits. Yet, despite policy pushes to drive resources into monetary economy circuits, thus expanding the market economy, on the ground, this process has been resisted, and many resources remain outside of, or poorly incorporated into, monetary circuits. The case of water (chapter 3) provides evidence of this. A resource revaluation approach can identify the continuities as well as the significant transformations and changes. In the end, continuity and change are mutually constitutive, as well as mutually transformative.

If capitalism can be characterized as a political-economic system that favors engagement through monetary circuits of exchange that are perceived as independent of human influence (depersonalized/dehumanized), then how can we distinguish contemporary capitalism from previous versions of capitalism? Is it simply that neoliberal reforms are quantitatively different from other forms of capitalism in terms of the degree of commodification? That the difference is a result of an increasingly larger number of resources, social and natural, being commodified (i.e., entering monetary exchange circuits), and that such commodification is being extended into domains of social life previously untouched by monetary forms of exchange? In short, that the creation and "mining" of social resources is being significantly expanded? There does appear to be some indications that the difference is quantitative rather than qualitative.[4]

However, significant distinguishing indicators may not be only quantitative in terms of the type and number of resources involved in the revaluation. There is also the question of access/control/ownership, and *who* is included or excluded in these exchange activities. The new land arrangements of former collective land (chapter 1) concentrated control over the resource into the hands of an elite few, excluding the majority from access to market exchange profits. The new private ownership configuration, alongside the new, noncooperative working of the land, resulted in a concentration of profits in the hands of just a few. This, then, is perhaps another marker of present-day capitalism: the increasing exclusion of a vast majority from profiting in any resource revaluation based on the concentration of the access/control/management (if not ownership) of resources in the hands of a few (reinforcing the "accumulation by dispossession" argument by Harvey [2004]). Such new ownership/management/control of resource arrangements create, in turn, different forms of inclusions and exclusions, as well as significantly higher levels of inequalities. In short, different versions of the same general form of political economy (e.g., welfare versus neoliberal forms of capitalism) are characterized not only as quantitatively moving more resources into commodified form (involving and increasing the number of resources in monetary exchanges), but also distinguished by the question of access/control/management and the concentration of these resources into fewer hands, serving to exclude a majority from participation in market relations. It is the increasing number of resources—material and immaterial—incorporated within monetary exchange circuits, *alongside* the exclusion of an increasing number of people from these circuits (or their inability to profit from such circuits), which distinguish contemporary capitalism from other forms of capitalism (as well as former socialist arrangements) and reinforces its unequal character.

In summary, such questions of the mobilization of resources in qualitative and quantitative terms, as well as questions relating to the distribution of the ownership/control/management of resources, corresponding tensions/alliances, and exclusions/inclusions, can be helpful in addressing some of these bigger comparative concerns relating to resource revaluation across different contexts, between different political economies or between different versions of similar political economies.

Ultimately, my focus on resource mobilization is much more than a theoretical endeavor, as the ethnographic chapters have highlighted. Resources and their valuation/revaluation were at the center of processes of social change, processes often accompanied by struggles and rising tensions that were played out daily at all levels of social life, from within households and communities, to national and international arenas. The proposed analytical framework is helpful for understanding the rising divisions and fragmentations that have been a feature of life in Brega (as in so many other east European sites) in recent decades. The tensions and struggles I have witnessed since 2000 in the village were grounded in access to, and control over, resources. Such tensions and divisions far outweighed any new solidarities, although these were also evident. We have seen in previous chapters some of these tensions and reorganizations within the village: between a new agricultural elite who retained most of the profits from the land and the majority of village landowners (chapter 1); within and between households and kin (chapter 2) that reinforced gender and generation distinctions while also establishing alliances between different households of kin exchanging labor; between neighbors (chapter 3) with unequal access to the vital resource of water; and between villagers and their priest (chapter 4), as the spiritual world and moral authority was divided between traditional and religious practitioners. Tensions between Bregans and outsiders were also laid bare (chapter 5): Villagers, as Ukrainian citizens, were marginalized from the Ukrainian state, while regional and transnational solidarities were reinforced and strengthened based on their historical associations (ancestral connections with the Republic of Bulgaria and a two-century heritage of Russian influence living in their adopted Bessarabian homeland).

In the post-Soviet and postsocialist contexts, a wide range of resources have been revalued, changing their ownership, control and management. This was and is part of a deliberate attempt to realize reform goals and the ultimate transformation of society. However, such processes are by no means limited to this region. The tensions resulting from struggles over resource valuation/revaluation, and the new exclusions, inequalities, and reorganizations generated as a result, are evident across communities far beyond the former socialist world, as resources take on new value (and meaning) in the ongoing dynamic project(s) of global capitalism.

# NOTES

## INTRODUCTION: RESOURCES AND SOCIAL CHANGE

An earlier version of some of the theoretical ideas presented in this Introduction can be found in Kaneff (2018).

1. Registration card for the village, Verkhovna Rada of Ukraine, official web.portal (http://w1.c1.rada.gov.ua/pls/z7503/A005?rf7571=22998). While I have decided on this official documentation, which is backed up by other publication sources (Institut Istorii (1978)), there is conflicting information as to the date that Brega was first settled. Archival documents I have seen in the village make it clear that by 1816 Brega was settled: letters dated from early in this year reveal correspondence between Russian generals (in the name of the Russian king) and Bulgarian settlers. However, both these earlier dates (1812 and 1816) are contested by a local history that provides the later date of 1820 (Mavrov and Bratkov 1967, 7 [DK translation]).

2. In 2000, when I first arrived in Brega, the population was approximately 3,000 but had fallen to 2,400 in 2014 (personal communication, Brega mayor).

3. Personal communication, Brega mayor, 2014.

4. This pattern generally held throughout the Izmail, Reni and Bolgrad regions: In most cases one ethnic group was in significant majority in the village (if we define "majority" as over 70 percent, although in most cases the ethnic group constituted 85–90 percent of the total population), although occasionally two ethnic groups together created a majority, with all other groups contributing only a few percent of the total (Ukrainian Population Census (2001), State Statistics Service of Ukraine (http://database.ukrcensus.gov.ua; Tronko [1978]).

5. Figures are based on information provided by the village mayor.

6. Wegren (2002, 15) identifies three main international organi-

zations which were prominent in implementing land privatization in Ukraine in the early years: International Finances Corporation (IFC), US Agency for International Development (USAID) and the British government's Know How Fund. It was the latter that was particularly influential in the case of Brega. The fund, which had a branch in Odessa in the late 1990s and early 2000s, worked closely with Brega village leaders between the years 1999 and 2004 (e.g., see Kaneff 2021).

7. The Know How Fund was a British government foreign aid program that assisted former Soviet bloc and former East European countries. The Fund in Brega primarily was involved in giving advice on agricultural matters and land reform. It also financed a number of small projects in the village, including a sewing center and providing assistance to various activities that supported private farming, such as offering help in the writing of business plans and legal documents. It was intermittently active in the village during the period 1999 to 2004.

8. Jarabik and de Waal (2018, 4).

9. Indeed, Jarabik and de Waal (2018, 3) report that more reforms have been implemented since 2014 than in the previous 25 years combined.

10. The other five priority areas are: privatization, the pension system, the educational system, healthcare and public administration. See Ukraine Reform Conference (2018).

11. "Postsocialism" was an attempt to move away from the arguably more problematic "transition" term (which is not a term considered here in any depth). Based on evolutionary notions of development, "transition" assumed social change to be the linear development of one social order into another (socialism to capitalism), where inevitably capitalism as exemplified in the West was seen as an end point/goal. Such a concept was rightfully dismissed as western-centric and ideologically/politically laden (Berdahl 2000) by anthropologists who preferred to focus on postsocialist "transformations" (Müller 2019; Rogers 2010). However, "transition" gained more prominence in other social science disciplines, such as economics and politics. (Rogers and Verdery 2013, 440–41).

12. The term is also used to simply designate a "historical condition" with emic importance (Borelli and Mattioli 2013, 4; Chari and Verdery 2009, 10). That is, "postsocialism" is a way to talk about the lived experiences of those in former socialist states. The term is still used in this way (Müller 2019; 536), although my interest here is in the term's analytical significance.

13. Discussions of the term's relevance, its problems and legacies continue (e.g., Hann 2002; Buchowski 2004; Skalník 2002; Chardi and Vedery 2009; Thelen 2011; Müller 2019; Gallinat and Kaneff 2022; Chelcea 2023).

14. Ganti (2014, 99) makes the point in passing, that while "neoliberalism" has come under scrutiny and its universality questioned, far less critical attention has been given to "privatization" and the associated movement of resources from "public to private."

15. If "privatization" is understood purely in the legal sense involving transfers of ownership from collective institutions (the state or agricultural collectives) to private individuals, then the resource has been privatized. However, if privatization is taken to mean that a land market must be developed and the resource incorporated into a monetary exchange circuit, then land privatization has not been completed. This raises the question: Can there be privatization without commodification or engagement in a monetary form of exchange, in other words, involvement in the market economy? In the case of Ukraine, we are told that privatization is not yet completed and will not be until land is commodified and can be bought and sold (Ukraine Reform Conference 2018, 2; World Bank 2018). Earlier pushes focusing on legal formalities no longer appear sufficient and evidently necessitate the development of a land market and the transformation of the land resource into a commodity.

16. However, see Ferry and Limbert (2008), Uchibori (2011), Richardson and Weszkalnys (2014), and Franquesa (2019).

17. Today, canals have gained new resource importance, having been transformed into places of leisure. The connection between resources and temporality is explored by Ferry and Limbert (2008).

18. Although Uchibori acknowledges the complexity of the interactive relationship between ecology and symbolism—and once or twice hints that symbolic resources may also come from social sources (2011, 148)—his focus is on the granting of meaning to ecological resources through symbolic resources and vice versa, rather than viewing the social world as a source of resources.

19. For example, Ferry and Limbert (2008, 15) note a tendency of resources, including "incorporeal" resources, to be objectified and "made tangible."

20. The exploration of natural resources in anthropology has a long tradition that can be linked back to neo-Marxist and political economy

approaches of the 1970s, as well as to the cultural ecology school (see Richardson and Weszkalnys 2014, 17, 9). Often overlooked, Ostrom's (1990; 1994) political-economy work on common pool resources has also had some influence in anthropology (e.g., see Acheson 2003). In contemporary times, natural resources have been the concern of economic and environmental anthropologists. The focus has been, and often remains, on the ways in which people engage with resources, for example, through conservation activities or property relations (e.g., Hann 1998). Resources are no longer assumed to be givens in the "natural" world to be "exploited" by humans; the "natural" world is attributed a far less passive role than in previous decades. Literature from other disciplines—development studies, and the interdisciplinary fields of political ecology and environmental studies—similarly give considerable attention to "natural" resources, although my explorations in these fields are not exhaustive or thorough. Uchibori (2011, 144) confirms that contemporary economic approaches tend to focus on material resources. This is not to say, however, that economists are not aware that immaterial resources are worthy of consideration. Indeed, most economists consider forms of human capital—knowledge, skills etc.—as resources (Personal communication, R. Hillebrand 2019).

21. There are some interesting parallels between recent attempts to theorize infrastructure and my own interest in theorizing resources. "Resources" and "infrastructure" are both seen to operate on multiple levels at the same time, to incorporate a wide range of actors, to be dynamic and be analyzable in many different ways as a result of their great diversity (see Larkin 2013 for a discussion of infrastructure). From my perspective, infrastructures are a particular type of resource—as "matter that enable the movement of other matter" (Larkin 2013, 329). Ultimately, I find resources a more fruitful concept because it can also focus attention on and accommodate "immaterial" phenomena. In other words, material resources need not be the starting point or basis for analysis, as is the case for explorations in infrastructure which tend to "privilege the technological" (Larkin 2013, 339).

22. But see Creed (2011), who talks about mumming rituals as cultural resources in the Bulgarian context.

23. There are exceptions. See Wallman (1979), who discusses identity as a resource.

24. While a lack of clarity in the "capital" concept (see Neveu 2018, 2) makes it hard to draw close comparisons with "resources," my reading

of Bourdieu (1986) suggests that his forms of capital are what I label immaterial resources (I later state a preference for the term "social resources"). This is suggested, for example, in the quote that grounds all his capitals, in the end, in the social world: "The structure of the distribution of the different types and subtypes of capital . . . represents the immanent structure of the social world" (Bourdieu 1986, 242). It includes Bourdieu's "economic capital," which applies to resources developed from the social environment (e.g., money, property rights) rather than from the physical world (Neveu 2018, 13).

25. The term's etymology is traced back to the 1600s, from the French verb *resourdre*, "to raise again," or to "recover" (Uchibori 2011, 143), which is itself from the Latin word *resurgere*, "to rise again, to be restored" (see online Etymology dictionary: http://www.etymonline.com).

26. See also Richardson and Weszkalnys (2014), who argue that viewing resources as simply "nature turned into culture," or as primarily "social constructs," is a reductive view that does not take into account the truly transformative power of resources.

27. See also Franquesa (2019, 76), who notes that while (natural) resources "are not complete or finished . . . and do not have stable boundaries," they are always in the making (i.e., a process) and have purpose. He develops this position, in turn, from Ingold's (2012) objects/materials distinction. There are different ways of theorizing this relationship between nature and culture, a task that lies outside my immediate concern, but see Ferry and Limbert (2008, 9–10).

28. The mining of the social world for resources may be a characteristic particularly associated with neoliberal capitalism, although it is by no means exclusive to it. Forms of knowledge (sacred and secular) and social networks, just to take two examples, can be resources in many other political economies.

29. We may also make a distinction between social resources and humans *as* resources. An example of the latter would be human slavery.

30. It is beyond the scope of this discussion to look at the difference between resources on the one hand, and "capital," "assets" and "property" on the other, although such a comparison would provide a further fruitful exploration and greater clarification of resources as a concept. Another interesting and potentially fruitful direction for further investigation, that also lies outside the scope of this study, is the consideration of the resources concept in terms of anthropological debates concerning gifts and commodities (see Gregory 2015).

31. In such an economy, resources are not judged simply on their use value, but through the medium of market price (itself dependent on supply and demand). "This brings in the factor of scarcity and materially changes or warps the method of appraisal" (Zimmermann 1933, 93).

32. Barter is yet another form of nonmonetary exchange that was practiced both in Soviet and post-Soviet times (Humphrey 1992; Stenning et al. 2010, 67–71; Collier 2011, 215).

33. Value as an anthropological concept has not received sufficient attention, but see Graeber (2001; 2005) and, more recently, Kalb (2024). These focuses on value diverge from my own central concern: to operationalize the traditional anthropological concepts of use and exchange value as an analytical tool for understanding processes of social change. This application of value stems from my conceptual concern with resources. Within the specific context of postsocialist anthropology, Verdery's 2003 work gives particular attention to "value," but her broad application of the term is very different from my own attempts to give value greater analytical precision.

34. The importance of value in terms of resources has been discussed in a very different way, and exclusively with respect to natural resources, by Franquesa (2019, 78–79).

35. From my perspective, to talk about the "loss" of value is less useful than conceptualizing the process as a revaluation. For something to really lose its value would mean it was no longer usable (in which case, it has ceased being a resource) or exchangeable.

36. "Bessarabia" (harking back to the administrative name it held while part of the Russian Empire "Bessarabskaya Guberniya" Schlegel 2016, 11), refers to the area between the Prut River in the west, the Danube River in the south, and the Dniester River in the east, covering territory that makes up present-day Moldova and southwestern Ukraine. My focus is on the area that lies within the contemporary borders of Ukraine, and which I refer to as "southern Bessarabia" following Schlegel, for all the appropriate reasons noted by him (2019, 18).

37. At the time, I was part of the first generation of researchers from the Max Planck Institute for Social Anthropology, whose research topic was "property."

38. In this book, the choice of language—that is, whether a word is provided in either Bulgarian and/or Russian—is determined by what the villager(s) used and the given context.

39. October 2000; July–October 2001; February–June 2003; and

November–February 2004. I returned again in September 2014 for a month.

## CHAPTER 1. ENTERPRISE LAND

1. The transactions are not considered an "exchange" because of the nature of the engagements as one-off, "dead-end" activities that did not enter any exchange circuit.

2. There was no exchange of land as a commodity (i.e., no land market) during either Soviet times or in the post-Soviet period covered by this book. Thus, the focus here is on produce from the land rather than land itself, which over the last three decades lay outside market exchanges and commodification (although occasional exchange took place through gifting or inheritance). A moratorium on agricultural land sales was initially imposed in 2001. It was extended numerous times over the last couple of decades, and only recently lifted, at least for Ukrainian nationals. The law abolishing the moratorium was officially passed on July 1, 2021, with restrictions relating to foreign ownership to continue until 2024 (See report by Ukrinform 2021). The moratorium has not succeeded in deterring foreign "land grabs" or a Ukrainian growth in "agro-oligarchies" (von Löwis 2019; Mamonova 2015).

3. For the earlier period after 1991, see Wegren (2002); for more recent initiatives, see, for example, Ukraine Reform Conference (2018, 13).

4. See also World Bank (2018).

5. As of 2021, the Ukrainian Parliament approved amendments to the agricultural land law that allowed Ukrainian citizens to buy and sell land of up to 100 hectares. From 2024, the land market has been opened up even further, widening the number of Ukrainian bodies who can engage in the market and the amount of land that can be traded, but there are still limitations in terms of possible owners and amounts of land involved (https://www.german-economic-team.com/wp-content/uploads/2024/01/GET_UKR_NL_183_2024_en.pdf and https://cms-lawnow.com/en/ealerts/2024/01/ukrainian-market-for-agricultural-land-opens-doors-for-additional-investments?format=pdf&v=14).

6. While I treat the land outside the village separately from household land it is important to note an interdependency between the two (see also Perrotta 2000, 170, 171; Wegren 2002, 11; and for Russia, Humphrey 1998, 196). In Brega, this relationship of interdependency goes back to the earliest pre-Soviet times.

7. Originally named after the village in Bulgaria, Varna District, from where many of the original migrants were thought to originate (Mavrov and Bratkov 1967, 18), the village's name was changed in 1947 to the name it currently holds today (Institut Istorii 1978).

8. The local arrangement as described to me by elderly villagers—some of whom were old enough to have experienced it—had some of the characteristics reminiscent of the mir system described by others (Gambold et al. 2003, 262–63), to the extent that it was a system of communal land tenure and in the control of local administration. However, I never heard the term "mir" used by villagers, and there were differences when compared with this system.

9. Meaning elderly gentleman or grandfather, "diado," is used as a term of respect.

10. Meaning elderly woman or grandmother, "baba," is used as a term of respect.

11. Humphrey (1998, 13, 14) provides a useful and detailed discussion of both kolkhozy and sovkhozy, although there were significant differences when compared to my Brega case. For example, in Brega, the sovkhoz was not established on the "basis of the estates of large landowners."

12. Sovkhozy had special status. Zina, a former kolkhoz economist working in higher levels of administration in the district capital from the early 2000s, told me that sovkhozy were meant to be "models . . . and examples of what the kolkhoz should aspire to," and when foreigners were shown around a collective, they were always shown a sovkhoz rather than a kolkhoz.

13. In the quite common situation of a "mixed" household, only one person in the household needed to be working at the kolkhoz, even if all the rest worked in the sovkhoz, for the household to be written down as a kolkhoznik household.

14. The term "khoziaistvo" or the plural "khoziaistva" referred to an economic organization that implied ownership, whether it was the household, collective/enterprise, or private farm. The term is explored in more depth in chapter 2.

15. Such alliances were also seen to influence employment decisions. For example, following the installation of a new head of the sovkhoz, a neighbor, Katya, discussed the new leader's appointment of non-sovkhoz workers: "Why," she asked rhetorically, "was he offering the head accountant position to a former kolkhoz accountant? Don't we [the sovk-

hoz] have enough unemployed sovkhoz people that he could take on?" The old sovkhoz/kolkhoz divisions continued to structure local identity, employment opportunities and loyalties.

16. "Enterprise" was not the word used by the villagers themselves, who preferred the term "cooperative." I have chosen not to use the emic term, as this did not reflect the true legal arrangement that existed between the lessees and landowners—and indeed was a source of village misunderstandings and discontent, as will become evident later in this chapter. However, I have retained the word "cooperative" in all quoted passages.

17. In this sense, Perrotta (2000, 169) is both right and wrong: Private ownership based on previous labor does maintain the Soviet land-labor nexus, although the historical connection to the land—on the basis of work—was significantly transformed through the new land arrangements.

18. Those who were pensioned or died before this date, no matter how long they had worked in the collectives, were not eligible. This raised resentment because in particular instances, young workers employed in the collectives only days before the cutoff date received land, while others, who had worked all their lives and yet died before the date, received nothing.

19. The perceived difference of quality of land between sovkhoz and kolkhoz meant that land titles *within* the enterprises of the former kolkhoz were "interchangeable," but they were not exchangeable *between* the former kolkhoz and sovkhoz, as the land was seen as "too different" in terms of quality. Thus, despite attempts to keep families together by allocating plots of land next to each other, such arrangements were restricted by the historical divisions of the land into "sovkhoz" and "kolkhoz" that kept these lands separate.

20. The reforms were carried out by the village council and its twenty elected representatives, and the Land Resources Committee in the district capital, with its local representative in the village who was not part of the village council. The kolkhoz and sovkhoz were first transformed, in 1989–1990, into Collective Agricultural Enterprises (CAEs). They were autonomous from the state and a true form of collective ownership in the sense that they had ownership rights and operated as independent organizations (Perrotta 2000, 157). In 1996–1997 (in the kolkhoz/ sovkhoz respectively) individuals were given land "certificates," which provided technical rights to landownership, or "shares." Brega had two

CAEs—one formed from the original sovkhoz, and one formed from the original kolkhoz. This situation continued until 1996, at which time Collective Village Enterprises (*Kollektivnye Sel'skokhoziaistvennye Predpriiatie*—KCP) were formed. The former kolkhoz was divided into four but had one leader, Petur. Three years later, in 1999, the legal formation of the Village Agricultural Productive/ion Collective (*Sel'skokhoziaistvennyi Proizvodstvennyi Kollektiv*—SPK) took place. This represented the establishment of the new four enterprises with their own separate leaders. The sovkhoz remained as one. See Allina-Pisano (2008), Ash (1998), Perrotta (2000), and Wegren (2002) for more details of the earlier period of land privatization and the problems encountered.

21. What the table does not show is the greater complexity resulting from inheritance issues. Villagers might—and sometimes did—have land certificates/titles in more than one enterprise. Those lucky enough to still have work, often had land titles in a different enterprise from the one in which they worked. This spreading of certificates across different enterprises seems to have been a deliberately employed strategy.

22. I have not included the "fifth" service cooperative in table 1.2. It supplied all the machinery and technology, as well as controlling the gas and electricity used by the kolkhoz. This organization did not possess land. In 2000 it had 98 workers (mechanics and others). Once disbanded in May 2003, all its machinery was divided between the four (former kolkhoz) enterprises that operated at the time.

23. In Brega, for example, cash was in such deficit that school fees (introduced in 2001) were payable as either 30 UAH or 100 kilograms of wheat (for the large number of families who could not pay in cash). The lack of cash and reliance on "payment in kind" was reported also in other parts of the former East Europe (e.g., see Humphrey 1998, x; Allina-Pisano 2008, 160, 161).

24. For example, Avant Garde gave the following to each holder of a land title in 2014: 600 kilograms of wheat, 100 kilograms of sunflower seeds (for oil) and 200 kilograms of corn.

25. Two of the enterprises (Dudza and the sovkhoz) raised pigs with the specific purpose of giving them to their workers in lieu of a cash salary during the winter months when the enterprises struggled to find cash, as they had little income from grain production in these lean months.

26. Enterprises continued to sponsor the community in more limited ways, although such support was wound down over the period of a number of years. Well into the early 2000s, they were still providing

milk (sovkhoz) and bread (kolkhoz) for school children's breakfasts; by 2014 one of the few gestures of community support remaining was the donation of prizes for the village day festival (see chapter 4).

27. The village council received 60 percent of the collected land taxes; the rest was divided between the district and oblast administrations. There was a renewed push by the government to ensure that all private farmers paid their taxes in 2014, something it had not pursued in earlier years, having focused on the operations of the much larger agricultural organizations. Such taxes posed a particular burden to smaller private farmers who did not have the same degree of security (capital and other) as the enterprises.

28. This opinion was voiced by the veterinary surgeon for the sovkhoz in 2003 at the peak of the tensions between the enterprise leaders.

29. While not the focus of this chapter, the sovkhoz also had its own internal leadership problems. The leader who headed the sovkhoz between the years 2001 and 2004 was appointed after an internal coup within the organization.

30. Connections played an important role in Ponte's appointment. Petur told me that it was the local wealthy businessman (Angelovski) who had asked Petur to include Ponte as a candidate for the position of an enterprise leader. Leadership positions in the village tended to be taken by individuals from within the same small circle of elite (see also Humphrey 1998, 336). Angelovski's local influence was unquestionable. He owned numerous business interests both in the village (including three shops, the village bakery, the petrol station and the only public transport [a minibus] between Brega and the district capital) and in the district capital (a mill, a café/bar and a shop). He employed 110 workers: 60 in Brega and 50 in the district capital. A word of support from him would have held a lot of sway in getting Ponte appointed.

31. In fact, in 2001, the three enterprises stored the wheat in one pile and paid the rent from the same pile, irrespective to which enterprise a lessor belonged.

32. The background to this story was that when the kolkhoz was divided into four, the lessees inherited a large debt. The debt was divided equally between the four enterprises. Unlike Ponte, the other enterprises paid off their debt, and this provoked the other three leaders to take action.

33. See Allina-Pisano (2004), who also highlights the importance of local connections in the success of new agricultural elites.

34. Although Ponte was not forthcoming, from what he said, I suspect that he was working for one of Ukraine's agro-oligarchs, who are known to rent out large tracts of land and make sizeable profits (von Löwis 2019).

35. At the time of his resignation, his workers were anxious to meet with him, seeking reassurances about their unpaid salaries amounting to thousands of UAH. However, Ponte avoided his workers by hiding at home, and refused to meet with any of them.

36. The sovkhoz's dire economic situation—it was on the verge of bankruptcy in 2011—and the moral pressure from villagers to give a similar rent as that obtained from the other enterprises, was probably a factor in ultimately driving the leadership to seek outside investment. The sovkhoz leadership signed a contract with an investor from Izmail. Former sovkhoz workers told me that behind the Izmail backer was "a rich man from Donetsk." Concerns were circulating in 2014, that when this takeover was sealed and the investors took control of the land, they would sack the village workers and instill their own Izmail people in the enterprise. The head of the sovkhoz, however, presented the situation in a different light, claiming that local employees would work alongside the Izmail investors and they would be partners. Some villagers were deeply disturbed by the idea of outsiders working and profiting from their land; others claimed it made no difference whether they worked for local "masters" or "outsiders," as long as there was work. Others queried whether it was even legal for the enterprise to sublease the land without the owners' permission.

37. For example, Pasha, Marusha's sister, worked part time as a cook for the kolkhoz on a casual basis. She received part of her salary for the year—175 UAH—plus the enterprise owed her another 160. They wanted to give her a bag of sugar in lieu of the salary still owed. But at 2.80 UAH/kilogram, Pasha didn't want to take it. "Of course you shouldn't," Marusha confirmed, "after all, it sells for 2.30/kilogram in Izmail." "That's exactly what I told the accountant who was trying to convince me to take the sugar," replied Pasha, "Why would I want to take sugar at 2.80?" The accountant had replied, "You could sell it." "Sure," Pasha responded cynically, "I'll buy at 2.80 and sell at 2.30." Despite this, she eventually agreed to be written down for a sack. The knowledge that the enterprises were cash poor and could not afford to pay salaries swayed her to accept the bad deal, which was better than not being paid at all.

Villagers were in a weak negotiating position, partly as a result of the united front by the leadership, and partly due to a lack of alternatives.

38. Villagers who were required to pay the enterprises for services rendered always paid a portion of their yield. Social sphere workers who relied on someone else to plow their land—an enterprise or private farmer—paid in kind from their harvest, rather than in cash. The village mill would accept money for grinding wheat into flour, but more often than not, it was paid in products (withholding a portion of the grain milled). Even at the institutional level, exchanges were often in kind: the sovkhoz frequently paid its debts in kilograms of wheat (that is, through a form of commodity credit). Indications from other places in the former Soviet Union reveal that barter was often used as a form of exchange (Humphrey 1998).

39. Yet, people need money. Marusha told me: "If only I got 30 UAH a month, and Kolyo [her husband] also got the same, then we'd be OK. People say we have everything and don't need money. It's true we have a lot, but still you need money for some things—for water, for electricity, for a gas cylinder, sometimes you feel like buying an ice cream or something . . . once or twice they've [the enterprise she works for on an irregular basis] given me 10 UAH for casual work, but nothing more."

40. For example, Sasho, the former head engineer at the kolkhoz who worked his own land, speculated that when sales became possible, the inequalities would increase even further, as Petur and the other enterprise leaders would buy up the land at a cheap price and become like "plantation owners," and the people would be working for them and become "like slaves (*robi*)." The situation would move from the present "land control grabbing" to "land grabbing" (Mamonova 2015, 629; see also Visser and Spoor 2011). In this context, distinguishing between local and outsider enterprise operations/ownership was of crucial importance, because the latter's activities, unlike the former's, were not restricted in the same way by the local moral economy of the community. Village natives who ran enterprises in Brega—and their families—were firmly embedded in the local moral structures of the community and influenced by it.

41. In the case of debt, leaders were responsible for any outstanding debts; however, it was clear from Ponte's example that leaders were not held to account, and everyone else ended up carrying the debt—the district government, the workers, the other enterprises and the landowners.

42. I was repeatedly told on different occasions what a mistake it was to break up the kolkhoz, and they blamed their leaders for this. "It is the leaders who determine which way things go, and here Petur has fragmented everything, while in other villages, the leaders have managed to protect their kolkhoz," Nadia, a pensioner from the sovkhoz, told me. "At the time that the sovkhoz and kolkhoz were disestablished, there was almost an uprising. Why did they destroy the collectives? What for? Not only did they destroy the sovkhoz, but they took all its equipment and building materials." She added, "They destroyed the kolkhoz, and with it the people's lives [*prusnakha kolkhoza i zhizn'iata na khorata*]."

43. For example, Kolyo described to me in 2003 how one of the female accountants in the sovkhoz motioned Kolyo and his friend over and asked them to sign their names on the piece of paper she placed in front of them. They did not even know what they were signing, as the rest of the document was not there, only the page with the required signature. While both men knew, through speaking to other sovkhoz members, that the papers were part of an agreement for a certain percentage of their certificate land (0.5 hectares) to be planted with vines by a company the sovkhoz was engaging for this purpose; they had not been told any details. Kolyo said he wanted to know exactly what the enterprise wanted from him, and also what they would give him in return, but he said, "There is no one to tell me." The lack of information and communication between the leadership and landowners was an ongoing complaint from villagers.

44. There were two independent bodies assigned to audit the operations of agricultural enterprises, but these were not (as of 2014) functioning as they should, according to district officials to whom I spoke.

45. This echoed concerns from other parts of Ukraine (e.g., Perrotta 2000, 163).

46. Others have noted similar growing divisions, arrangements with questionable democratic worth that concentrate profits into the hands of a few Ukrainian oligarchs and foreign agribusiness corporations at the expense of the already impoverished rural inhabitant landowners (see Loewis 2019; Fraser 2015; Amosov 2019). Nevetheless, it is important to distinguish between different types of large farming enterprises on the basis of whether the investors are "outsiders"—foreign or Ukraine nationals—or local lessees. Murky land arrangements make it sometimes difficult to discover the details of management/control operations. While in the case of the former sovkhoz in Brega, it is likely that since

2014 some outsider (if not foreign) investment was involved, in the case of former kolkhoz lands, which were still managed by Brega natives, the working of the land continued to be subject to the local moral community in a way that outside investors were not. Even if responsibility to owners was minimal from a legal viewpoint, the dissatisfaction of the villagers and their moral condemnation could not be totally ignored by enterprise leaders. As discussed above, those still working in the enterprise retained some clout. Petur and the other lessees had lived and worked their entire lives in the village and were immersed in kinship and other relationships. While they gave very little away to the landowners, the enterprises did continue, for example, to contribute occasionally to community events—see chapter 4.

47. For example, Perrotta 2000; Wegren 2002.

48. Rising inequalities in rural sites have been observed in a wide range of postsocialist locations across eastern Europe and the former Soviet Union (e.g., Allina-Pisano 2008; Humphrey 1998; Kaneff 2009; among others).

49. I do not include the sovkhoz leader in this discussion, because his circumstances were less clear, given the sovkhoz's ongoing financial problems that led ultimately to "outsiders" being involved in the running of the organization.

## CHAPTER 2. HOUSEHOLD LAND

1. The exception was for public organizations, such as the village school, that continued to own land under "permanent use."

2. To reflect full ownership rights, household land—the house and additional amount in the fields—was renamed from "Lichnoe Podsobnoe Khoziaistvo," to "Lichnoe Krest'ianskoe Khoziaistvo," that is, from "personal usage farm/economy," to "personally owned farm/economy."

3. There were a few cases in which homeless families were given houses (by the village council) if they were empty and unused, or houses were signed over to new owners on the condition that they provided care to the elderly resident until his/her death.

4. In Soviet times, household land was restricted to the land surrounding the house and limited to 0.25 hectares for kolkhoz members and 0.15 for sovkhoz workers. After 1991, when full ownership rights were phased in, household land was granted in terms of "family" units. Family was understood as a married couple and their children. This meant that households had rights to more land than previously, since

households were usually made up of more than one family (i.e., different generations) who lived under the same roof. For example: In my household, where Valentina lived with her teenage daughter and parents, having separated and then later divorced from her husband, her parents constituted one family, Valentina and her teenage daughter a second. This was a case of two families living under one roof, with two land titles for household land; between them, they had the right to own up to four hectares of household land, which was made up of the land around the house (0.25 ha) and additional land located outside the village. Marusha's household next door held three such titles because she lived with her parents-in-law, who constituted one family (the house was in their name, they owned the land around the house and a further plot outside the village, making up their total entitlement); Marusha and her husband were the second family (and thus owned their land outside the village); and her youngest son and his second wife and their child were the third family (again, their land was located outside the village). Marusha's elder son and his family lived in another house and therefore constituted a separate household and family. In other former Soviet republics, land was privatized in terms of households, not families, as was the case in Azerbaijan (see Yalcin-Heckmann 2010, 11, 76.)

5. This was for a few reasons: household land in the fields was located far away, not easily accessible and petrol costs were high; over a period of a few years, the enterprises gradually withdrew their previously free services relating to this land (plowing, planting, etc.); the land was viewed as of poor quality; and there were taxes associated with this land. Although there was no law requiring the land to be worked, villagers could be fined if they left it to go fallow. Therefore, many preferred to give up their rights of ownership to this land. The small number of households that had the capacity to expand their production preferred to buy empty houses and the surrounding blocks of land within the village boundary (usually next door or across the road from themselves) or work the land of deceased relatives where the house was no longer inhabited. For example, a second cousin of Valentina's worked three household plots together with her husband: their own plot, the plot next door that belonged to the deceased grandfather (on her husband's side) and across the road, which was the house and land of her mother-in-law (also deceased). Neither of the latter two houses were occupied, but the land surrounding the houses were planted with corn (for animal feed), and the grapes were cared for and harvested.

6. A "selsko khaziaistvo" refers to the village as a total economic unit: its agricultural enterprises, private farms, and households.

7. Despite usually being a "private" organization, a khoziaistvo could also be a collection of individuals operating collectively (such as the three agricultural enterprises leaders acting as one khoziaistvo). Or it could be an organization responsible for publicly owned resources that were privately managed, such as the "komunalno khaziaistvo"—the (Brega Bulgarian) official name for the company that, as we will see in chapter 3, operated as a public-private organization, to manage the water. For more on different variations of meanings of khoziaistvo in different contexts, see also Collier (2011), and Humphrey (1998), among others.

8. Godparents.

9. The association between the household plots and former collectives in Brega was different from that portrayed by Mamonova (2015, 613) where the relationship seems to be one of greater tension and contrast. However, differences could be due to either the difference in academic methods (the macro perspective versus my ethnographic perspective) or due to regional differences, as Mamonova's focus was on western and central parts of Ukraine.

10. During Soviet times, households did not make their own cheese. Sheep were milked by the collective and the cheese brought to them ready-made. Villagers paid for this service in cash and cheese.

11. There were no professional fishermen in the village—in the sense that no one in Brega had a license to fish—and thus formally at least, catches were limited to a few kilograms at a time.

12. In 2002, the mean household size was 2.99 persons (figures obtained from the village council). More than a decade later, the village population had declined from 3,000 to 2,400, and high unemployment had forced many younger villagers to migrate. However, many did not transfer their registration to their new place of residence, so official village statistics did not reflect the extent of the decrease. One can realistically expect that the average number of persons per household would also have fallen, placing even greater demand on inter-household relations discussed in a following section of this chapter.

13. "Delianki" (the plural of "delianka"), as discussed in chapter 1, are land plots rented from the enterprise that have been planted with a labor-intensive crop (e.g., vines). Families looked after the crop, sold the harvest and kept the profits (after paying the enterprise a predetermined fee). A delianka was 25 "sotka" (1 sotka is 10 m x 10 m).

14. Even full-time employees were not paid regularly. In February 2003, the sovkhoz veterinary surgeon came home with a partial payment of his salary, 50 UAH. It was the first time in 10 months that he had received any monetary payment for his work. His wife said that the only way they survived was that they kept sheep and pigs, which they sold for cash, plus she received a pension as a retired nurse.

15. As my neighbor and kindergarten teacher Luba said to me and Marusha one evening: "They are saying at work that the elderly are supporting the household. It is their pensions that allow the household to survive, so if you have pensioners at home, you are OK." Marusha, a week earlier, had told me how her mother was depressed and crying, because all her contemporaries were dying or dead, and she did not want to live anymore. Marusha had responded, "Don't you dare die, we need your pension!" They both laughed and realized the truth of this, and that cheered her mother up. The importance of state pensions in the survival of households is documented for many parts of the former socialist world, for example, see Clarke (2002) for urban Russia.

16. No matter how self-sufficient a household was in food production, cash was needed in order to pay for the land taxes, electricity bills and so on. Marusha once told me: "If only I got 30 UAH a month and Kolyo also got the same, then we'd be OK. People say we have everything and don't need money. It's true we have a lot, but still, you need money for some things—for water, for electricity, for a gas cylinder, sometimes you feel like buying an ice cream or something."

17. Animal food was a combination of the husks of the wheat, with milled wheat. One neighbor estimated that one pig eats more than one ton of wheat before it can be sold. Thus, household need for wheat was high, and often, when wheat was not plentiful, keeping animals for sale was not economically prudent.

18. The symbolic importance of wheat and bread went far beyond the brief list provided here. The Ukraine flag, for example, incorporates the yellow color of the wheat fields against the blue sky. During Soviet times, Ukraine was known as "the breadbasket" of the USSR, in recognition of the central importance of wheat production in the country. For an extensive view of the importance of bread across a range of countries, see Arutynov and Voronina (2004).

19. The building has always been either a mill/bakery or both. The building was a mill in pre-Soviet times that was converted by the sovk-

hoz into a bakery. In 2000, Mitko (a private farmer) extended the building a little, removed the ovens, and turned it back into a mill.

20. Bread was also fundamental to local identity and a metaphor used in daily life to describe changes in their lives since 1991. Villagers often spoke wistfully about the "wonderful bread of past times," methaphorically contrasting these previous days with the contemporary declining importance of their village. Marusha pointed out, "Before [in Soviet times], our bread would be sent to the district capital and a few other villages would also sell it, but now this is not the case." Said with pride about their production successes and local capacities of the past, it was a commentary on the reversal of fortunes, a reversal that seemed to underline the decline of the village. By 2014, bread made in the city was sold in the villages, in contrast to previous Soviet times, when village-produced bread was sold throughout the district.

21. According to the women on my street, bread and flour were always available during Soviet times. The kolkhoz ran a bakery, and another bakery in the district capital would also deliver bread. Villagers did not keep sacks of flour in the attic for safekeeping, as they did in more recent times. For special occasion baking (such as Easter), flour was bought at the kolkhoz shop. Or it could be bought from the kolkhoz—although then the buyer would have to find a means to mill the grain into flour. So, Baba Mina preferred, as did most women with whom I spoke, to buy (just a few kilograms of flour) from the shop and keep it for those special baking occasions.

22. In the very different context of Bulgaria, where Rhodope households were never as fully integrated into collective agriculture, Meurs (2002, 223) argues a similar case.

23. The newly opened, privately owned village bakery made bread for the school, and this bread was also sold in the village shops. However, there was no one in our neighborhood who bought the bread. From what I saw, it was only bought in exceptional emergency situations, when there was no opportunity to bake at home and no one to ask for a loan of a loaf. The vast majority continued baking at home.

24. There was only one bakery in the village during this time, privately owned, which charged one UAH for a loaf, a sum far beyond what most villagers could afford, given the cash-starved economy and high quantity of bread eaten at home. In 2014, there were three options villagers had for obtaining bread: buying loaves from the shop, using the

coupon system with the mill (i.e., households gave 100 kg of wheat to the mill and in return received 60 coupons and were charged 50 UAH for the service. The 60 coupons entitled the recipient to 60 loaves of bread) or milling the wheat and making bread at home. Marusha and I calculated that the latter remained the cheapest option, even after the cost of electricity and milling was factored into the account.

25. Unlike the case described by Pine (1999), where women negotiated between two worlds—waged labor and the household domain—in my Ukrainian case, the world of waged work was no longer an option for most.

26. Holding back some flour for safekeeping was not only due to a lack of certainty as to the quality of next year's yield, but also a sign of more insecure times, as households recognized that from year to year, they were more at risk of not having enough flour for their bread needs.

27. Marusha pointed out that a loaf of bread was also called a "bulka" of bread, that is, "a bride," in an explicit association between bread and the young women on whose shoulders rested the reproduction of the household, both through being responsible for feeding the household as well as in terms of bearing and raising children.

28. In the very different context of Poland, Pine (2003, 285) notes a similar trend.

29. It is likely that pre-Soviet traditional gender and generation hierarchies have been modified in contemporary times by Soviet ideologies of equality.

30. He worked approximately 70 hectares of land from family and friends and was in all but legal terms a private farmer.

31. I prefer to use, where possible, the emic word "kum" to the rather inadequate English translation of "godparents," which does not reflect the full meaning and responsibility of kum. Traditionally, kum were actively involved in the marriage of the betrothed in an Orthodox church: They held the crown over the heads of the couple getting married, which was seen as a significant honor that bound the two couples over a lifetime. Kum were accepted as close family: They christened the children of the couple, and at least traditionally, the newborn took on the name of the kum, or the name suggested by them. Also, when the godchildren married, it was the kum who organized and led the wedding; the parents played a secondary role.

32. I know of only one case (2014) in which onions were used for ritual/treatment purposes: A traditional healer (Ponte's wife) used an onion

cut in half as part of a remedy, applying it to the stomach of Valentina's ailing granddaughter.

33. Often, the market developed via social networks that extended between individuals in Brega and their contacts in other parts of Ukraine. For example, it was through the connections of an ethnic Ukrainian woman who had married into the village that one lorry came to trade potatoes for onions.

34. Marusha stopped working onions in 2005.

35. For example, in 2003, one worker in the enterprise Avant Garde received a total harvest of 1,250 tons of grapes from his one delianka of vines and paid the agricultural enterprise a fee of 250 kg of the harvest for plowing and spraying.

36. In 2003, a Ukrainian government initiative by the Institut Proektvannya sadiv i Vinogradnikiv (i.e., Institute for the Planning of Gardens and Viticulture) created a credit scheme with the long-term aim of expanding the wine industry. The enterprises planted vines on hectares of land owned by their members who agreed to part of their land being used in this way (it meant that the member would receive correspondingly less grain as rent). Avant Garde planted 30 hectares that year; the sovkhoz was also hoping to plant new vines to add to the 60 hectares it already had under cultivation.

37. If Kolyo had had siblings, they too would have been potential helpers. However, he had only one sister, who had died at a young age.

38. It was a loan offered by the Odessa Oblast at a low interest rate, specifically available to villagers to improve their lives, according to Valentina.

39. On one occasion, it was our household's turn to collect our share of the sheep's milk (80 liters, which was made into feta cheese for home consumption) from the shepherd who was looking after the livestock over the summer. Valentina asked one of her deceased father's sisters and husband, but they were unable to assist, as they were attending a christening on that particular day. A second sister of Valentina's father, with whom she did not have close ties, was willing to help, but Valentina explained, "They won't do it for nothing," meaning they would only help if Valentina paid them. Valentina said that the former aunt was more willing to help than the latter who is "po stodena" (colder, i.e., holds herself at a greater distance).

40. The literal translation of "dvoiurodnyi brat/sestra" reflects the closeness of the relationship: These kin were "qualified siblings."

41. See Caldwell (2005, 22), who in a very different context, also

notes that the "revival" of religion is driven by strong, pragmatic reasons (alongside possible spiritual ones).

42. Land allocation on the basis of kin and kum ties provided further evidence of the importance of these social relations in production activities. During the privatization process, when land was allocated, officials advised villagers, "to get together with brothers, sisters and kum, so that the land is located all together in the one site, so that if a family wishes to leave the agricultural enterprise, it will be easier" to work the land. Family and kum worked the land and made decisions concerning it together. Neighbors, despite being part of each other's daily lives and sharing everyday tribulations, were not asked for help in activities that were directly linked to the reproduction of the khoziaistvo.

43. This makes my case quite different from other examples across the former Soviet world, such as the case described by Yalcin-Heckmann (2010) for Azerbaijan, where household plots were primarily used for cultivating cash crops.

44. Pine (2002, 103) makes a related point, arguing for the case of Poland, that waged work outside the domestic space allowed women to "realise a sense of individual autonomy." Individual autonomy and relations of equality are not the same thing, but in both cases waged work created new forms of relatedness outside of the traditional age and generational hierarchies of the household.

45. Serious divisions between women of different generations could and did occasionally result in the splitting of households and the creation of new khoziaistva as young couples moved out to establish a new home. However, from what I witnessed, senior women went out of their way to play down their new authority in the household in order to avoid potential conflicts.

## CHAPTER 3. WATER

1. See Article 6 of the Water Code.

2. Policy reversals applied only to those companies servicing over 100,000 inhabitants, and not to smaller companies such as in Brega. Decentralization remained a central focus of Ukrainian reforms and a new drive for devolution was triggered following Euromaidan in February 2014 (Kucheriv no date).

3. This bears similarities to reforms in other places in the world. For example, see Bolivian case, in Salman et al. (2014, 271).

4. Boelens, Getches, and Guevara-Gil (2012, 10) point out that en-

gagement in the market requires a "universalising bias by offering blanket prescriptions for the vast diversity of local contexts." It is in this sense that water is commodified, through the ability to meter water usage, and thus allow the imposition of a standard price per unit consumed.

5. Ostrom (1990, 8–15, 135–36) provides an important early reminder of the complex mix of public, private and local influences in the consideration of natural (in her case, common pool) resources.

6. Households that remained unconnected included houses only occupied on a temporary/seasonal basis, or households occupied by single, elderly occupants who could not afford (financially or in terms of finding the labor) to lay the pipes and connect to the mains.

7. Lake water comes from a combination of rainwater, the underground water table and the Danube River. Water from the latter source can be directed to flow into the lake via a lock system.

8. Here, to avoid confusion with the agricultural enterprises that are also "khoziaistva," I translate the latter term as "company," rather than "enterprise." The communal company was usually referred to by villagers as a "cooperative," although in the same way that the so-called "agricultural cooperatives" were not actually cooperatives in a legal sense or actual practice, the "water cooperative" was also not a cooperative. As with the agricultural enterprises, there was some local confusion as to the actual legal status of the communal company. While the mayor, in speaking to me, called it a "khoziaistvo," one of the workers in the company said he believed it was legally a "kommunal'noe predpriiatie," a "communal company," which is the term I use here. In all quoted passages, I remain true to emic terminology and use "cooperative."

9. The various mayors to whom I spoke over the years all agreed that the company was both "separate" and "tied" to the council. It was "tied" to the extent that the company leader was usually appointed by the mayor (in its early period of 2001–2004, three different men held the position). Also, annual profits (assuming there were any) were shared with the council. The company was required to hand in an annual report to the council. Any complaints from villagers concerning the company would be dealt with by the council, which planned to form a commission to examine any complaints. In other ways, the company was supposedly autonomous. According to the company statutes, an election and change in mayor or council need not bring about a change in company personnel. In actuality, the situation was different: The first company head (Ivan) told me that he had been removed from his posi-

tion following the elections, when the new mayor appointed "his own person" to the job.

10. Venu reinforced what everyone knew: The people who put down the main pipelines made a big mistake—they should have laid them on the upper side of the street. "Water will always run down to the lower end."

11. Other technical problems facing the company included the malfunctioning of the pumps. One of the pumps in the previous kolkhoz quarter was powerful, providing strong pressure, but overheated easily and thus could not be used for long periods of time. This exacerbated access problems for inhabitants in different parts of the village. Household location was crucial: Households located close to the lake were never without water, because they were serviced by two pumps, one that fed directly from the street, and one directly from the lake; most other locations were not so lucky.

12. Village streets were long (ours was almost 1 km in length), but in the couple of blocks that constituted our neighborhood, our household, along with our next-door neighbor Marusha's household and Luba's (on the lower side of the street, directly opposite Marusha), constituted a core social circle. We were the regulars who meet nightly on the street to share our daily trials and tribulations and exchanged knowledge and advice about household production. We shared birthdays and other significant social occasions. We also relied on each other in the case of need: help to transport seeds to the agricultural enterprise to be turned into oil, requests to "borrow" part or a whole loaf of bread when there was no time to bake at home that day, etc.

13. As a point of comparison: Despite geographical proximity, relations with the next-door neighbor on our other side (from Marusha) had broken down as a result of a boundary dispute some years earlier, and there was thus no sharing between the two households, despite living literally next door. Relations were so strained that verbal communications were rare, and even when we all happened to be on the street at the same time in the evening, there was no direct conversational exchange between the neighbor and Valentina.

14. This reference related to the mysterious death of Katya's husband, who was found dead one morning. His cause of death was never resolved, leaving room for gossip and speculation.

15. Some of these were individuals with privileges granted to them by national legislation, such as war veterans (see Institute of Urban Eco-

nomics 2004, 18). Notably, these individuals were not the target of village resentments.

16. We see from the Brega case how intimately linked political economy is to the infrastructure that provides the technical backbone to a system. A society's infrastructure is always shaped in terms of the political economy for which it is designed, and of which it is a product. Collier (2011, 205) makes a similar point when he writes, "Collective life . . . is articulated by infrastructure." This topic requires far more attention but is beyond the scope of this chapter.

17. Unlike other cases in the world where there is a concern for maintaining the collective order of water usage (e.g., see Vium 2016), in the Brega instance, there was an open disregard for (distant) neighbors' access to the resource.

18. Presumably this refers to the leaders of the agricultural collectives who disestablished the kolkhoz, although she might also have had in mind higher level officials in the district or even the national capital responsible for the reforms.

19. It is tempting to speak here of a "moral economy." After all, neighbors applied pressure to their fellow neighbors in the hope that they would make a self-sacrifice for the greater good. However, I hesitate to use the term, because of a number of crucial factors that meant that this case did not easily fit within the moral economy literature. First, there was no collective unified response to the commodification of water; to the contrary, the response was fragmented and created greater divisions between different neighboring households. Second, households only acted collectively when it was in their interests to do so; thus, mutual obligations and sharing took a back seat to individual household considerations and their fundamental requirement of water. Third, and lastly, Bregans—like other rural Ukrainians—were not traditional peasants. Following 50 years of Soviet industrialization and collectivization, they could not be seen as coming from a "traditional peasant society," despite the contemporary priority households gave to their subsistence and survival needs.

20. Those villagers who supported the commodification of water and the activities of the company through their willingness to install meters and pay for water were not showing blind faith or belief in a market economy. Any willingness to engage in the water market was driven by immediate concerns to gain better access to the resource through bringing about a fairer or more equitable distribution of it; it was not a reflection of any deeper commitment or preference for a particular form

of political economy. Indeed, many of the people who were critical of the reforms and often spoke favorably of previous Soviet arrangements—such as my neighbor Marusha—at the same time placed their hopes in the commodification of water as an equitable means of resolving the contemporary water problems, through the installation of meters and water payments. Likewise, householders who refused meters were not necessarily pro-Soviet times or against the reforms. They were merely making the most of an opportunity to protect their household interests above those of their neighbors. The opting out of using meters, as much as a reliance on them, was an instrumental decision taken by individual households in order to secure their livelihoods; it was not a display of preference for one form of political economy above another.

21. Political science literature presents decentralization as evidence of growing corruption at the local level (e.g., Khmelko 2012, 8) due to the local elite's rising powers. Admittedly, the selection of operators/managers and the setting of tariffs for the water was a highly politicized process, something also noted in passing in some of the literature (see OECD 2006, 10; Institute of Urban Economics 2004, 14, 23). However, what might appear to be "corruption" from an outsider's perspective is often, from another viewpoint, about relations embedded in local reciprocity and obligations. Decentralization and the transfer of resources from national to lower levels of state administration are never simple or straightforward, as macro perspectives often assume, because communities are rarely sites of solidarity and unity (see Burns, Hambelton and Hoggett 1994). Further, my study reveals that new divisions emerged from the very process of decentralization itself, as a result of the combination of water being locally run and yet at the same time needing to operate in a market context that was supposed to be "autonomous," "free," and "impersonal." Decentralization embedded management and control of the resource in local social relations of which it was a part. As one main component of the water reforms, decentralization thus operated against another reform agenda—the creation of a "free" market. The contradiction was built into the reform process.

22. As across much of the world where water reforms have been implemented, the "existing social organization of water" has been severely disrupted and resulted in "social dramas and inequalities" (Boelens et al. 2012, 48). The situation is much the same in my example, although as is often the case, the significance is in what can be gleaned from the particularities of different contexts.

## CHAPTER 4. MORAL AUTHORITY

1. See Kaneff (2017).

2. As my fieldwork was not carried out in Soviet times, it is difficult to ascertain the degree to which contemporary traditional/pagan practices were shaped by the "domestification of religion" (Dragadze 1993), in other words, how much traditional practices changed during the Soviet decades due to the transfer of various previously religious practices into the home. Nor is this an objective of the chapter. However, it is clear that post-1991, there was little evidence of a reversal of the domestification of religion processes (suggested by Dragadze in 1993 in the case of Georgia and other parts of Eurasia), as Bregans were unwilling to give unlimited influence to the priest.

3. While significant upheaval within the Orthodox Church in the country has led to the granting of independence to the Orthodox Church of Ukraine (OCU), the Moscow Patriarchate of the Ukrainian Orthodox Church (UOC MP) did not recognize the decision of the *tomos* signed by Patriarch Bartholomew of Constantinople in 2019 (Deutsche Welle 2019). Although over 400 UOC MP parish churches transferred to the OCU after the 2019 signing, in Bessarabia—including the Izmail, Bolgrad, and Reni Districts—there was a reticence to leave the Moscow Patriarchate, and the churches refused to join the Orthodox Church of Ukraine (Svetlichnyi 2019). All these political intricacies bypassed villagers, who simply saw their church as being ROC. I continue to refer to it as the ROC, because that is how the villagers understood and spoke about it.

4. Halemba (2015, 181–202) identifies a number of strategies used by priests in Transcarpathian Ukraine to legitimate their authority. Later in this chapter, I explore some of the strategies deployed locally, more from the villagers' rather than the priest's perspective.

5. It is probably worth emphasizing that while "religious pluralism" (Wanner 2003, 274) may characterize Ukraine when considered at the national level, regional situations vary, and at the local level, often one religion dominates. The vast majority in Brega identified with the ROC. However, there were very small numbers of other religious followers: There were eight Jehovah's Witnesses (a family of four, and another four individuals); there were also a handful of Baptists (I was unable to ascertain exactly how many). Most villagers confused the two, referring to everyone who was something other than ROC as "the Baptists."

6. The local naming system can be cited as one example of the dual cultural arrangements. From the earliest times, villagers held two names: a formal Russian name with which they were christened, and a Bulgarian name. The former appeared in all official documents; the latter was used in everyday village life (see Kaneff 2018).

7. Traditions provided continuity with the past, connecting migrants with their Bulgarian heritage, and in this sense distinguished the community from other villages in the district, as well as helping define their position in the new Ukrainian state as a Bulgarian minority. In the many post-Soviet contexts where religion was used to "restore" national identity and thus served as an important nation-building block—such as the Georgian case discussed by Dragadze (1993)—a shift of boundaries to give more prominence to religion was welcome. However, in the context of Brega, where local identity was dependent as much on ancestral traditions as organized religion, the priest's attempts to deter villagers from traditions was unwelcome.

8. Undoubtedly, the fundamental conflict between traditional practices and the ROC lay in a number of important opposing features. Lindquist (2000, 271) notes that magic practices enable a person to be an active agent in their environment, in terms of their health/illness concerns and in managing their web of social relationships. This is in contrast to the ROC, where worship is carried out according to liturgy, and thus is very formularistic and structured. It gives a passive role to the individual, since agency is with God and his representatives on Earth, priests.

9. Moreover, the priest's lack of knowledge of the region became apparent to me in the first year of his tenure. In one conversation, Priest Alexei told me that in 1924, "Lenin had taken all the churches and tried to turn people away from them, but "thank god, Lenin had not succeeded"." I was momentarily taken aback and then pointed out that this part of the country was not under "Lenin," but part of Romania at the time. It was then his turn to look uncertain, and he said, "Well, I'm not sure exactly of the dates, maybe it was 1934 or later." A priest's training clearly did not include educating him for service in any particular locality.

10. Traditions were precisely about defining local identity and belonging. In emphasizing the particularity of the tradition, the priest was not, as he believed, arguing against the validity of the practice and delegitimating it. To the contrary, in the villagers' eyes, he was actually reinforcing uniqueness and, therefore, the centrality of the practice in the reproduction of their specific local identity.

11. Priest number four was similarly against the practice of lighting fires at grave sites. He reportedly said: "Why do people do this? Don't they realize that the fires attract the devils?"

12. Olya (and many others like her), an occasional churchgoer, kept her options open, carefully conducting her affairs in order not to anger the priest, but at the same time carrying on with her traditional practices. A day before the predawn trek to the cemetery, at the church, while at the booth selling candles, Olya whispered to me, "The priest forbids it, but Vito and I are going to the cemetery at 6 a.m. Do you want a lift?" At the same moment we were having this conversation, she bowed her head and crossed herself as the priest—in the middle of a service—passed us, waving his incense!

13. Although small in number, they were an important mouthpiece, instrumental in spreading the priest's word throughout the village. Through kinship networks his followers were also able to mobilize higher numbers of people to support the priest when necessary, such as in helping establish and maintain the church's vineyard that brought in a regular income for the church.

14. The priest actively spoke against a whole range of other "traditions," for example, the use of music at a funeral and wine at the cemetery, the use of traditional healing methods and "white magic" practices.

15. For example, the priest said that you should not bring wine to any place associated with the dead, such as a cemetery. This is because wine had sacred significance, and its traditional use was an affront to the church. Baba Sonia, a singer in the village folklore group, scoffed and said: "Can you imagine a *pomenina* [anniversary of someone's death that is recognized with a wake] where you serve water rather than wine?" The entire notion was ludicrous and incomprehensible.

16. I was told on numerous occasions that in the village there were no babi who practiced "black" magic, only a couple who performed "white" magic. There were also one or two who read fortunes by means of melting wax or bullets. The melted material was poured into cold water, and the form taken by the hardened substance was read by the teller.

17. In the following years, Angelica went even further. She ended up marrying a ROC priest who was serving in Crimea. To my knowledge she and her husband still live there.

18. Tocheva, in discussing the ROC economy in the Russian context, noted that the "church economy has always been controversial" (2014, 7) but was given new impetus in the post-Soviet situation (2014, 21) that

raised issues of moral legitimacy. (See also Halemba 2015, 174, 180.) It seems likely that it was high unemployment and the growing reliance on household economies (see chapter 2), in the context of post-Soviet economic insecurity, which gave villagers a new and additional reason to be wary of the material demands made by the church.

19. Such tensions were evident far beyond Brega. While visiting the Bulgarian Cultural Association in Odessa, the director told an audience of parents—whose children were attending weekend language classes—that in Bulgaria, the state pays church salaries, which is a good thing because "they [priests] cannot grab all they can, like they do here." From the nods in the audience, there was general agreement on this point.

20. Church income was spent on the priest's salary, as well as on other costs, such as maintaining the church and contributing to the salaries of those who worked for the church. The church did not pay taxes to the government, because it was considered a nonprofit organization (see Ishchenko 2019).

21. In this respect, the Brega priest seemed less generous than other priests, who expressed the view that they would never refuse a funeral or baptism to someone who could not afford it, and would carry out the service for free (see Tocheva 2014, 14).

22. Vito and Olya recalled their wedding engagement in the early 1980s, when they went to a church in Bolgrad, just before Easter during Lent, to be blessed. When they arrived, they found the three priests eating chicken. "They tell people not to, but then they do eat these forbidden foods." Another memory from Soviet times supported this view: Venu told me that when he was a student in Odessa, he "saw the front and back entrances of the church, and in the front, all is normal, and in the back rooms the priests are there with women and playing cards. So, I don't respect them, and I just can't bring myself to kiss their hands. Why should I? They represent God, but they aren't God, so there's no need to kiss their hands." This type of story was repeated in many variants by other villagers.

23. If "belonging without believing" can be seen as a reaction to those who simply associate with the church as a way of supporting a national legacy (Halemba 2015, 11), then in Brega we see the opposite: Many villagers claimed to be "believers" (in God) but without "belonging" (to the church).

24. The history of Den' Sela is interesting, although only tangentially relevant here. The celebration of the foundation of cities has a long tradi-

tion. Moscow celebrated its 800th birthday in 1947 (Alekseevskii 2010, 375). Kiev first celebrated its anniversary (1,500 years since foundation) in 1982 (Izbusheva 2015, 26–27). In both cases, celebrations included concerts, festivals, museum and sporting events. Odessa first celebrated its City Day in 1849 (55 years after it was first founded), and at least in this pre-Soviet period, the celebrations were a mixture of religious and secular activities (see for example: http://odesskiy.com/chisto-fakti-iz-zhizni-i-istorii/den-rozhdenija-odessy-ili-kak-etot-den-otmechali-v-19-veke.html last accessed 23.7.2020). Contemporary celebrations appear to be purely secular and "cultural" in nature (see, for example, with respect to the 2019 celebrations: https://omr.gov.ua/ru/acts/mayor/175541/ [especially paragraphs 1–3]). I could find no mention in the literature of Village Days being celebrated during Soviet times (or earlier), something confirmed in Brega when I was told that they had only introduced such a celebration in the mid-1990s. Valentina justified the introduction of the event by saying: "Odessa and Kiev had a 'City Day,' so why shouldn't we have a 'Village Day?'"

25. Termed in Russian "khramovyi prazdnik" (church holiday) and sometimes also known as "prestol'nyi prazdnik" (temple holiday) some researchers claim that the old Christian Orthodox holiday goes back to the thirteenth century in Russia (Chernykh 2014, 25–26). The holiday is practiced across Slavonic Orthodox sites, including Russia, Ukraine and Belarus (Chernykh 2014, 27). Anecdotal evidence (personal communication from Ms. Bershak when speaking about the Luhansk Region) suggests that the practice continued during Soviet times in places which had an operational church. However, in villages such as Brega, where the church was shut, the holiday only resurfaced in the post-Soviet period after the reopening of the church. Most villages in the region celebrated Den' Sela and their church's holiday on the same day. This was because most villages did not know their precise day of foundation and thus chose to commemorate Den' Sela on the same day as the saint's day after which their church was dedicated. The two celebrations have been mutually interconnected from the beginning.

26. Support for the paparuda tradition from all the main officials (school, agricultural cooperatives and council) was long-standing, extending back to Soviet times (and undoubtedly before). One of the elderly paparuda participants recalled how one year, pre-1991, the women had been given a car and driver from the kolkhoz to take them from house to house. The village council, even in Soviet times, was openly and actively

supportive of local traditions. Binns (1980, 177) recounts the incorporation of various "folk customs" into state-authorized ceremonies, and he notes the role of Soviet ceremonies in "preserving," and sometimes "reviving" some customs (184).

27. The term "kurban" denotes a special meal that is held as a thanksgiving for good health (following illness). It usually involves the slaughter of a large animal—in this case, a lamb. Sometimes the prepared food can be blessed by the priest, but this is not a requirement for it to be called a kurban. For example, on St. Nikolai Day, a kurban was held not only at the church but also in individual households where there were men who shared the same name, "Nikolai." In the case of Marusha, where not only her husband, but also the husbands of both her sisters were named "Nikolai," the whole family—along with kum (godparents)—feasted together on the day from a lamb slaughtered by Marusha's household. Marusha did not take a plate of the kurban meal to the church to be blessed and donated to others, but some other households did.

28. Anya was of the opinion that she should have been included in the relevant organizational council meetings, so that decisions about the prizes could have been made in a more timely fashion. Valentina confided in me, however, that the meetings were intended only for the leaders who were donating resources to the event. In the council workers' view, it was not appropriate for Anya to attend.

29. The main focus of disagreement concerned the exclusion of the priest and church followers from the village feast. However, some of the churchgoers also had misgivings about the moral worth of some of the particular activities of Den′ Sela. For example, Tanya did not participate in the raffle, and from her pursed lips and tone of voice, it was clear that she did not approve, seeing it as a form of gambling.

30. As far as I could ascertain, neither the mayor nor agricultural leaders were to blame for the delays. Rather it was as Valentina told me: The source of delay was due to the disagreement between Anya and the council workers.

31. Mass participation was also a feature of Soviet ceremonies: It was a means to show ideological support for the state and a way that loyalty to the Party and leadership was demonstrated and even broadened (Binns 1979, 597; Lane 1981, 265). At the same time, participation highlighted the egalitarian principles through mass involvement: Everyone had a role to play by "manifesting" or participating in events (Kaneff 2004; Lane

1981). Such secular public rituals were designed to create a "common faith" in the community, promote the ideal of equality, and encourage "devotion to the common good" (Steinberg and Wanner 2008, 6, 8). In much the same way after 1991, leaders and the organizations they represented still very much relied on displays of support through participation. Thus, Den′ Sela, in some ways reminiscent of Soviet ceremonies, provided an entertainment program by mainly amateur artists, but also included other activities that attracted "mass participation." What was dropped from the contemporary ceremonies was the "official/ideological" content that was a fundamental part of Soviet ceremonies (Binns 1979, 593). The new added dimension was the material incentive where performances were rewarded with prizes. No longer were the rewards confined to medals or certificates that acknowledged the achievement of socialist workers—a form of symbolic capital that provided a currency for those engaged in socialism. Instead, participation was driven by rewards/prizes that held material advantages but also functioned as a redistribution of goods within the community. Egalitarian values remained: Everyone who partook won something.

32. As Tocheva (2014, 18) shows in the different context of Russia, the boundary between gift/donations and commerce in the ROC are often blurred, and this is encouraged so that transactions between the church and its followers are not seen as profitable activities, which can lead to accusations of moral impropriety.

33. For example, the district capital's Day of the City celebrations included the active participation of the church and priest.

34. Although Lindquist (2000, 252) notes that the division between magic and religion has gained importance in post-Soviet times—and this may be particularly true in the case of rural sites where churches were not previously active—given the significance of tradition in anchoring local identity, it is likely that tensions have always existed between the church and the community in Brega. I suspect that the removal of organized religion in Soviet times was in some ways convenient, since the inactivity of the church in Brega would have created fewer reasons for local confrontation. If and when villagers wanted to engage the services of a priest, they traveled to the district capital. The binary spiritual world of traditional practices and organized religion, which had been clearly delineated in spatial terms during Soviet times, was challenged by the return of organized religion to the community. In Brega, it was not so much, as Halemba (2015, 177) argued for Transcarpathian Ukraine,

that the laity believed that they should have a "decisive voice in religious matters and that priests were their servants and subordinates," but rather that a healthy separation made the practice of traditions easier: "You get on with your job, and we will get on with ours."

35. Priests have come and gone in two senses: first, because the ROC was inactive in the village during Soviet times; second, because after 1991, the village went through four priests in quick succession before priest number five (Alexei) settled in Brega.

36. As we saw from the predawn cemetery visit, every household was responsible for the practice and for the details of how the practice was carried out: whether the householders went to the cemetery at 3 a.m. or 5 a.m. or 7 a.m., or not at all, what they took with them, etc. Traditional practices in this sense are egalitarian, and every participant conducts the practice as they wish.

## CHAPTER 5. IDENTITY

It is particularly important to remind the reader that this chapter—as all others—is based on fieldwork carried out up to (and including) 2014. I do not make claims that the Bregan views expressed here remain the same today. See note at the beginning of the book.

1. Orthodox Christians who spoke a Turkic language and traced their historical roots to Bulgaria.

2. I choose to use the terms used by Bregans when referring to different groups or places. For example, they distinguished "Romanians" from their Bessarabian neighbors who were "Moldovans." I use whichever term Bregans used, in order to convey their perspective.

3. Village statistics for 1983 (collected from the village council) show that from a total population of 3,194, the vast majority (3,097) were self-designated Bulgarians. The rest was made up of 49 Moldovans, 25 Ukrainians, 13 Russians and 10 Gagauzi; that is, 1.5%, 0.7%, 0.4% and 0.3% of the total population, respectively. Non-Bulgarian ethnicities thus made up less than 5% of the total population. In 2014, the numbers of non-Bulgarians had increased proportionately to about 10% of the total 2,400 population: Moldovans made up about 3%, Gagauzi about 2% and Ukrainians and Russians about 2.5% each. The rise is likely a result of the increased emigration of ethnic Bulgarian Bregans.

4. The importance of language and identity in the Ukrainian context is also the central theme of many excellent studies on the topic, for

example, see Bilaniuk (2005), Dickinson (2010), Kulyk (2006), among others.

5. This is unlike the case of other non-Russian speakers in the USSR where the choice of Russian as the lingua franca felt like "Russification" and colonization. To the contrary, Russian was a crucial part of Bregan history that was associated with liberation from their historical oppressors, the Ottomans.

6. For a general discussion of how a Russian Empire and Soviet identity differed, see Kulyk (2006, 288, 289).

7. According to the National Census of 2001, of a total population of just over 48 million, 37 million were Ukrainians (77.8%), 8 million were ethnic Russians (17.3%), Moldovans, Crimean Tatars, and Belarusians had populations of approximately one quarter of a million each, and there were just over 200,000 Bulgarians. The share of national minorities was just over 22 percent of the total population. See Number and composition of the population of Ukraine (2001), Ukrainian Population Census of Ukrainian State Statistics Service, http://2001.ukrcensus.gov.ua/rus/results/general/nationality/. Importantly, identification with a particular ethnicity (or language) did not correlate with language usage, which explains the far larger proportion of Russian speakers in the country that included millions of ethnic Ukrainians (e.g., see Kulyk 2013, 282; Kulyk 2006, 294), as well as the people of my study.

8. For discussion, see Richardson (2008, 6). See also Schlegel (2016, 11) and Golczewski (2011, 194), among others.

9. The statistically most significant ethnic groups can be broken down as follows: Bolgrad District—Bulgarian, 58%; Gagauz, 18%; Moldovan, 1%; Russian, 16%; and Ukrainian, 5%. Izmail District—25%, 0.2%, 26%, 22%, and 26%, respectively. Reni District—8%, 7%, 49%, 15%, and 17%, respectively. Other minorities included Belarussian, Armenian, Roma, German, Polish, Slovak, and Jews, among others. If I define a mono-ethnic village as having 70% or above of any one self-designated ethnic group or when any combination of ethnic groups together amounted to over 70%, then the following findings apply: Bolgrad District had 21 villages, of which 12 were Bulgarian, 3 Gagauz, 1 Russian, 2 Russian-Bulgarian, 1 Russian-Bulgarian-Gagauz, 1 Russian-Bulgarian-Moldovan, and 1 Bulgarian-Gagauz. In the Izmail District, there were 23 villages: 7 Bulgarian, 5 Ukrainian, 4 Russian, 4 Moldovan, 1 Bulgarian-Russian, 1 Russian-Ukrainian, and 1 Bulgarian-Russian-Moldovan. In the Reni District, there were 7 villages, of which 5 were Moldovan, 1 Bulgarian,

and 1 Gagauz. This meant that 43 of the 51 villages that constituted this region were dominated by one ethnicity. The remaining 8 were a combination of 2–3 ethnicities (Ukrainian Population Census 2001, State Statistics Service of Ukraine, http://database.ukrcensus.gov.ua).

10. Much like laws relating to land privatization, language laws have been the subject of ongoing amendments and additional reform (for summary of the first two decades since independence, see Kulyk 2013, 281–86).

11. See Verkhovna Rada of Ukraine (2019), Law of Ukraine No. 2704-VIII. The law includes requirements that all state organizations use only the Ukrainian language; civil servants must have certification to prove their knowledge of the language; the media should predominantly use Ukrainian (a minimum of 75 percent in the case of TV and radio); and businesses must serve customers in the Ukrainian language unless the customer requests otherwise. The language of interethnic communication must be exclusively in Ukrainian. There were no prohibitions of the use of Russian—or other national "minority" languages—for private communications and religious rites, but it was mandatory for any broadcasting or publications in the minority language to be accompanied by a Ukrainian translation. There were hefty fines for breaking the law. The Ukrainian language was also obligatory in schools and higher education institutions. Since this original law of 2019, there have been numerous amendments that have strengthened the role of Ukrainian even further. For example, TV and radio must be 90 percent in Ukrainian as compared to the original 75 percent. Recent amendments have made some concessions in certain areas for English, official languages of the EU, and minority languages, but they do not include Russian where further laws have been passed to restrict its usage. Human Rights Watch, among other commentators, has expressed concern about the 2019 law's failure to protect the linguistic rights of Ukrainian minorities (see https://www.hrw.org/news/2022/01/19/new-language-requirement-raises-concerns-ukraine).

12. Although history can be a resource in its own right, in the way I discuss it here, its importance lies in its service to identity, which is the resource under discussion. Others have discussed history itself as a resource and shown how, as such, it is used in different ways during different periods in the past (e.g., Eiss 2008).

13. The ongoing war in east Ukraine, and the escalating tensions, makes many of the views held by individuals noted in this chapter par-

ticularly sensitive. In order to protect identities, I have deliberately given many of the villagers quoted in this chapter extra anonymity, avoiding names or other identifying features altogether.

14. There was considerable anger directed at the mayor at the time, who invited district officials to help themselves to the collected items that were described by a neighbor as "village treasures." Valentina and the schoolteachers were especially annoyed, expressing the view that the items should have all remained in Brega for their own museum collection. The mayor made it clear that Brega efforts had been slow off the mark, and that he felt justified giving the selected items to the more proactive district officials for their center.

15. Since ancient times, the region has come under various influences: Thracian in BCE times, then Roman, and following their retreat (in early centuries CE), Goths, Huns, Slavs, Avars, Bulgarians, Magyars and eventually the Vlachs (who were seen as predecessors to the Romanians) have all left their mark (Van Meurs 1994, 35–36). Yet as Van Meurs points out, the lack of primary evidence means that any historical narratives concerning this time are contentious and most likely "inaccurate" (1994, 38).

16. Apart from Bulgarians, Bessarabia also became the home during this time to increasing numbers of Moldovans, Albanians, Russians, and Ukrainians from central Russia, as well as to Gagauzi and those escaping serfdom (a system never introduced in Bessarabia) (Van Meurs 1994, 47). Jews and Germans were also part of the diverse population of the region (Schlegel 2017, 3–4). Estimates of Bessarabia's population in 1812 ranged between 240,000 and 275,000 (Van Meurs 1994, 115). For additional details of the ethnic makeup of the region in this early period, see Van Meurs (1994, 115–16).

17. For the role of Bulgarian Bessarabians in alliance with the Russians in the war of independence from the Ottomans and also contemporary examples of the continued relevance of the Russo-Turkish War of 1877-1878, see Schlegel (2017, 214).

18. Unlike the situation in urban areas in the nineteenth century, "Russian literature and education never reached the rural masses who remained illiterate and loyal to their folk culture and language" (Van Meurs 1994, 48).

19. The situation in different parts of Bessarabia during different times of Romanian rule was far more complicated than I am able to convey here. From some accounts, at least, it seems that revolutionary

movements—especially coming from large Slavic and Jewish minorities—plagued the Romanian government (Van Meurs 1994, 75–77). Unsurprisingly, Bessarabia was strategically important to Soviet-Romanian relations during the interwar period (Van Meurs 1994, 79).

20. Meanwhile, Moldovan independence led to ethnic strife that resulted in the proclamation of the Transnistrian Republic in 1990 (made up largely of Russian-Ukrainians) and the Gagauz Autonomous Republic by the Orthodox population speaking a Turkic language (Van Meurs 1994, 98, 99).

21. In addition, see Schlegel (2016, 182–85); Golczewski (2011, 201, 204). As Marples' (2007, 255) study makes abundantly clear, such a history also found its way into school and university history books (see also Wanner 1998).

22. For a discussion of this, see Richardson (2008, 7–8).

23. A view propagated by the Ukrainian North America diaspora, many of whom originated from west Ukraine (Marples 2007, xi–xii, 304).

24. Arguments that the private ownership of the land meant that collectivization "remained alien to Ukrainian peasants" (Vasyl' Marochko, in Marples 2007, 45) was contrary to the situation in Brega where land was worked under a collective rotation system since the village's foundation in the early 1800s, over a century before incorporation into the USSR (see chapter 1). The point being that response to collectivization—and many other Soviet reforms—was location-specific.

25. Had this part of Bessarabia been under Soviet control pre–World War II, it is likely the Bulgarians would have undergone a change of status from full Soviet citizens in the 1920s and early 1930s to being designated a diaspora nationality in 1939 (with questionable allegiance to the USSR given Bulgaria's alliance with Germany during the war) and deported to other parts of the Soviet Union away from the strategically sensitive border zones. Such was the fate of Bulgarians and other diasporas in the Soviet Union in the lead up to the war (Hirsch 2005, 274–75). However, southern Bessarabia was not part of the USSR at this time, and thus Bregans were spared this fate.

26. One book records that nine Brega residents were in the Soviet Army (Tronko 1978, 678–93).

27. To add further complexity, even in southwestern Ukraine, there are local and regional differences, as Dickinson (2010, 61) makes abundantly clear in her study of the Zakarpattia region, where the people

maintained a "positive orientation" toward the USSR (as their liberator from Hungarian oppression).

28. The complaints from eastern and (other parts of southern) Ukraine that "the west Ukraine version of history predominates in Ukraine today" (Marples 2007, 287) echoed sentiments I heard in Brega. Bregan views cannot be dismissed as a result of 70 years of "subjection" to the USSR (Marples 2007, xvii), since this area was incorporated into the Soviet Union far later (1944) and had fundamentally different experiences of Russian engagement—as a historical savior, not an oppressor.

29. The Russia versus "the West" alliance (the latter in this case a term used by the villagers), which has been a central tension since Ukrainian independence, continued to divide the country. Euromaidan, it may be recalled, was at least in the early phase, triggered by the government's hesitation to sign an Association Agreement with the EU, thereby bringing Ukraine more in line with Western interests (Marples 2015, 9–10).

30. In 2014, stories abounded of recent visits to the Republic of Bulgaria, where there was ample evidence of how little conditions had improved in Bulgaria since its admittance into the EU. This in turn gave impetus to villagers' critical questioning of Kiev's steering of their own country toward "the West" and EU, and away from Russia.

31. See also Boneva (2006, 53).

32. The Russian equivalent for "Marusha" is "Masha"(a diminutive form of "Maria").

33. See, for example, Bilaniuk (2005) and Kulyk (2006). Apart from the head of the sovkhoz, I can think of several others I knew, such as Anya, the village's cultural coordinator (an ethnic Russian), and agricultural worker Dzenya (an ethnic Ukrainian who married into the village) who had not learned Bulgarian well despite years of living in the village. They were able to continue in this way because of the dominant value given to Russian/Ukrainian above other languages, giving them less incentive to learn Bulgarian. However, lack of good Bulgarian-language skills came at a cost: the ongoing reinforcement that they were "outsiders." One such example concerned Valentina and Anya, who never got on well, and yet as workers with official positions were often forced to work together. After a particularly bad argument, when both lost their tempers, Valentina said to me afterward of Anya, "One of ours would not have behaved in such a way," clearly attributing Anya's bad behavior to her "outsiderness."

34. See also Dickinson (2010, 72–74) for a similar point made with respect to a different part of Ukraine.

35. The dual language practices in Brega were reflected in the kinship system that also made use of Russian and Bulgarian terminology, denoting greater or lesser degrees of relatedness in particular contexts. For example, villagers used two terms for "aunt," one from Bulgarian, one from Russian. The Bulgarian word "lelia" was used when talking about biological aunts, while the Russian "teta" was used to refer to "fictive" kin in order to denote closeness between villagers that was a step removed from the biological relationship. Marusha's grandchildren, for example, who lived next door, addressed me as "teta," not "lelia." It reflected our non-biological but nevertheless close relationship. Which terms were used, and on which occasion, was related to context and the particular (educational) history of the user, among other factors.

36. This same point from a different perspective is made by Schlegel (2017, 205) who writes how despite the considerable mixing of the ethnic mosaic in Bessarabia, the boundaries remained "clear and stable," and there were good political and economic reasons for maintaining these distinctions.

37. Wanner (2014), for example, noted how many citizens were able to easily navigate between Russian and Ukrainian, and this was determined by context and the particular people conversing. Bilaniuk (2005) also focused on the language mixes in Ukraine, on notions of purity and hierarchies that influenced when, where, how and who used Russian and Ukrainian. The almost exclusive attention to Russian-Ukrainian experiences (see also Fournier 2002), where the two cultures and two languages were interwoven and shaped multiple layers of identity (from individual, to community, to national and international), presented an important insight into many regions of Ukraine, although it was not applicable to the southern Bessarabian region discussed here.

38. In this sense, the difference in response when compared to other locations where such name changes were also implemented, such as Odessa, was notable. In contrast to the rather low-key response in Brega, in Odessa, my Jewish landlady was livid as she recounted the process in 2003 by which her Russian name was changed to a Ukrainian one in her internal passport. To add salt to the wound, her Russian name could have been translated perfectly into Ukrainian (as the letters involved were the same), but instead she had been given a Ukrainian equivalent. A translation would have given her the name "Turchinskaya,"' but in-

stead she was given the Ukraine equivalent of "Turchinska"' which was, as she said, "a different name." As she pointed out, there was no need for this; many names like hers could have been transliterated without a problem, as the two languages have the same necessary letters, "but it is done on purpose to impose Ukrainian names on the people." My landlady proceeded to list a number of other people, who like her, had been given an "equivalent" Ukraine name, when a perfect translation of the Russian name was possible. In one case, her acquaintance took her passport to the head of the passport division and complained angrily, "See this name, there is no such person at this address." Finally, after kicking up a huge scandal, the officials relented and changed her name back to a truer translation. Another of her friends who had similarly stormed into the offices of the authorities and taken her complaints to a higher level was eventually allowed to have her name changed back. It suggests that the name changes were not legally binding but pushed through in such a way as to attract less public commentary or scrutiny.

39. External passports (i.e., for international travel), which used at this time both Russian and Ukrainian names, were not changed.

40. Those villagers in their sixties, seventies, and eighties (in the early 2000s), such as Baba Mina, spoke or at least understood some Romanian because they had attended school during the period when Romania controlled the region.

41. Tanya added that now you can "go where you like and there are no privileges or extra help," and as a consequence graduates do not go to villages or rural areas. She said that at present (2003), Brega had no physics teacher at the school, and at the end of the year the math teacher was also leaving, with no prospect of being replaced.

42. Van Meurs notes a similar occurrence for Moldovan villagers who in the late 1950s and 1960s went to work in Kazakhstan and "other distant republics" (1994, 124).

43. Before this, the village group's repertoire was more limited, having performed Bulgarian songs only at informal gatherings (not state-sponsored events). To quote Anya, the cultural coordinator, who spoke at the annual village meeting in 2003: "We want the young generation to know the Bulgarian customs and traditions of their grandmothers and grandfathers." Not a native of Brega, Anya would consult books on Bulgarian customs to check that they were doing the practices "correctly," while documents in the museum from the 1800s attested to the "genuine" Bulgarian nature of the customs practiced.

44. I also made a token contribution to this collection when Alyona asked me if on my return trip I could bring her a map of Bulgaria to hang up in the classroom, as there were no government funds for this. On another occasion, the village librarian requested I bring Bulgarian books for the children. The Brega library—merged from the three once operating during Soviet times—contained 27, 000 books.

45. Desire to remain uninvolved in the war was reinforced by the firsthand witness accounts given by the handful of young men from Brega—already serving in the army in 2014 and thus drawn into the fighting—on their return from the front, who confirmed the horrors of the war. One recent returnee was said to have gone first to the church, still in his uniform, fallen on his knees and sobbed. Another refused to speak or watch television or use the internet or anything that reminded him of the war. He said, "I just want to forget."

46. A few women from Brega worked in Italy, Greece and Turkey as caregivers or domestic helpers. Their language skills determined their migration paths: Moldovan speakers were most likely to go to Italy; Gagauz speakers went to Turkey. The vast majority of Brega migrants ended up in Russia or Odessa. Statistics on village migration were hard to come by, as such mobility was not recorded; villagers remained registered in Brega even after they moved. However, an official from the village council estimated that 20–25 percent had left the village in search of jobs by the end of 2003. Personal observations indicated that most Brega households were touched by migration, and many younger adults no longer lived permanently in the village.

47. These labor migrations became a way to establish additional transnational connections: "Fictive" marriages for the sake of gaining continued access to work in Russia were discussed openly and were evidently not an uncommon occurrence. Valentina's cousin was searching precisely for such marriage opportunities in order to hold on to his job in Russia.

48. While Russia's active role in the separatist cause in the east of the country was undeniable, the selective and exclusionary linguistic and historical criteria on which Ukrainian identity was constructed (among other factors) also played a part in alienating some citizens.

## CONCLUSION: A MODEL FOR ANALYZING SOCIAL CHANGE

1. With no possibility to carry out fieldwork in Ukraine in recent years, I cannot speculate on the value of my analytical approach in the

very specific case of war in which Russia and Ukraine are tragically currently locked.

2. A significant proportion of the produce from the collective land that fulfilled the state plan was traded within the Soviet market. The contemporary agricultural enterprises sold their produce on the Ukrainian market, either to the government or private buyers from outside the region. Thus, in both periods, the produce from this land had exchange value for the agricultural organizations.

3. This is perhaps an example of a reverse flow of exchange, from monetary to nonmonetary: Salaries were replaced by "rent" paid with grain by the agricultural enterprises to the landowners.

4. See, for example, Harvey, who notes that the monetization of exchange, commodification, is an aspect of the privatization process and opens up "new fields for capital accumulation" (2005, 160–61; 2004, 75). He understands the process to go beyond just the "wholesale" commodification of nature and includes the commodification of "cultural forms" (here, he seems to mean "culture" in the specific sense of various traditions/handicrafts/food/music, as well as histories and intellectual creativities). In this respect, neoliberalism differs from previous forms of capitalism, in that "it embraces the production of social life itself, seeking to commoditize the most intimate of human relations and production of identity and personhood" (Gledhill 2004, 340; Stenning et al. 2010, 68).

# REFERENCES

Abrahams, Ray, ed. 1996. *After Socialism: Land Reform and Rural Social Change in Eastern Europe*. Oxford: Berghahn Books.

Acheson, James. 2003. *Capturing the Commons: Devising Institutions to Manage the Maine Lobster Industry*. Hanover: University Press of New England.

Alekseevskii, M.D. 2010. "Den′ Goroda v Sovremennoi Prazdnichnoi Kul′ture" ["The Day of the City in Contemporary Festive Culture"]. In *Traditsionnaia Kul′tura Sovremennogo Goroda, Slavianskaia Traditsionnaia Kul′tura i Sovremennyi Mir*, Vypusk 13 [*Traditional Culture of the Contemporary City, Slavonic Traditional Culture and the Contemporary World*, Issue 13], compiled by M. D. Alekseevskii, V. E. Dobrovol′skaia and A. B. Ippolitova, 370–90. Moscow: Gosudarstvennyi Respublikanskii Tsentr Russkogo Fol′klora, Ministerstvo Kul′tury Rossiiskoi Federatsii.

Allina-Pisano, Jessica. 2004. "Land Reform and the Social Origins of Private Farmers in Russia and Ukraine." *The Journal of Peasant Studies* 31 (3–4): 489–514.

Allina-Pisano, Jessica. 2008. *The Post-Soviet Potemkin Village. Politics and Property Rights in the Black Earth*. Cambridge: Cambridge University Press.

Amosov, Myhailo. n.d. "The Land Question: Land Concentration and the Agricultural Land Moratorium in Ukraine." *TNI Longreads*. http://longreads.tni.org/the-land-question-ukraine.

Anand, Nikhil. 2018. "A Public Matter: Water, Hydraulics, Biopolitics." In *The Promise of Infrastructure*, edited by Nikhil Anand, Akhil Gupta, and Hannah Appel, 155–72. Durham, NC: Duke University Press.

Arutynov, Sergej Aleksandrovic, and T. A. Voronina. 2004. *Bread in Popular Culture: Studies in Ethnography*. Moscow: Nauka.

Ash, Timothy. 1998. "Land and Agricultural Reform in Ukraine." In

*Land Reform in the Former Soviet Union and Eastern Europe*, edited by Stephen K. Wegren, 62–86. London: Routledge.

Bassin, Mark, and Catriona Kelly, eds. 2012. *Soviet and Post-Soviet Identities*. Cambridge: Cambridge University Press.

Benovska-Sabkova, Milena, Tobias Köllner, Tünde Komáromi, Agata Ladykowska, Detelina Tocheva, and Jarrett Zigon. 2010. "'Spreading Grace' in Post-Soviet Russia." *Anthropology Today* 26, no. 1 (February): 16–21.

Berdahl, Daphne. 2000. "Introduction: An Anthropology of Postsocialism." In *Altering States: Ethnographies of Transition in Eastern Europe and the Former Soviet Union*, edited by Daphne Berdahl, Matti Bunzl, and Martha Lampland, 1–13. Ann Arbor: University of Michigan Press.

Bilaniuk, Laada. 2005. *Contested Tongues: Language Politics and Cultural Correction in Ukraine*. Ithaca, NY: Cornell University Press.

Binns, Christopher. 1979. "The Changing Face of Power: Revolution and Accommodation in the Development of the Soviet Ceremonial System: Part I." *Man, n.s.* 14, no. 4 (December): 585–606.

Binns, Christopher. 1980. "The Changing Face of Power: Revolution and Accommodation in the Development of the Soviet Ceremonial System: Part II." *Man, n.s.* 15, no. 1 (March): 171–87.

Boelens, Rutgerd, David Getches, and Armando Guevara Gil. 2012. "Water Struggles and the Politics of Identity." In *Out of the Mainstream: Water Rights, Politics and Identity*, edited by Rutgerd Boelens, David Getches and Armando Guevara-Gil, 3–7. Abingdon: Earthscan.

Bohannan, Paul. 1955. "Some Principles of Exchange and Investment Among the Tiv." *American Anthropologist* New Series 57, no. 1, Part 1 (February): 60–70.

Boneva, Tanya. 2006. "Continuity and Identity in the Local Community: A Long Term Perspective." *Anthropology of East Europe Review* 24 (1): 51–58.

Borelli, Caterina, and Fabio Mattioli. 2013. "The Social Lives of Postsocialism." *Laboratorium* 5 (1): 4–13.

Bourdieu, Pierre. 1986. "The Forms of Capital." In *Handbook of Theory and Research for the Sociology of Education*, edited by John George Richardson, 241–58. Westport, CT: Greenwood Press.

Brandes, Detlef. 2011. "Bulgarian and Gagauzian Settlers in New Russia and Bessarabia Since the 18th Century." In *The Encyclopedia of*

*Migration and Minorities in Europe: From the 17th Century to the Present*, edited by Klaus J. Bade, Pieter C. Emmer, Leo Lucassen, and Jochen Oltmer, 271–74. Cambridge: Cambridge University Press.

Buchowski, Michal. 2004. "Hierarchies of Knowledge in Central-Eastern European Anthropology." *Anthropology of East Europe Review* 22 (2): 4–13.

Burns, Danny, Robin Hambleton, and Paul Hoggett. 1994. *The Politics of Decentralisation: Revitalising Local Democracy*. London: Macmillan.

Cahill, Damien, Cooper, Melinda, Konings, Martijn, and David Primrose. 2018. "Introduction: Approaches to Neoliberalism." In *The Sage Handbook of Neoliberalism*, edited by Damien Cahill, Melina Cooper, Martijn Konings, and David Primrose, xxv–xxxiii. London: Sage.

Caldwell, Melissa. 2005. "A New Role for Religion in Russia's New Consumer Age: The Case of Moscow." *Religion, State and Society* 33 (1): 19–34.

Chari, Sharad, and Katherine Verdery. 2009. "Thinking Between the Posts: Postcolonialism, Postsocialism, and Ethnography After the Cold War." *Comparative Studies in Society and History* 51 (1): 6–34.

Chelcea, Liviu. 2023. "Goodbye, Post-Socialism? Stranger Things Beyond the Global East." *Eurasian Geography and Economics* (July): 1–27. doi:10.1080/15387216.2023.2236126.

Chernykh, Aleksandr V. 2014. *Russkii Narodnyi Kalendar' v Prikam'e: Prazdniki i Obriady Kontsa MX [sic]–Serediny XX Veka.* Chast IV [*Russian Folk Calendar in Prikamie: Holidays and Rites of the Late Twentieth to the Mid-Twentieth Century.* Part 4. Local Holidays Mestnye Prazdniki]. St. Petersburg: Mamatov.

Clarke, Simon. 2002. "Sources of Subsistence and the Survival Strategies of Urban Russian Households." In *Work, Employment and Transition: Restructuring Livelihoods in Post-Communism*, edited by Al Rainnie, Adrian Smith, and Adam Swain, 195–212. London: Routledge.

CMS Law-Now. 2024. "Ukrainian Market for Agricultural Land Opens Doors for Additional Investments." January 31. https://cms-lawnow.com/en/ealerts/2024/01/ukrainian-market-for-agricultural-land-opens-doors-for-additional-investments?format=pdf&v=14.

Collier, Stephen. 2011. *Post-Soviet Social: Neoliberalism, Social Modernity, Biopolitics*. Princeton, NJ: Princeton University Press.

Creed, Gerald W. 2011. *Masquerade and Postsocialism: Ritual and Cultural Dispossession in Bulgaria*. Bloomington: Indiana University Press.

Dale, Gareth, and Adam Fabry. 2018. "Neoliberalism in Eastern Europe and the Former Soviet Union." In *The Sage Handbook of Neoliberalism*, edited by Damien Cahill, Melina Cooper, Martijn Konings, and David Primrose, 234–47. London: Sage.

Davis, John. 1992. *Exchange*. Minneapolis: University of Minnesota Press.

De Waal, Thomas, and Balazs Jarabik. 2018. "Bessarabia's Hopes and Fears on Ukraine's Edge." *Carnegie Endowment for International Peace*. May 24. https://carnegieeurope.eu/2018/05/24/bessarabia-s-hopes-and-fears-on-ukraine-s-edge-pub-76445.

Deutsche Welle. 2019. *Varfolomei Podpisal Tomos ob Avtokefalii Ukrainskoi Tserkvi* [Bartholomew Signed the Tomos of Autocephaly for the Ukrainian Church]. January 5. https://p.dw.com/p/3B48w.

Dickinson, Jennifer. 2010. "Languages for the Market, the Nation, or the Margins: Overlapping Ideologies of Language and Identity in Zakarpattia." *International Journal of the Sociology of Language* 201: 53–78.

Dikhan, Mikhail. 2001. *Preselvane na Bulgarite v Iuzhna Ukraina* [The Migration of Bulgarians to Southern Ukraine]. Odessa: Maiak.

Dragadze, Tamara. 1993. "The Domestication of Religion Under Soviet Communism." In *Socialism: Ideals, Ideologies, and Local Practice*, edited by Chris M. Hann, 148–56. London: Routledge. https://www.etnologia.uw.edu.pl/sites/default/files/tamara_dragadze.pdf.

Eiss, Paul K. 2008. "The Claims of El Pueblo: Possessions, Politics, and Histories." In *Timely Assets: The Politics of Resources and Their Temporalities*, edited by Elizabeth Emma Ferry and Mandana E. Limbert, 191–214. Santa Fe, NM: School for Advanced Research Press.

Ferry, Elizabeth Emma, and Mandana E. Limbert. 2008. "Introduction." In *Timely Assets: The Politics of Resources and Their Temporalities*, edited by Elizabeth Emma Ferry and Mandana E. Limbert, 3–24. Santa Fe, NM: School for Advanced Research Press.

Fontein, Joost. 2008. "The Power of Water: Landscape, Water and the State in Southern and Eastern Africa: An Introduction." *Journal of Southern African Studies* 34 (4): 737–56.

Fournier, Anna. 2002. "Mapping Identities: Russian Resistance to Linguistic Ukrainisation in Central and Eastern Ukraine." *Europe-Asia Studies* 54 (3): 415–33.

Franquesa, Jaume. 2019. "Resources: Nature, Value and Time." In *A Re-*

*search Agenda for Economic Anthropology*, edited by James G. Carrier, 74–89. Cheltenham: Edward Elgar.

Fraser, Elizabeth. 2015. "Who Owns Agricultural Land in Ukraine?" *Oakland Institute*, May 8. https://www.newcoldwar.org/who-owns-agricultural-land-in-ukraine/.

Gallinat, Anselma, and Deema Kaneff. 2022. "The Anthropology of Postsocialism: Theoretical Legacies and Conceptual Futures." *Critique of Anthropology* 42 (2).

Gambold Miller, Liesl L., and Patrick Heady. 2003. "Cooperation, Power, and Community: Economy and Ideology in the Russian Countryside." In *The Postsocialist Agrarian Question: Property Relations and the Rural Condition*, edited by Chris Hann and the "Property Relations" Group, 257–92. Muenster: Lit Verlag.

Ganti, Tejaswini. 2014. "Neoliberalism." *Annual Review of Anthropology* 43: 89–104.

Gledhill, John. 2004. "Neoliberalism." In *A Companion to the Anthropology of Politics*, edited by David Nugent and Joan Vincent, 332–48. Malden, MA: Blackwell.

Golczewski, Frank. 2011. "Ukraine." In *The Encyclopedia of Migration and Minorities in Europe: From the 17th Century to the Present*, edited by Klaus J. Bade, Pieter C. Emmer, Leo Lucassen, and Jochen Oltmer, 193–207. Cambridge: Cambridge University Press.

Government of Ukraine. 1995. "The Water Code of Ukraine." N 214/95-BP, June 6. http://www.transport-ukraine.eu/en/docs/water-code-ukraine. No longer available.

Graeber, David. 2001. *Toward an Anthropological Theory of Value: The False Coin of Our Dreams*. New York: Palgrave.

Graeber, David. 2005. "Value: Anthropological Theories of Value." In *A Handbook of Economic Anthropology*, edited by James G. Carrier, 439–54. Cheltenham: Edward Elgar.

Gregory, Chris. 2015. *Gifts and Commodities*. Chicago: Hau Books.

Grek, Ivan, and Nikolai Chervenkov. 1993. *Bulgarite ot Ukraina i Moldova: Minalo i Nastoiashte* [Bulgarians from Ukraine and Moldova: Past and Present]. Sofia: Hristo Botev.

Halemba, Agnieszka. 2015. *Negotiating Marian Apparitions: The Politics of Religion in Transcarpathian Ukraine*. Budapest: Central European University Press.

Hall, David, and Vladimir Popov. 2005. *Privatisation and Restructuring of Water Supply in Russia and Ukraine*. London: PSIRU.

Hann C. M., ed. 2002. *Postsocialism: Ideals, Ideologies and Practices in Eurasia*. London: Routledge.

Hann, Chris. 1998. "Introduction: The Embeddedness of Property." In *Property Relations: Renewing the Anthropological Tradition*, edited by Chris Hann, 1–47. Cambridge: Cambridge University Press.

Hann, Chris. 2006. "Introduction: Faith, Power, and Civility After Socialism." In *The Postsocialist Religious Question: Faith and Power in Central Asia and East-Central Europe*, edited by Chris Hann and the "Civil Religion" Group, 1–26. Muenster: Lit Verlag.

Hann, Chris. 2006a. "Introduction." In *"Not the Horse We Wanted!" Postsocialism, Neoliberalism, and Eurasia*, edited by Chris Hann, 1–13. Muenster: Lit Verlag.

Hann, Chris, and the "Property Relations" Group. 2003. *The Postsocialist Agrarian Question*. Muenster: Lit Verlag.

Hann, Chris, Caroline Humphrey, and Katherine Verdery. 2002. "Introduction: Postsocialism as a Topic of Anthropological Investigation." In *Postsocialism: Ideals, Ideologies, and Practices in Eurasia*, edited by C. M. Hann, 1–28. London: Routledge.

Harvey, David. 2004. "The 'New' Imperialism: Accumulation by Dispossession." *Socialist Register* 95: 63–87.

Harvey, David. 2005. *A Brief History of Neoliberalism*. Oxford: Oxford University Press.

Harvey, Penny, and Hannah Knox. 2015. *Roads: An Anthropology of Infrastructure and Expertise*. Ithaca, NY: Cornell University Press.

Henig, David, and Nicolette Makovicky, eds. 2017. *Economies of Favour After Socialism: A Comparative Perspective*. Oxford: Oxford University Press.

Hirsch, Francine. 2005. *Empire of Nations: Ethnographic Knowledge and the Marking of the Soviet Union*. Ithaca, NY: Cornell University Press.

Humphrey, Caroline, ed. 1992. *Barter, Exchange and Value: An Anthropological Approach*. Cambridge: Cambridge University Press.

Humphrey, Caroline. 1995. "Introduction." *Cambridge Anthropology* 18 (2): 1–12.

Humphrey, Caroline. 1998. *Marx Went Away—But Karl Stayed Behind*. Ann Arbor: University of Michigan Press.

Ingold, Tim. 2012. "Toward an Ecology of Materials." *Annual Review of Anthropology* 41: 427–42.

Ingram, Helen, John M. Whiteley, and Richard Warren Perry. 2008. "The Importance of Equity and the Limits of Efficiency in Water

Resources." In *Water, Place and Equity*, edited by John M. Whiteley, Helen Ingram, and Richard Warren Perry, 1–32. Cambridge, MA: MIT Press.

Institute of Urban Economics. 2004. *Review of Key Reforms in the Urban Water Supply and Sanitation Sector of Ukraine. Final Report*. Moscow: OECD.

Ishchenko, N. N. 2019. Bozh'ia Plata: Kto Platit Zarplatu Sviashchennikam v Ukraine? [God's Tariff: Who Pays Wages to Priests in Ukraine?] *Etcetera*, Kyiv. Last accessed 28 January 2019.

Izbusheva, A. M. 2015. "Podgotovka i Provedenie Iubileia Goroda v Sovetskoi Istorii kak Sposob Sokhraneniia i Zakrepleniia Istoricheskoi i Kul'turnoi Pamiati" [Preparing and Conducting the Anniversary of the City in Soviet History as a Way to Preserve and Consolidate Historical and Cultural memory]. *Vestnik Omskogo Universiteta. Seriia "Istoricheskie Nauki"* 3 (7): 24–35.

Kalb, Don. 2024. *Insidious Capital: Frontlines of Value at the End of a Global Cycle*. New York: Berghahn Books.

Kaneff, Deema. 1996. "Responses to 'Democratic' Land Reforms in a Bulgarian Village." In *After Socialism: Land Reform and Social Change in Eastern Europe*, edited by Ray Abrahams, 85–114. Providence, RI: Berghahn Books.

Kaneff, Deema. 1998. "Negotiating the Past in Post-Socialist Bulgaria." *Ethnologia Balkanica* 2: 31–45.

Kaneff, Deema. 2004. *Who Owns the Past? The Politics of Time in a "Model" Bulgarian Village*. New York: Berghahn Books.

Kaneff, Deema. 2009. "Property and Transnational Neoliberalism: The Case of British Migration to Bulgaria." In *Accession and Migration: Changing Policy, Society and Culture in an Enlarged Europe*, edited by John Eade and Yordanka Valkanova, 59–74. Surrey: Ashgate.

Kaneff, Deema. 2017. "Making History, Making Politics: Socialist and Postsocialist Elite Economies of Favour in Bulgaria and Ukraine." In *Economies of Favour After Socialism: A Comparative Perspective*, edited by David Henig and Nicolette Makovicky, 140–60. Oxford: Oxford University Press.

Kaneff, Deema. 2018. "Religion, Customs and Local Identity: Bi-Spirituality in Rural Ukraine." *Religion, State and Society* 46 (2): 139–55.

Kaneff, Deema. 2018a. *Resources and Their Re/Valuation in Times of Political-Economic Reform*. Halle/Saale: Max Planck Institute for Social Anthropology.

Kaneff, Deema. 2021. "'The Market Is Far Away': Global Connections and Economic Remoteness in Rural Ukraine." *Europe-Asia Studies* 73 (3): 451–71.

Kaneff, Deema. 2021a. "Property, Resources and Gauging Social Change." In *Explorations of Economic Anthropology: Key Issues and Critical Reflections*, edited by Deema Kaneff and Kirsten Endres, 169–81. New York: Berghahn Books.

Kaneff, Deema. 2022. "Extending the Reach of 'Postsocialism,'" *Critique of Anthropology* 42 (2): 209–18.

Kaneff, Deema, and Monica Heintz. 2006. "Guest Editors' Note: Bessarabian Borderlands: One Region, Two States, Multiple Ethnicities." *Anthropology of East Europe Review* 24 (1): 6–16.

Khmelko, Irina. 2012. "Administrative Decentralization in Post Communist Countries: The Case of Water Management in Ukraine." *Journal of Political Science, Government and Politics* 1 (1): 1–12.

Kideckel, David A., ed. 1995. *East European Communities: The Struggle for Balance in Turbulent Times*. Boulder: Westview Press.

Kisse, Anton Ivanovich. 2006. *Vzrazhdane na Bulgarite v Ukraina* [The Resurgence of Bulgarians in Ukraine]. Odessa: Optimum.

Kulyk, Volodymyr. 2006. "Constructing Common Sense: Language and Ethnicity in Ukrainian Public Discourse." *Ethnic and Racial Studies* 29 (2): 281–314.

Kulyk, Volodymyr. 2013. "Language Policy in Ukraine: What People Want the State to Do." *East European Politics and Societies and Cultures* 27, no. 2 (May): 280–307.

Lane, Christel. 1981. *The Rites of Rulers: Ritual in Industrial Society—The Soviet Case*. Cambridge: Cambridge University Press.

Larkin, Brian. 2013. "The Politics and Poetics of Infrastructure." *Annual Review of Anthropology* 42 (October): 327–43.

Ledeneva, Alena V. 1998. *Russia's Economy of Favours: Blat, Networking, and Informal Exchange*. Cambridge: Cambridge University Press.

Lindquist, Galina. 2000. "Not My Will but Thine Be Done: Church Versus Magic in Contemporary Russia." *Culture and Religion* 1 (2): 247–76.

Magocsi, Paul Robert. 1996. *A History of Ukraine*. Toronto: University of Toronto Press.

Mamonova, Natalia. 2015. "Resistance or Adaptation? Ukrainian Peasants' Responses to Large-Scale Land Acquisitions." *Journal of Peasant Studies* 42 (3–4): 607–34.

Marples, David R. 2007. *Heroes and Villains: Creating National History in Contemporary Ukraine*. Budapest: Central European University Press.

Marples, David R. 2015. "Introduction." In *Ukraine's Euromaidan: Analyses of a Civil Revolution*, edited by David R. Marples and Frederick V. Mills, 9–26. Stuttgart: ibidem.

Marx, Karl, ed. 2015 [1887]. "Volume I, Book One: The Process of Production of Capital." In *Capital: A Critique of Political Economy*. Translated by Samuel Moore and Edward Aveling, edited by Frederick Engels. Moscow: Progress. https://www.marxists.org/archive/marx/works/download/pdf/Capital-Volume-I.pdf.

Mavrov, D. F., and M. A. Bratkov. 1967. *Istoriko-Ikonomicheski Ocherk na s. Nagornoe, gr. Reni, Odeska Oblast* [Historical and Economic Insights into Village Nagorna, Reni, Odessa Oblast]. Translated by Irina Dimotrova from Russian to Bulgarian. Translated from Bulgarian to English by Deema Kaneff (2006). Unpublished manuscript.

Meurs, Mieke. 2002. "Economic Strategies of Post-Socialism: Changing Household Economies and Gender Divisions of Labour in the Bulgarian Transition." In *Work, Employment and Transition: Restructuring Livelihoods in Post-Communism*, edited by Al Rainnie, Adrian Smith, and Adam Swain, 213–30. London: Routledge.

Mosse, David. 2008. "Epilogue: The Cultural Politics of Water—A Comparative Perspective." *Journal of Southern African Studies* 34 (4): 939–48.

Müller, Martin. 2019. "Goodbye, Postsocialism!" *Europe-Asia Studies* 71 (4): 533–50.

Neveu, Erik. 2018. "Bourdieu's Capital(s): Sociologizing an Economic Concept." In *The Oxford Handbook of Pierre Bourdieu*, edited by Thomas Medvetz and Jeffrey J. Sallaz, 347–74. Oxford: Oxford University Press.

Nikulin, Alexander M. 2011. "From Post-Kolkhoz to Oligarkhoz." *Bulletin of the Peoples' Friendship University of Russia. Sociology* (2): 56–68.

Nivievskyi, Oleg, and Roman Neyter. 2024. "Further Liberalisation of the Farmland Sales Market in Ukraine." *Newsletter Ukraine*, no. 183 (January). https://www.german-economic-team.com/wp-content/uploads/2024/01/GET_UKR_NL_183_2024_en.pdf.

OECD. 2006. *Guidelines on Performance-Based Contracts Between Municipalities and Water Utilities in Eastern Europe, Caucasus and Central Asia (EECCA)*. Paris: OECD. Last accessed August 31, 2016.

Orlove, Ben, and Steven C. Caton. 2010. "Water Sustainability: Anthropological Approaches and Prospects." *Annual Review of Anthropology* 39: 401–15.

Ostrom, Elinor. 1990. *Governing the Commons: The Evolution of Institutions for Collective Action*. Cambridge: Cambridge University Press.

Ostrom, Elinor, Roy Gardner, and James Walker. 1994. *Rules, Games, and Common-Pool Resources*. Ann Arbor: University of Michigan Press.

Perrotta, Louise. 2000. "Politics, Confusion and Practice: Landownership and De-Collectivisation in Ukraine." In *Land, Law, and Environment: Mythical Land, Legal Boundaries*, edited by Allen Abramson and Dimitrios Theodossopoulos, 156–75. London: Pluto Press.

Petras, James, and Henry Veltmeyer. 2011. *Beyond Neoliberalism: A World to Win*. London: Ashgate.

Pine, Frances. 1999. "Incorporation and Exclusion in the Podhale." In *Lilies of the Field. Marginal People Who Live for the Moment*, edited by Sophie Day, Evthymios Papataxiarchis, and Michael Stewart, 45–60. Boulder: Westview Press.

Pine, Frances. 2002. "Retreat to the Household? Gendered Domains in Postsocialist Poland." In *Postsocialism: Ideals, Ideologies and Practise in Eurasia*, edited by C. M. Hann, 95–113. London: Routledge.

Pine, Frances. 2003. "Reproducing the House: Kinship, Inheritance, and Property Relations in Highland Poland." In *Distinct Inheritances: Property, Family and Community in a Changing Europe*, edited by Hannes Grandits and Patrick Heady, 279–95. Muenster: Lit Verlag.

Polanyi, Karl. 1957. "The Economy as Instituted Process." In *Trade and Market in the Early Empires: Economies in History and Theory*, edited by Karl Polanyi, Conrad M. Arensberg, and Harry W. Pearson, 243–70. Chicago: Henry Regnery.

Pradhan, Rajendra, Franz Benda-Beckmann, and Keebet Benda-Beckmann, eds. 2000. *Water, Land and Law: Changing Rights to Land and Water in Nepal*. Proceedings of a Workshop, Kathmandu, March 18–20, 1998. Kathmandu: Legal Research and Development Forum.

Richardson, Tanya. 2008. *Kaleidoscopic Odessa: History and Place in Contemporary Ukraine*. Toronto: University of Toronto Press, 2008.

Richardson, Tanya, and Gisa Weszkalnys. 2014. "Introduction: Resource Materialities." *Anthropological Quarterly* 87 (1): 5–30.

Rogers, Douglas. 2009. *The Old Faith and the Russian Land: A Historical*

*Ethnography of Ethics in the Urals.* Ithaca, NY: Cornell University Press.

Rogers, Douglas. 2010. "Postsocialisms Unbounded: Connections, Critiques, Comparisons." *Slavic Review* 69, no. 1 (Spring): 1–15.

Rogers, Douglas, and Katherine Verdery. 2013. "Postsocialist Societies: Eastern Europe and the Former Soviet Union." In *The Handbook of Sociocultural Anthropology*, edited by James G. Carrier and Deborah B. Gewertz, 439–55. London: Bloomsbury.

Salman, Ton, Salvador Marti i Puig, and Gemma van der Haar. 2014. "David Versus Goliath in Cochabamba: Water Rights, Neoliberalism, and the Revival of Social Protest in Bolivia." In *Dignity for the Voiceless: Willem Assies's Anthropological Work in Context*, edited by Ton Salman, Salvador Marti i Puig, and Gemma van der Haar, 269–91. New York: Berghahn Books.

Schlegel, Simon. 2016. "Making of Ethnicity in Southern Bessarabia: Tracing the Histories of an Ambiguous Concept in a Contested Land." PhD diss., Martin Luther University, Halle-Wittenberg.

Schlegel, Simon. 2017. "Ukrainian Nation Building and Ethnic Minority Associations: The Case of Southern Bessarabia." In *Transnational Ukraine? Networks and Ties That Influence(d) Contemporary Ukraine*, edited by Timm Beichelt and Susann Worschech, 203–24. Stuttgart: ibidem.

Schlegel, Simon. 2019. *Making Ethnicity in Southern Bessarabia: Tracing the Histories of an Ambiguous Concept in a Contested Land.* Leiden: Brill.

Sikor, Thomas, Stefan Dorondel, Johannes Stahl, and Phuc Xuan To. 2017. *When Things Become Property: Land Reform, Authority and Value in Postsocialist Europe and Asia*. New York: Berghahn Books, 2017.

Skalník, Peter, ed. 2002. *A Post-Communist Millenium: The Struggles for Sociocultural Anthropology in Central and Eastern Europe.* Prague: Roman Míšek-Set Out.

State Statistics Committee of Ukraine. 2001. "Main Points in Brief." http://2001.ukrcensus.gov.ua/eng/.

Steinberg, Mark D., and Catherine Wanner, eds. 2008. *Religion, Morality, and Community in Post-Soviet Societies.* Washington, DC: Woodrow Wilson Center Press.

Stenning, Alison, Adrian Smith, Alena Rochovska, and Dariusz Swiatek. 2010. *Domesticating Neo-Liberalism: Spaces of Economic Practice and Social Reproduction in Post-Socialist Cities*. Sussex: Wiley-Blackwell.

Svetlichnyi Andrei. 2019. *V Pravoslavnuiu Cherkov' Ukrainy Pereshlo Bolee 480 Prikhodov, v Bessarabii Vsego Dva* [More than 480 Parishes have Transferred to the Orthodox Church of Ukraine, with Only Two in Bessarabia]. March 18. https://bessarabiainform.com/2019/03/v-pravoslavnuyu-tserkov-ukrainy-pereshlo-bolee-480-prihodov-v-bessarabii-vsego-dva/.

Swain, Nigel. 1992. *Hungary: The Rise and Fall of Feasible Socialism*. London: Verso.

Sydorchuk, Oleksii. 2015. "Decentralization Reform in Ukraine: Prospects and Challenges." Policy Brief. Ilko Kucheriv Democratic Initiatives Foundation, November 29. https://dif.org.ua/en/article/decentralization-reform-in-ukraine-prospects-and-challenges.

Taussig, Michael T. 2001. *The Devil and Commodity Fetishism in South America*. Chapel Hill: University of North Carolina Press.

Thelen, Tatjana. 2011. "Shortage, Fuzzy Property and Other Dead Ends in the Anthropological Analysis of (Post)socialism." *Critique of Anthropology* 31 (1): 43–61.

Tocheva, Detelina. 2014. "The Economy of the Temples of God in the Turmoil of Changing Russia." *European Journal of Sociology* 55 (1): 1–24.

Tronko, Petro, ed. 1978. *Istoriia Gorodov i Sel Ukrainskoi SSR Odesskaia Oblast'* [History of Cities and Villages of the Ukrainian SSR: Odessa Oblast]. Kiev: Institute of History of Ukraine, The National Academy of Sciences of the Ukrainian SSR, 678–93. https://malorus.ru/igsu/Odesskaja.obl/Izmailxskij.rajon/.

Uchibori, Motomitsu. 2011. "Theoretical Themes for an Anthropology of Resources." *Social Science Information* 50 (1): 142–53.

Ukraine Reform Conference. 2018. *Reforms in Ukraine: Progress and Priorities*, June. Reforms Delivery Office, Cabinet of Ministers of Ukraine. https://www.kmu.gov.ua/storage/app/sites/1/reform%20office/Ukraine_Reform_Conference_II_web.pdf.

Ukrainian Population Census. 2001. State Statistics Service of Ukraine. https://2001.ukrcensus.gov.ua/eng/

Ukrinform, Ukrainian Multimedia Platform for Broadcasting. 2021. "Ukraine Abolishes Moratorium on Sale of Agricultural Land. July 1. https://www.ukrinform.net/rubric-economy/3273209-ukraine-abolishes-moratorium-on-sale-of-agricultural-land.html.

Van Meurs, Wim. 1994. *The Bessarabian Question in Communist Historiography: Nationalist and Communist Politics and History-writing.*

New York: East European Monographs, distributed by Columbia University Press.

Verdery, Katherine. 1999. *The Political Lives of Dead Bodies: Reburial and Postsocialist Change.* New York: Columbia University Press.

Verdery, Katherine. 2003. *The Vanishing Hectare: Property and Value in Postsocialist Transylvania*. Ithaca, NY: Cornell University Press.

Verkhovna Rada of Ukraine. 2019. On Supporting the Functioning of the Ukrainian Language as the State Language. Document 2704-VIII. April 25. https://zakon.rada.gov.ua/laws/show/en/2704-19/#Text.

Verkhovna Rada of Ukraine. N.d. Registration Card for the Village, official web portal. http://w1.c1.rada.gov.ua/pls/z7503/A005?rf7571=22998. Accessed October 30, 2021.

Visser, Oane, and Max Spoor. 2011. "Land Grabbing in Post-Soviet Eurasia: The World's Largest Land Reserves at Stake." *Journal of Peasant Studies* 38 (2): 299–323.

Vium, Christian. 2016. "Moral Valves and Fluid Properties: Water Regulation Mechanisms in the Badia of South-Eastern Mauritania." In *Waterworlds: Anthropology in Fluid Environments*, edited by Kirsten Hastrup and Frida Hastrup, 219–46. New York: Berghahn Books.

Von Benda-Beckmann, Franz, Keebet von Benda-Beckmann, and Rajendra Prasad Pradhan. 2000. "Introduction." In *Water, Land and Law: Changing Rights to Land and Water in Nepal*, edited by Franz Benda-Beckman, Keebet Benda-Beckmann, and Rajendra Prasad Pradhan, 1–16. Kathmandu: Legal Research and Development Forum.

Von Löwis, Sabine. 2019. "The Sale of Agricultural Land in Ukraine." *ZOiS Spotlight*, January 9. https://en.zois-berlin.de/publications/zois-spotlight-2019/the-sale-of-agricultural-land-in-ukraine/.

Von Schnitzler, Antina. 2008. "Citizenship Prepaid: Water, Calculability, and Techno-Politics in South Africa." *Journal of Southern African Studies* 34 (4): 899–917.

Wallman, Sandra. 1979. "Introduction." In *Social Anthropology of Work*, edited by Sandra Wallman, ASA Monographs, 1–24. London: Academic Press.

Wanner, Catherine. 1998. *Burden of Dreams: History and Identity in Post-Soviet Ukraine*. University Park, PA: Pennsylvania State University Press.

Wanner, Catherine. 2003. "Advocating New Moralities: Conversion to Evangelicalism in Ukraine." *Religion, State and Society* 31 (3): 273–87.

Wanner, Catherine. 2007. *Communities of the Converted: Ukrainians and Global Evangelism*. Ithaca, NY: Cornell University Press.

Wanner, Catherine. 2014. "Fraternal Nations and Challenges to Sovereignty in Ukraine." *American Ethnologist* 41 (3): 427–39.

Wanner, Catherine, and Mark D. Steinberg. 2008. "Introduction: Reclaiming the Sacred After Communism." In *Religion, Morality, and Community in Post-Soviet Societies*, edited by Mark D. Steinberg and Catherine Wanner, 1–20. Washington, DC: Woodrow Wilson Center Press.

Wegren, Stephen K. 2002. *The Land Question in Ukraine and Russia*. Seattle: Henry M. Jackson School of International Studies, University of Washington.

Wittfogel, Karl A. 1957. *Oriental Despotism: A Comparative Study of Total Power*. New Haven, CT: Yale University Press.

World Bank. 2018. *Ukraine Economic Update*. Washington, DC: World Bank.

Yalcin-Heckmann, Lale. 2010. *The Return of Private Property: Rural Life After Agrarian Reform in the Republic of Azerbaijan*. Muenster: Lit Verlag.

Zigon, Jarrett. 2011. "Multiple Moralities: Discourses, Practices, and Breakdowns in Post-Soviet Russia." In *Multiple Moralities and Religions in Post-Soviet Russia*, edited by Jarrett Zigon, 3–15. New York: Berghahn Books.

Zimmerman, Erich Walter. 1933. *World Resources and Industries: A Functional Appraisal of the Availability of Agricultural and Industrial Resources*. New York: Harper and Brothers.

# INDEX

*Note:* Page numbers in **bold** indicate tables, page numbers in *italics* indicate figures, and references following "n" refer notes.